HITLER'S BLACK CHARIOTS

CHARIOTS

The Legend & Reality
of Germany's Tiger Tank
in World War Two

HITLER'S BLACK CHARIOTS

The Legend & Reality of Germany's
Tiger Tank in World War Two

by
Logan Kaine

Library and Archives Canada Cataloguing in Publication
Kaine, Logan, author
Hitler's Black Chariots / Logan Kaine

Issued in print and electronic formats.
ISBN: 978-1-990644-97-9 (paperback)
ISBN: 978-1-990644-98-6 (ebook)

Cover Design: Pablo Javier Herrera
Interior Design: Muhammad Tahir

Double Dagger Books Ltd.
Toronto, Ontario, Canada
www.doubledagger.ca

CONTENTS

ACKNOWLEDGMENTS

In the process of writing this book a number of people provided invaluable assistance, for which I will be forever indebted. First among them is Dr. Alexander Hill who has been a steadfast and eagle-eyed advisor throughout this entire journey. Without his efforts this book would be much longer and much less interesting. My Parents, Brian and Sandy have also made an immense contribution. Their encouragement has been vital in pursing my passion for history in general and this thesis in particular. They have also acted as editors and sounding boards throughout this process. Their willingness to tolerate the nearly endless discussions about these vehicles is greatly appreciated.

The good people at the Digital History Archive must also be thanked for without their efforts in providing the relevant German documents electronically this thesis could not have been completed in the midst of the COVID-19 Pandemic.

Last, but not least, my editor Chuck Oliviero, Phil Halton and the rest of the team at Double Dagger Books, who have with great skill and patience turned a promising a thesis into a viable book.

Any remaining errors and omissions remain mine alone.

PREFACE

rowing up I developed an enduring interest in World War Two. In the fashion of youth this interest encompassed all aspects of the conflict, and in all honesty my interest still has much of that broad enthusiasm today. One element that certainly consumed much of my attention though were tanks. These massive metal beasts storming across the battlefield belching fire captured my imagination. Being able to hop into the virtual turrets of these vehicles in video games was fantastic, putting me in the driver's seat of these legendary monsters.

As I became a teenager, I kept playing these games and was increasingly drawn into the age-old debates. What tank was your favorite? Which tank was best? My answer to the first question was easy, even if the answer changed over the years, right now it is the *M4 Sherman* but the answer to the second question was always harder. Certainly, the most common answer and one that I gave myself more than once was that the best tank had to be German, typically one of the "big cats", the *Panther* or the *Tiger*, either the *Tiger I* or the *Tiger II*, better known as the *King Tiger*. Looking at the statistics provided in references books, everyone involved in these discussions had supported this conclusion. The *Tiger* 88mm gun could reach out and destroy *T-34* and *Sherman* at two thousand meters while the Allied tanks had to close to within 500 meters to even have a hope of penetrating German armour. There was a wrinkle, however. There was always someone in these discussions who would disqualify these mighty German cats from contention as the best tank of the war because of their lack of mechanical reliability.

Getting a conclusive answer to these questions was not something that concerned me then, but they bounced around in the back of my head as time marched on and I spent less time driving virtual tanks and more time building plastic ones, including a number of *Tiger* tanks (seven at the time of writing). While this modelling ensured that I could never truly forget these questions, they were hardly front and center. What brought them to the forefront, and produced this book, was my growing professional interest in the German military in the Second World War that developed over the course of my bachelor's degree at the University of Calgary. As I thought about the Germans and the contradictions that made them both one of the most successful militaries in the world and one of the most badly flawed brought me back to the tanks. When I did, it was the *Tiger* that loomed the largest, both literally and metaphorically and so it became the focus of my research when I took the academic plunge and started my masters under Dr. Alexander Hill at the University of Calgary. My aim was to determine which of the two *Tiger* reputations was correct and determine if it could even be considered for the title of the best tank of World War Two.

Our initial discussions and my initial research echoed all of my childhood debates about the *Tiger*. Some works praised its thick armour and powerful gun while others condemned its lack of mechanical reliability. It was also clear that while the case for the tank's fame and infamy were well laid out in broad strokes, few works had ever attempted to tell the full story of these vehicles, with books by Christopher Wilbeck, Hilary Doyle and Thomas Jentz being noteworthy exceptions.

Even these works did not fully answer my question. As good as they were, they all proved too narrowly focused on either the technical aspects of the vehicles or upon the combat effectiveness of the *Tiger* units themselves.

So, if I was going to really answer these questions, I could not rely on the traditional metrics by which I had assessed what a good tank was. The size of the gun, the thickness of the armour, and the number of enemy tanks destroyed were not sufficient. I would have to step away from all the hobbyist's metrics and dig deeper, placing the *Tiger* within the broader context of the German war effort. Only by determining what effect the *Tiger* had on German armoured doctrine, the wartime economy, and the battles in which they fought could its true effectiveness be assessed.

As a final note, I want to explain the use of German words and phrases as well as the naming conventions used for weapons and vehicles. Whenever possible, I have elected to use the original German designations. I have done so partly to better reflect the language that surrounded these vehicles and their use and because a number of words and phrases like *Klotzen, nicht kleckern*, lose something in translation. As for naming conventions, these vehicles, particularly the two tanks, had a number of different official names attached to them over the course of their production and use. I have settled on *Tiger I* and *Tiger II* as the best names partly for convenience but also because referring to the *Tiger II* as the *King Tiger*, while historically and thematically appropriate serves to unduly distance it from the *Tiger I*. As readers will see, the two vehicles share far more than a name. Also, all vehicle and weapon names have been italicized.

Further, I usually introduce the German term, translate it, and then switch to English for ease of reading. Usually, but not always. Also, the reader will note that I try to obey rules of German grammar where I can. For instance, the plural of *Tiger* in German remains *Tiger* and the plural of *Kampfgruppe* is *Kampfgruppen*.

Logan Kaine, MA
Calgary, Alberta, 2023

FOREWORD

Tanks fascinate people. From their terrifying introduction in France in 1916 to fields littered with destroyed *T-90s* in the current Russo-Ukrainian war, steel behemoths raging across battlefields hold most people in their thrall. I understand it; how could I not? I was myself a tank commander and have had the pleasure of sitting in most NATO tanks and commanding an entire regiment (59 tanks) of German-built *Leopard A5*. But I see the tank not as a romantic successor to Sir Walter Scott's *Ivanhoe*, riding in a royal tournament. They are master weapon systems. Deadly killers. Tanks – of all stripes – are the modern battlefield's most flexible weapon system. The five characteristics of armour, namely, speed, firepower, protection, flexibility, and communications, make these steel beasts the ultimate tools of modern ground combat. But only if those tools are employed correctly. In the right hands, tanks dominate the modern battlespace. In the wrong hands, they are scrap metal.

This brings us to Logan's investigation of the German Army's *Panzer Mark VI*, more commonly known as the *Tiger*. As young officers undergoing tank training, we all held this legendary machine in great esteem. It nearly swept the European battlefields of all comers. It was practically invincible. Unmatched firepower. Unparalleled protection. Had the Nazis been able to bring more of them into service we may well all be speaking German today. Or so the stories went. The truth is not quite so breathtaking. Not quite so one-sided.

Logan has done a deep dive into archives and historical records to uncover the reality behind the myth. He has done what all good historians endeavor to do. He is looking for the facts. He is striving for the truth. Was the *Tiger*, in all its iterations, really the fabled super weapon of countless breathless stories? Was it invincible? Even if it was as powerful as many believe it was, did it fulfil its promise?

The greatest tank ace among the Allied armies of World War Two was a Canadian major: Sydney Valpy Radley-Walters CMM, DSO, MC, CD. Rad, as we called him, was a tank commander in the Sherbrooke Fusiliers, an infantry unit re-rolled to armour for the invasion of Normandy. Rad was credited with destroying 18 German tanks and many other armoured vehicles. He carried a photo in his wallet of a tank that was shot out from under him. It was a *Sherman* with over a dozen holes in it, courtesy of a *Tiger* in Normandy. Nonetheless, he and three of his four crewmen survived the encounter and went on to trap and kill the *Tiger*. How so? How could a lowly *Sherman* crew defeat the mighty *Tiger*? You'll see.

Warfare is much more than technology and weaponry. Inevitably, there are untold parts of every story and in this volume, Logan digs to uncover some of those hidden parts. Through the course of his investigation, Logan uncovers aspects that were either unknown or have been forgotten. In the end, we are left with a much better picture of what this fabled weapon meant to Germany's war effort.

In popular military memory, the *Tiger* was the scourge of the battlefield from Normandy to the gates of Stalingrad. Or was it? I won't spoil the story; read on!

Colonel (Ret'd) C.S. Oliviero, CD, PhD
8th Canadian Hussars (Princess Louise's)

INTRODUCTION

n September of 1942, a new German *Panzerkampfwagen* (Armoured Fighting Vehicle, AFV, or more commonly a tank) the *Panzer VI*, entered combat outside Leningrad. Better known as the *Tiger I*, by the time the war ended, it and its successor the *Tiger II* had gained a formidable reputation. Their thick armour and high velocity 88mm guns allowed them to penetrate the armour of any Allied tanks they encountered at over 1,000 meters. As *Generalmajor* (Major General) Friedrich von Mellenthin wrote in his post war memoir *Panzer Battles*, the *Tiger* with its powerful gun and heavy armour was the most effective tank used during the war. This reputation for battlefield mastery contrasted sharply with their other reputation as being overly complex and mechanically unreliable.[1]

With the exception of a few notable authors like Wilbeck, Doyle, and Jentz who consider both aspects of the tank's history, the majority of the historiography is split into works that deal with either the vehicles' mechanical complexity or their combat performance. Further, none of these works are set within the context of the Germans' wider use of tanks or Germany's wartime economy. Without the ability to combine the technical, operational, doctrinal and economies of the vehicles' history, assessing their value to the *Reichsheer* (German Army) has been a considerable challenge.

Combining these four elements demonstrates that although there is certainly truth to the *Tigers'* much vaunted combat performance, this performance was overshadowed by their mechanical unreliability and limited numbers as well as by the fact that they were designed not to fill a pressing doctrinal or combat need but instead to satisfy Adolf Hitler. Consequently, the *Tigers* were in no way capable of fulfilling the roles they were given in the latter half of the war, at a time when the *Reichsheer* did not have the resources to employ them as designed.

This study covers the entire *Tiger* family of variants, including not only the *Tiger I* and *II,* but also the specialized vehicles based on their chassis, the *Ferdinand* and *Jagdtiger* tank destroyers as well as the *Sturmtiger*, an urban assault gun. These vehicles are discussed both for the sake of completeness and because their stories, while unique, demonstrate interesting parallels to the vehicles upon which they were based.

In combat, the Tigers were organized into independent *schwere Panzer Abteilungen*[2] (heavy tank formations or battalions) rather than being added to the panzer divisions. This decision was made by the *Oberkommando des Heeres* (OKH or Army High Command). It was a concession to low production numbers as well as a realization that the units could be shuffled to provide additional combat power to key sectors.[3]

The vehicle's combat record from September 1942 to May 1945 showed its effectiveness and limitations in not only its intended role as a breakthrough tank but also as a defensive weapon when the Germans were forced onto the defensive across all fronts from 1943 onwards. Its service also occurred amidst the ongoing decline of the army and the ever-growing effectiveness of Allied anti-tank weapons, two long term trends which had dire consequences on the effectiveness of the *Tiger* as the war went on.

The early deployments of the *Tiger* in the Soviet Union in the fall 1942, and the winter of 1943, as well as in North Africa during 1943, led to the creation of its legendary reputation with its armour and armament proving to be more than a match for any Allied vehicle. However, these initial employments also demonstrated the vehicle's weaknesses, especially regarding its lack of mechanical reliability and poor mobility. In both North Africa and the Soviet Union, the Allies captured *Tiger* tanks, paving the way for improved weapons and tactics to counter them in the battles to come, leaving the *Tiger* with an all too brief moment of battlefield superiority.

Operation Zitadelle (Citadel) in July of 1943, also known as the Battle of Kursk, was in theory at least, a high-water mark for the *Tiger*. The tanks were to be employed in the breakthrough role with all the supporting weapons the Germans could muster. Unfortunately, extensive Soviet defences and a growing understanding of the tank's strengths and weaknesses, combined with more powerful anti-tank weapons like the *SU-152* "beast killer" self-propelled guns, allowed the Soviets to counter the *Tiger* far more effectively than they had at the beginning of year.[4] The depth of the Soviet positions also robbed the formations supporting the *Tiger* units of the strength to exploit whatever breakthroughs the tanks were able to achieve.

Subsequent operations on the Eastern Front in 1943 and 1944 saw German forces largely on the defensive. During this period the *Tiger* was not only used in its counter attack role, which was the intended defensive role for all armour, but also as so-called *Korsettstange* (corset stays). In this role, the *Tiger* occupied positions in the German front line to support infantry divisions, which had neither the numbers nor morale to hold their positions alone. While the Germans achieved some successes in this period, with small numbers of well-handled *Tiger* units defeating larger Soviet units, it was generally a period that placed ever more strain on the unreliable vehicles than previous offensive operations had. These strains ensured that their effectiveness was limited, especially in the face of the overwhelming superiority of the Red Army.

The Normandy Campaign in the summer of 1944 saw the *Tiger* facing many of the same problems it had faced in the Soviet Union, with the vehicle's poor mechanical reliability and the Allied materiel superiority limiting its effectiveness. It also saw the introduction of the *Tiger II* and the Allies' significantly improved anti-tank capabilities, most famously the *Sherman Firefly*, which sported the high-velocity 17-Pounder anti-tank gun.[5]

The operations of the *Tiger II* in Hungary from October 1944 to March 1945, provided the vehicle with a much more effective showcase for its abilities, with its improved armour and armament further contributing to the *Tiger* legend. That said, the vehicle did not improve upon the poor mobility and lack of reliability of the *Tiger I*. Operations in Hungary also provided the *Tiger* with its last victories, demonstrating that in the right circumstances, the heavy tank could still be used with great effectiveness, though German weakness and Soviet strength ensured that those victories were both few and fleeting.

The combat experiences of the assorted *Tiger* variants, the *Ferdinand, Sturmtiger* and *Jagdtiger* bear many similarities to their better-known relations. Like the *Tiger*, they suffered from poor mobility and reliability, but it is in their combat performance where there were some differences. The *Ferdinand* was the most successful, but only when employed as a long-range tank destroyer. Attempts to use them outside of this role, most famously in their first use, which saw them employed as assault guns during Operation Zitadelle, proved that the vehicles were too specialized to be used in any way other than designed. This was a stark contrast to the relative flexibility of the *Tiger*. The *Sturmtiger* and *Jagdtiger* also suffered significantly from being overly specialized. Their even greater weight (65 tons and 75 tons respectively) severely limited their use, which meant that they enjoyed very little success, and were easily the worst vehicles in the entire *Tiger* series.

Putting together the different elements of the *Tiger* story, it is clear that the vehicles were technically impressive and that their combat performance did sometimes live up to their post-war reputation, but overall the story is one of failure. The *Tiger* proved too complex to produce in sufficiently large numbers, and its mechanical unreliability made it a vehicle of questionable value. Already lacking a clear doctrinal role, it becomes even less valuable when its high production costs and limited numbers are considered. In the end, whatever success it had was overshadowed by its weaknesses.

TIGER TANK DEVELOPMENT

he *Tiger I* and *Tiger II* were remarkable creations. What was more remarkable was that they were ever built at all. Their development, and the development of other vehicles based on their chassis, was a long and torturous one because of a vehicle selection system that was extremely inefficient. It was marred by the lack of a clear role for a heavy tank, and political interference in the design and the development of vehicles that reflected Hitler's personal whims. His desire to have the biggest vehicles possible, even if those vehicles had little operational value, acted as a drain on an already stressed system. These themes were present throughout the development of the five vehicles that made up the *Tiger* family and each will be dealt with separately, in chronological order. The creation of the *Tiger I* saw an indecisive German Army spend seven years on numerous prototypes without result. Only with Hitler's intervention in 1941, was a clear design chosen. His interference proved more curse than blessing, as his meddling continually led to the modification of proposals from the leading heavy tank designers, Henschel und Sohn and Dr. Ing. h.c. F. Porsche KG. Once Henschel won the production contract for the *Tiger I*, Porsche's design became the basis for the *Ferdinand* tank destroyer. The final vehicle to be based on the *Tiger I*, the *Sturmtiger*, featured an awe-inspiring 380mm rocket launcher. But such a heavy vehicle was not really necessary for urban combat, particularly when the Germans were on the defensive. Even before the *Tiger I* entered service, Hitler wanted a *Tiger II* with more armour and a more powerful gun, despite the fact that there was no indication that the *Tiger I* faced any foe that it could not destroy. The *Jagdtiger*, based on the *Tiger II* chassis was, like the *Sturmtiger*, a testament to the trend Hitler had established to create vehicles that were bigger and better than any conceivable rival even though the vehicle had little to offer a resource strapped army.

To understand why the vehicles of the *Tiger* family became the behemoths that they were, it's important to understand the vehicles that preceded them. Plotting the lineage of the *Tiger* means starting with the first German tanks produced after the First World War. In 1925, the *Heereswaffenamt* (Army Weapons Office), of the Weimar era German army, commissioned Daimler Benz, Rheinmetall and Friedrich Krupp to build the first German tanks since 1918. These vehicles were referred to as the *Grosstraktor* (heavy tractor), in an effort to convince Allied inspectors looking at company records that the Germans were not defying the Treaty of Versailles. Had any inspector seen these tractors for themselves, they would have had no illusions regarding their actual purpose.

Tractors didn't usually weigh 16 tons and most certainly did not have 14mm of armour and a turret with a 75mm gun. The *Grosstraktor* was intended to act as an infantry support tank while the *Leichtetraktor* (light tractor), which was commissioned in 1928, was to be a tank killer.[6] In 1929, while the vehicles were still being developed, the Weapons Office called for a heavier infantry support tank with multiple turrets, imitating the 1926 British Vickers A1E1 *Independent*. Rheinmetall completed two prototypes in 1934, and a further three production vehicles finished in 1935. Since it was being produced at a time when the Nazis were still pretending to abide by the Treaty of Versailles it was christened *Neubaufahrzeug* (new build vehicle). The 23-ton vehicle retained the 14mm of armour found on the *Grosstraktor* but featured three turrets. In the central turret a 75mmgun was fitted along with a coaxial 37mm gun. Two other turrets, one in front of and the other behind the central one, were fitted with machine guns. Once these vehicles were completed, interest in the venture quickly waned as the Germans discovered the same faults with multi-turreted tanks that other powers either already discovered or would discover in the next few years. Vehicles of this type proved to be impossible for commanders to coordinate effectively. Managing the fire of multiple turrets proved impossible. As a result, the *Neubaufahrzeug* was relegated to propaganda duties, with one exception. In April 1940, the three production vehicles were assigned to Panzerbataillon 40, a special unit, for operations in Norway. In their only combat use, one of the vehicles was destroyed after bogging down in a swampy area. They were soon scrapped.[7]

Despite the inauspicious life of the *Neubaufahrzeug*, interest in a heavy tank, both in infantry support and anti-tank roles, continued. In 1935, as the *Neubaufahrzeug* left Rheinmetall, the life of the *Tiger* was beginning. On the 30th of October, General Kurt Liese, head of the *Waffenamt*

[8] authored a report on *Offensive Abwehr von Panzerwagen* (Offensive Defence of Tanks). This report called for a 30-ton tank mounting a high velocity 75mm gun, with over 20mm of armour to counter heavy French tanks of the period. This included the *Char 2C*, a 76-ton tank with 45mm of armour and a 75mm gun, developed by the French in 1917, the heaviest tank in world at the time.[9]

This hypothetical heavy tank posed some engineering problems from the start. It would have been considerably heavier than any other tank the Germans had produced up to that point. Their heaviest tank in 1935, the *Panzer II*, was a light tank of just 8.9 tons and the heavier *Panzer III* and *Panzer IV*, weighing 16 and 17 tons respectively were still in development and wouldn't be ready for testing for another year.[10] Given this much greater weight, there were concerns over the sort of engine needed to move this vehicle. In October and December, representatives of the *Waffenamt* met with Dr. Wilhelm Maybach of Maybach Motorenbau (Maybach Engine Works). Maybach was already providing the rest of the German tanks with their engines and the *Waffenamt* wanted a 700-horsepower V12 engine for this proposed heavy tank. The company's engineers deemed such an engine to be impossible, but a longer sixteen-cylinder engine was considered feasible, although this engine would add an additional half-meter to the tank's length. This additional length also increased the weight, thus removing any horsepower advantage. While Maybach eventually supplied 700-horsepower engines for the *Tiger*, producing such an engine was beyond the firm's capabilities at the time.[11]

Without an engine, the *Waffenamt* abandoned the idea of a heavy tank but not for long. In January of 1937, *Waffen Prüfen 6* (weapons design), the agency responsible for the design of tanks for the army approached Henschel to develop a 30-ton tank. They had previously been one of the manufacturers of the *Panzer I* and were also prominent manufactures of locomotives. This prior experience with both tanks and heavy steel locomotives made them ideal as the designers of a heavy tank. As with the 1935 proposal, this tank was to mount a 75mm gun in a turret to be provided by the famed German gun manufacturer Krupp AG.

Since this vehicle was formally tendered to a company for construction, it was graced with a name, the *Begleitwagen (verstärkt)* (escort vehicle, strengthened). *Begleitwagen* was the same designation given to the *Panzer IV* when that tank had been in development, implying a similar role of infantry support but *verstärkt* denoted a more heavily armoured vehicle. This name was not used for long. On the the12ᵗʰ of March, 1937, it was renamed as the *Durchbruchswagen* (breakthrough vehicle) or *DW*, reflecting its new role. With this third tank, the panzer divisions would have the two faster tanks, the *Panzer III* and *IV*, optimized for the destruction of enemy tanks and infantry support respectively, while the *DW* would facilitate the breakthrough, taking full advantage of its heavier armour, in the process allowing the other two to surge through the hole blasted in the enemy's defences.[12]

To perform this role, the *DW* was to mount the Krupp 75mm Kwk L/24. [13] The same gun was mounted on the *Panzer IV*. This was a sensible decision since the tank's support roles made the short-barreled, lower velocity gun more useful than the higher velocity 37mm gun on the *Panzer III*. It would also have 50mm of hull armour, a significant improvement over the 15mm of hull armour on the *Panzer III* and *IV*.[14]

Once the *DW* design had been finalized in 1938, Henschel had the design approved by the *Waffenamt*, which gave it the designation *VK 30.01* (*Versuchs Kraftfahrzeug*, experimental vehicle). The first pair of numbers referred to the intended weight, while the second two designated different prototypes. The *VK 30.01* came to weigh 32 tons but otherwise had the same attributes as the *DW*, with only one other substantial difference. The *VK 30.01* was the first Henschel tank designed with interleaved road wheels, rather than the five separated road wheels used on the *DW*. This configuration of road wheels became standard not only for the *Tiger* but also the majority of mid-to-late war German armoured vehicles. It better distributed the vehicle's weight across the length of the tracks, which made it easier for the tracks and the suspension to bear the load. It also had the effect of making the vehicle less likely to bog down as the larger surface area of the wheels spread the weight.[15] The big problem with this system was that changing interleaved road wheels was incredibly time consuming. On the *Tiger I* it required between twelve and twenty-four hours to effect repairs, depending on the severity of the damage.[16]

Beginning in June of 1939, the *Waffenamt* asked Krupp to design a turret to take a 105mm gun and in mid 1940, Henschel was ordered to build a hull to mount this turret. Since the *VK 30.01* was too small for this task, a larger vehicle christened *VK 36.01* was created. This new tank featured 80mm of armour on its front plate, with 50mm on the sides and rear. The decision to abandon the *VK 30.01* in favor of the *VK 36.01* was based in part on experience gained in Poland and France, which indicated that the 75mm guns available were inadequate for the breakthrough role. The 105mm gun could certainly be used to great effect against enemy tanks, but as a comparatively low velocity gun, the inclusion of this artillery piece as the tank's main armament suggested that destruction of fortifications was the main role of the *VK 36.01*.[17]

As the first hulls for *VK 30.01* were being built and the *Waffenamt* was calling for a 105mm gun to smash enemy fortifications, another company was working on a heavy tank designed for a very different role. Dr. Ferdinand Porsche had a solid reputation as a carmaker. But his resume obscured Porsche's earlier experience with tank design. While working at Daimler he was the chief designer and project supervisor for that company's *Grosstraktor*, making Porsche a man with significant knowledge of tank design. He was convinced that he could not only build a heavy tank but a vastly superior one. It was the power plant – a pair of gas engines – each of which powered an electrical generator to propel the tank, which would make it superior to the single gas engine used on the Henschel vehicle.[18] This 30-ton tank, known internally as the *Type 100*, was soon under development. Owing to its dual engine design, the power train occupied a considerable amount of space in the rear of the vehicle. It had an unconventional layout with the turret located not in the center of the vehicle as was the norm for German tanks, but much further forward, giving the Porsche design a distinctive look. In April of 1941, Krupp was awarded a contract to provide a turret for *Type 100* sporting the 88mm, a tank gun based on the company's 88mm *Flak 36* anti-aircraft gun.[19]

While no turrets and only one hull for the *Type 100* were ever completed, it nevertheless marked the introduction of the "damned 88s", as the Allies called them, to the *Tiger* fleet.[20] While the weapon's fearsome reputation was largely made later in the war, by April of 1941 it was already a well-established tank killer. During the conquest of France the previous year, the gun had proven itself during the Battle of Arras on the 21st of May. The battle was a British led counterattack against the 7th Panzer Division, the 7th Infantry Regiment and SS Totenkopf Division under *Generalmajor* Erwin Rommel. [21] The 58 *Matilda I* and 16 *Matilda II* from the 4th and 7th Battalions of the Royal Tank Regiment led the British force. Thanks to poor coordination and a lack of reconnaissance, the British tanks quickly outpaced their supporting infantry from the 6th and 8th Battalions of the Durham Light Infantry. The *Matildas* then attacked the German positions unsupported. With 60mm of frontal armour on the *Matilda I* and 78mm of frontal armour on the *Matilda II*, the tanks proved to be immune to fire from the 37mm *Pak 36*, the standard German anti-tank gun. As their shells bounced off the British tank hulls the men of Totenkopf fled. Seeing the need for greater firepower, Rommel personally directed a battery of four Flak guns to fire on the oncoming British. Thanks to Rommel's swift intervention and the high velocity of the Flak guns 88mm shells, over thirty British tanks were destroyed, and the counterattack was defeated.[22] In the process, the 88mm Flak gun's status as a weapon capable of destroying even the best protected Allied tanks was established.

The conflicting designs from Henschel and Porsche in this period spoke to an army that had no clear role for a heavy tank. Henschel's designs were intended for infantry support, with either the 75mm of *VK 30.01* or the 105mm gun of *VK36.01*. By contrast, the high velocity 88mm gun to be mounted to Porsche's *Type 100* – a gun that was best suited to an anti-armour role suggested a vehicle designed more explicitly as a tank killer.

Clarity about the main role of Germany's heavy tank was not obtained until the 26th of May, 1941. On this date Hitler outlined his requirements for a heavy tank, finally committing the *Waffenamt* to a single set of design priorities.[23] After reviewing the vehicles then in development, Hitler ordered that any new heavy tank would be used in a spearhead role and must have a gun with greater penetration capability and heavier armour than any previous tank.[24] These design parameters allowed the new heavy tank to deal not only with the British *Matildas* encountered in France but also Soviet heavy tanks, which had been identified and described in detail by German intelligence in December of 1940.[25]

The 88mm mounted on the *Type 100* was considered acceptable, but Hitler also wanted to explore the possibility of fitting a version of the *Flak 41*, a higher velocity 88mm gun designed by Rheinmetall-Borsig [26] As well, Henschel's *VK 36.01* was to be redesigned to mount the *Waffe 0725*, a tapered bore gun. This gun was similar to the *Pak 41*, a gun with a 75mm breech that narrowed to 55mm at the muzzle. By squeezing the projectile down the barrel, it gained greater velocity and penetration while requiring lighter projectiles. But there was one major problem. This ammunition required tungsten and all of Germany's supplies of this rare metal came from neutral Spain and Sweden. Consequently, Hitler ordered that the gun only be used if sufficient tungsten was available for mass production.[27] Hitler also decreed that both tanks should have 100mm of frontal armour and be ready for testing by the spring of 1942.[28] At this point the parameters for Germany's heavy tanks were finalized at last, creating a fusion of the breakthrough oriented *VK 36.01* and Porsche's tank killing *Type 100*.

Fulfilling Hitler's requirements meant that both companies had to modify their designs to accommodate the armour and weapons required and do so quickly. The final date for submission of the new designs was the 20th of April 1942, Hitler's birthday, less than a year away. Porsche's new design, which the *Waffenamt* dubbed *VK 45.01 (P)* and which the company christened the *Type 101* received the 100mm of frontal armour called for by Hitler, leading to a considerable increase in the vehicle's weight, now tipping the scales at 59 tons.[29] Visually the tank was identical to the *Type 100*, even inheriting the earlier tank's turret, as Porsche and Krupp concluded by September of 1941 that the turret ring was too small to allow the *Flak 41* to be mounted. This fact saved Krupp from the embarrassment of having to mount the Rheinmetall gun in their turret, allowing the company to retain its virtual monopoly on tank guns.[30]

Henschel's entry, the *VK 45.01 (H)* underwent a similar process. The new vehicle retained the final drives, suspension, steering gear, and the interleaved road wheels of *VK36.01* – a valuable addition given the tight time frame the company was working under. As with the Porsche tank, the weight of the vehicle increased significantly to 56 tons in order to accommodate the increased armour. The most substantial change came in September of 1941. Henschel, like Porsche, was forced to reconsider their armament. Fritz Todt, *Reichsminister für Bewaffnung und Munition* (Minister for Armaments and Munitions) had concluded in July of 1941 that out of an available stockpile of 700 tons of tungsten, only 260 tons could be allocated for weapons, with the rest required for tool steel. As each *0725* shell required a kilogram of tungsten, the *Waffe 0725* was not feasible. Henschel and the *Waffenamt* remained wedded to the *Waffe 0725*, nevertheless. Hitler had to intervene personally, forcing them to accept that the weapon was impossible to use, refuting the common trope that "Hitler was solely responsible for the technical dead ends that plagued the armoured forces during the war's second half."[31] With their desired turret unavailable and time running short, Henschel modified the *VK 45.01 (H)* to accept the same Krupp turret, with the 88mm gun as the Porsche tank.[32]

With only eleven months to complete the vehicles, it was a testament to the skill of Porsche's and Henschel's engineers that they were able to redesign their vehicles to accommodate Hitler's wishes. In their initial tests before the Führer on his birthday, no clear winner was determined and both vehicles showed the strain of their rushed production. They both broke down repeatedly and during a speed test in which the Porsche tank reached 50 kilometers per hour and the Henschel 45, the latter vehicle's engine temperature was so high that the company's engineers feared it would burst into flames. Thankfully it didn't, and the tank went on to prove its superior maneuverability.[33] Despite the inconclusive results of the initial testing, both companies handed over their vehicles to the *Waffenamt* for further testing in July. In these tests the Henschel vehicle proved to be superior, especially since the Porsche tank frequently bogged down and broke down.[34]

Henschel may have emerged victorious, but Hitler continued to have an interest in the Porsche vehicle. His interest, combined with the fact that the company had already contracted for 100 tanks, led to a desire to find a role for them. Since the Porsche vehicles were air-cooled Hitler decided in the summer of 1942 that they should be sent to North Africa, though none were dispatched before the Axis position in the region collapsed.[35] In the meantime the first company of *schwere Panzer Abteilungen* 503 (1.503) was equipped with the Porsche *Tiger* for additional testing.[36] While they only kept the vehicles until December, their experiences provided an excellent view of the vehicle and its flaws.

Dr. Franz Wilhelm Lochmann described the vehicle as being very smooth and easy to drive, "like a streetcar."

The 88mm gun was also considered excellent. There were a number of problems as well. With the turret being placed so far forward on the hull, the driver and radio operator lacked hatches of their own. While the vehicle did feature escape hatches in the bottom of the hull, Lochmann was not overstating things when he said that "in the event of trouble, the driver and radio operator had drawn very bad cards." [37] They also experienced the same problems that the *Waffenamt* had in July. Porsche's tank had a greater tendency to bog down, owing to the great weight of the turret over the front of the vehicle. It was also cursed with abundant engine fires, never a glowing recommendation to attach to any vehicle.[38] As the negative reports about the Porsche *Tiger* piled up, Hitler's confidence in the vehicle began to wane. Since 100 vehicles were already being manufactured, and with Hitler's regard for Porsche, a cost and face-saving measure was needed. On the 2nd of September 1942 Hitler declared that the Porsche tanks were to be converted into tank destroyers. At this point Henschel had, for all intents and purposes, won but a formal decision was still considered necessary to placate Porsche. So, in October of 1942, Albert Speer, who had replaced Todt after his death in February, created a *Tiger* Commission. After meeting from the 26th to the 31st the commission became the second and final organization to endorse the Henschel vehicle, as the *Tiger*. The next month, production of the Porsche *Tiger* was halted. This timing worked well. The hulls had been completed and were ready for conversion.[39]

Thus ended the basic development of the *Tiger*. The numerous proposed vehicles and prototypes that preceded it were a testament to an army that struggled to define a clear role and attributes for a heavy tank. Only Hitler's authority ended this uncertainty but as Hitler gave, Hitler also took away and he injected more uncertainty into the proceedings as Henschel and Porsche vied for the *Tiger* contract. His clear preference for the Porsche tank meant that the final decision was delayed for months. Only the many failings of the Porsche vehicle and the early availability of the Henschel vehicle prevented the process from being dragged out further.

At the 2nd of September 1942 meeting where the Porsche tank was ordered to be converted into a tank destroyer, Hitler again called for some changes. He wanted 200mm of frontal armour, and the mounting of the Rheinmetall *Flak 41*, the gun Hitler had wanted to be fitted to the *Tiger*. Krupp provided this in the form of the 88mm *Pak 43 L/71* in March of 1943.[40] This gun had a higher velocity than the previous 88mm, allowing it to penetrate the frontal armour of a *T-34* from over 3,500 meters, rather than the 1,500 meters possible with the earlier gun.[41] Fulfilling Hitler's orders required the work of three firms: Altmärkische Kettenwerk GmbH (Alkett), Nibelungenwerk and Eisenwerk Oberdonau.

Design of the vehicle went to Alkett. This firm had extensive experience with tank destroyers and assault guns, having been the primary manufacturer of the *StuG III* since 1940 (*Sturmgeschütze*, assault gun).[42] To accommodate the much larger gun, the vehicle was designed as a casemate tank destroyer, with the gun mounted in a non-rotating fighting compartment. While this design decision limited the vehicle's flexibility, since the entire vehicle needed to turn to traverse the gun outside of the limited degree of rotation, it allowed the vehicle to be produced more quickly. Further, it allowed the mounting a larger gun unencumbered by the additional machinery needed for a turret. For balance, the fighting compartment was placed over the rear of the vehicle, with the gun extending out over the front of the hull. Nibelungenwerk in St. Valentin Austria had been awarded the original Porsche contract and had completed the vehicles' hulls and running gears, which were to be retained. But these hulls needed to be reconfigured before being used since the original vehicle had the engines and electrical generators mounted in the rear. To make room for the new fighting compartment, the engine compartment was moved forward into the middle of the vehicle.

This work was completed by Eisenwerk Oberdonau, a steel workshop in Linz, near the Nibelungenwerk. Once the hulls had been modified, they were initially to be sent to Alkett for final assembly, but Speer ordered them to be returned to Nibelungenwerk in February of 1943 to simplify production. The 200mm armour thickness was achieved by adding another 100mm armour plate onto the hull's original 100mm thick front plate. This addition, along with the new gun and the new fighting compartment gave the vehicle a weight of 68.5 tons.[43] On the 6th of February 1943, during a Führer conference the name *Ferdinand* was chosen for the vehicle, to acknowledge Dr. Porsche's contributions.[44]

The development of the *Ferdinand* certainly reflected the desire on Hitler's part to compensate Porsche for the loss of the *Tiger* contract but there were other factors involved in making their conversion an attractive prospect. Normally when a vehicle was not accepted, any completed prototypes, even if they were only finished chassis, were retained either by the company for testing or by the army for training purposes. Porsche kept a sole *Type 100* chassis for testing purposes, especially for insights into air-cooled tank engines.[45] Henschel's *VK 36.01* prototype had a similar fate, being given to Maybach for engine trials.[46] With the very limited production of these failed prototypes, retaining them as training or test vehicles made sense, to avoid wasting materiel and with the possibility of gleaning valuable insights for future production.

When more vehicles were finished before production was halted however, their fates became more varied. Henschel's *VK 30.01* had eight hulls finished by July of 1940, before production was halted in favor of the heavier *VK 36.01*.[47] One of the hulls remained at Henschel as a test vehicle, while another five were used as training vehicles. Two were handed over to Rheinmetall, which lengthened the chassis and fitted them with a 128mm gun. These vehicles, named the *Sturer Emil*, were test beds for the mounting of 128mm guns and went on to see service on the Eastern Front. One was destroyed in 1942 and the other was captured.[48] The two *VK 30.01* hulls converted into the *Sturer Emil* would be the only of the *Tiger* predecessors from Henschel to see combat service.

These precedents were of little use in the case of the *VK 45.01 (P)*. Porsche had produced 100 vehicles and since the Porsche's dual engine, electrical generator powertrain was unique it was of dubious value as a training vehicle, so another role needed to be found. Their conversion into tank destroyers was the best available option because by the time development started in September of 1942, it was clear that the war would last for at least one more year if not more, and that Germany was being out-produced by her enemies.

That year Germany produced 6,094 AFVs, while Great Britain, the United States and the Soviet Union produced a combined 60,364 AFVs.[49] Thus, the potential for 90 new tank destroyers (the other ten were finished to the original *VK.45.01 (P)* specifications and were used mostly for testing and training purposes), was not something that could be passed up. As *Generaloberst* (Colonel General) Heinz Guderian put it after inspecting the finished vehicles in May of 1943, before their first use during Operation Zitadelle in July, "I also had to use it, even though from a technical standpoint, I could not share Hitler's enthusiasm over the creations of his favorite Porsche." [50]

After the development of the *Ferdinand* there would be a final vehicle connected to the *Tiger I*, the 380mm *Sturmmörserwagen* (assault mortar vehicle), better known as the *Sturmtiger*. This vehicle emerged from a 5th of August 1943 meeting where Hitler agreed to create a "Tiger Mortar." It was to be a heavy assault gun, with the armour and armament to support infantry in urban environments. [51] Two previous vehicles had already been built along the same lines. The *Sturminfanteriegeschütze 33B* (infantry assault gun) developed in the fall of 1942, which was a modification of the *StuG III*, mounting the 150mm *sIG 33* howitzer. Mounting such a weapon was intended to give the *StuG* greater firepower. This focus was the result of the ongoing Battle of Stalingrad, where the majority of these vehicles were used and lost. [52] A second vehicle, the *Sturmpanzer* (assault tank) was developed in the same period, using the *Panzer IV* hull, and sporting a short-barreled 150mm *StuH 43* gun in a ball mount, a weapon using the same shell as the 150mm *sIG 33*. [53]

While both of these vehicles served fairly well, the *Sturmtiger* was born out of a belief that these previous vehicles were not sufficiently armoured for close-range engagements in urban environments and that the gun should be capable of toppling buildings with a single round. Given that by this time the Germans were increasingly on the defensive, the wisdom of constructing such a vehicle was debatable. The fact that production was pursued, despite Germany's reversal of fortune, reflects a sense of desperate optimism that Hitler insisted upon until the war's end.

To create this vehicle Alkett was given 18 *Tiger I* hulls in 1944. These were recycled hulls, remnants of tanks that were so badly damaged that they had been returned to Germany for repair or scrapping. This decision was not an effort at recycling per se, but was done at the behest of the army, which was extremely reluctant to give up any *Tiger* production for the project. Alkett built a superstructure atop the hulls, with a 150mm thick front plate, creating a 65-ton vehicle. The gun was the 380mm *Raketenwerfer 61* (rocket launcher). This weapon, originally designed for the German navy as a depth charge launcher, was more than powerful enough to level virtually any building it hit. However, the rounds were so large that only 12 could be carried. The vehicle had to have a crane attached to the engine deck to facilitate its resupply. This was not considered a serious drawback given the nature of the vehicle's task since, unlike a conventional tank, it was unlikely to venture far from its supply base.[54] The *Sturmtiger* was the most exotic of the *Tiger* variants, although far from the most useful.

Turning now to the development of the *Tiger II*, it is necessary to return to the summer of 1941. As discussed previously, the 26th of May 1941, meeting between Hitler and senior armaments officials had seen Hitler's requirements for a heavy tank outlined, requirements that led to the production of the *Tiger I*. The invasion of the Soviet Union, less than a month after this meeting helped to spur the development of another heavy tank, which became the *Tiger II*.

On the 22nd of June 1941, Germany invaded the Soviet Union in Operation Barbarossa. Soon after, the Germans began to encounter two new Soviet tanks, the *T-34* medium tank and the *KV-1* heavy tank. These vehicles were superior in armour and armament to the Germans tanks. The OKH had been aware of the *T-34* since the previous December but had no knowledge of the *KV-1* prior to the invasion.[55]

Encounters with the *KV-1* and the *T-34* demonstrated the shortcomings of German tank weapons in dramatic fashion. The 6th Panzer Division encountered the *KV-1* during its defence of Raseiniai on the 24th of June. A lone *KV-1* broke through the division's lines and sat astride the road acting as the division's sole supply line. The 3rd Battery of *Panzerjäger* (anti-tank) Battalion 41 arrived with the new 50mm *Pak 38* guns. After scoring eight hits at 600 meters, the *KV-1* responded, destroying two of the guns and badly damaging two others. As one of the division's officers, Erhard Raus recalled, "Deeply depressed, *Leutnant* Wegenroth [the *Pak* commander] returned to the bridgehead with his soldiers. His newly introduced weapon, in which he had felt absolute confidence, had proven completely inadequate against the monster tank." [56]

An effort to destroy the Soviet tank using a nighttime attack by engineers with satchel charges failed, and the next day an 88mm Flak was brought in, with cover provided by fire from the division's *Panzer 35(t)*s. Even this heavy weapon proved insufficient, and the Soviet crew was finally dispatched by a grenade lobbed through the hatch. Once the crew had been removed from the vehicle and buried with full honours befitting their dogged defiance of an entire division their battered tank was inspected. Only two penetrating hits were found, unsurprisingly both were from the 88mm Flak. What was surprising was that five of the rounds had failed to penetrate, leaving deep gouges in the armour. Eight "blue spots" marked the impacts of the 50mm *Pak* rounds. The engineers' charges had damaged one of the tracks and had left a "slight dent in the gun barrel." Most frightening of all was the fact that no trace of any of the 37mm rounds fired by the *Panzer 35(t)* could be found.[57]

Encounters like these eroded the confidence that many German tankers had in their tanks and more specifically their guns. *Gefreiter* (Corporal) Robert Pönsgen of the 9th Panzer Division, a loader in a *Panzer III* armed with the short 50mm gun, the best tank gun available for most of 1941, said that this tank was "popularly and properly known as the army doorknocker." [58] Comments like these spurred the development of longer barreled and higher velocity guns in the same calibres for the *Panzer III* and *Panzer IV*. In December of 1941 the first of these, the *Panzer III ausf J* (*Ausführung*, version) was introduced.[59] In early 1942, the *Panzer IV ausf F2* followed.[60]

These improvements did much to restore the confidence of the average soldier. They also had an impact on the nascent *Tiger*. Reports coming back from the front lines reinforced the wisdom of developing a heavy tank to deal with the *KV-1*, something that *VK45.01 (P)* and *VK45.01 (H)* could do thanks to the armour and armament requirements outlined in May. Even though Hitler's requirements for the *Tiger* had provided a vehicle that could take on the new Soviet tanks, he was not entirely satisfied. By September of 1941 he began to call for a higher performance weapon. The change in Hitler's views resulted from consideration of a number of different factors. One was that while the *Flak 37* had performed very well against the new Soviet tanks, there were exceptions, including the decidedly mixed performance of the gun as noted by Raus. However, it was Hitler's personal philosophy of tank design that proved to be a decisive factor. After the appearance of the *T-34*, the initial plan proposed was to either copy the *T-34* wholesale or produce a vehicle that could outmaneuver the Soviet tank. Neither solution satisfied Hitler, who had determined that it was not speed and maneuverability that were decisive, but rather armour and armament. In his memoir, Speer recalled that Hitler's favorite way to describe this philosophy was to use the analogy of warships:

> *In a naval battle the side having the greater range can open fire at the greater distance. Even if it is only half a mile. If along with this he has stronger armour... He must necessarily be superior. What are you after? The faster ship has only one advantage: to utilize its greater speed for retreating. Do you mean to say a ship can possibly overcome heavier armour and superior artillery by greater speed? It's exactly the same for tanks. Your faster tank has to avoid meeting the heavier tank.[61]*

With such a philosophy, Hitler was dissatisfied with the attributes of the *Tiger I* and called for a more heavily armed and armoured version in keeping with his beliefs. By September of 1941, Porsche and Krupp had already informed the *Waffenamt* that there was no way to fit the *Flak 41* into the *Tiger I* turret. The *Flak 41* not only required a larger gun mount, but the engineers also needed to find ways to balance this larger, longer weapon, protect the recoil cylinders, traverse the gun, and find space in the turret to handle the larger projectiles. These problems proved to be insurmountable given the space available in the *VK 45.01* vehicles.[62] Hitler was not satisfied with this answer and pressured Fritz Todt to get the *Flak 41* into the *Tiger*. The letter that Todt sent to General Emil Leeb, the head of the *Waffenamt*, on the 23rd of September 1941 is an excellent example of the pressure Hitler was exerting to achieve this dream:

> *I must inform you that every time I see Hitler, he repeatedly asks if in reality the highly effective Flak 41 will be installed... Hitler does not feel confident that*

> *another 88 mm gun design can be used instead of the*
> *Flak 41. Hitler wants the Flak 41 installed in the new*
> *heavy panzer without any degrading modifications. I*
> *bring to your attention today that we will have to expect*
> *the strongest objections from Hitler if one day during*
> *the first demonstration, the Panzer has a gun other*
> *than the Flak 41.*[63]

With this less than subtle encouragement, the *Waffenamt* turned to Porsche and Henschel to begin to develop a tank that mounted a tank gun based on the *Flak 41*. Porsche was the first to respond in January of 1942. Their vehicle, known internally as the *Type 180* and as *VK.45.02 (P)* by the *Waffenamt,* was effectively an enlarged *VK 45.01 (P)*. It retained the engine and suspension of the earlier vehicle. The only major changes were the new turret, which was to be another Krupp design, featuring a rounded front plate and a modification to the armour. Instead of the 100mm vertical plate of frontal armour, the *VK 45.02 (P)* featured a 55-degree angled plate of 80mm. This change in the layout was inspired by Porsche's knowledge of the designs being submitted for *VK 30.02*, which would later become the *Panther*. This was insider knowledge stemming from his position as the head of the *Panzerkommission*, which was overseeing the design of German tanks at the time.[64]

While Porsche was developing *VK 45.02 (P)*, Henschel lagged behind, only starting work on their *VK 45.02 (H)* in April of 1942. This delay was due to the continued work on the *VK 45.01 (H)* and on the *VK 36.01*, which was halted only in March of 1942 with one hull finished for testing purposes. These delays badly affected the Henschel prototype, which never progressed past a few drawings, and the company abandoned the project quickly. In November, work on *VK 45.03* began. This was a more serious effort by Henschel to develop a new heavy tank. The new tank retained the suspension and drive train of *VK 45.01 (H)*. Like the Porsche vehicle, *VK 45.03* featured a new turret from Krupp, with a unique design featuring a flat frontal plate. Henschel also followed Porsche's lead and sloped the frontal armour on the tank's hull to 50 degrees while retaining the 100mm thick plates found on their previous vehicle.[65]

As Henschel began to work on their second attempt to create a new heavy tank, Porsche was well on its way to exiting the competition. It lacked a viable engine. To power the 65-ton vehicle, Porsche designed a power plant similar to one in the *VK 45.01 (P)* with two Porsche Type 101/3 ten-cylinder engines connected to a pair of electrical generators, which would in turn powered two electrical motors, each connected to a drive sprocket. These engines proved to be insufficiently powerful and so in October of 1942, Porsche began design work on five different engines in an effort to extract as much horsepower as possible. Just one month later, Porsche was forced to concede that none of his company's engines were sufficiently powerful, and contracts placed with Krupp to provide turrets and armour plate were cancelled, as were contracts with Nibelungenwerk. Ferdinand Porsche's efforts to build a heavy tank had ended unceremoniously The only company left that could fulfill Hitler's wishes was Henschel.[66]

Before Henschel could provide Hitler with a new heavy tank, he once again changed its specifications. During a conference with Speer on the 3rd of January 1943, Hitler decided that while he was satisfied with the longer 88mm gun being developed by Krupp, he was dissatisfied with the 100mm front plate that Henschel was proposing for *VK 45.03* and instead wanted a 150mm front plate. In keeping with Hitler's wishes, the plans for *VK 45.03* were duly modified to accommodate a 150mm thick front plate, sloped at 50 degrees. This change added 1,760 kilograms to the tank's weight, helping to turn what was to be a 45-ton vehicle into a 68-ton vehicle.[67]

It is a testament to Hitler's fixation on a replacement for the *Tiger I* that this discussion was taking place just six months after the operational debut of the *Tiger*. At this point only 111 *Tiger* had been built and just two units, Panzerbataillonen 502 and 503 were using them in the field. The limited experience of these units had been sufficient to demonstrate the vehicle's strengths, especially in the areas of armour and armament. Raus recalled that after the *Tiger* was introduced, German troops remarked, "the *T-34* tips its hat whenever it meets the *Tiger*", a reference to the ability of the 88mm guns to blow the turrets off the *T-34*, something that could be done at ranges of over 1,000 meters.[68]

The armour, too, had been well proven at this point. Richard *Freiherr* von Rosen described the armour on the *Tiger* as "almost a life assurance." [69] This was a far cry from the way Otto Carius described the armour on his first tank, a *Panzer 38(t)*, "[it] would only serve as moral support. If necessary, it would stop small arms fire." [70] Despite these endorsements, Hitler remained fixated on the purely hypothetical *Tiger II*. Guderian recalled that Hitler nominally conceded to the experts, including himself, that armour was a secondary consideration, with armament and speed being the first and second considerations in tank design, "but he was a paradoxical man, and he continued to insist that heavy armour was also a primary requirement." [71]

This fixation on armour did not stop with the *Tiger II* but lasted until the end of the war, becoming in Guderian's words, "[a] fantasy [which] led him into the realms of the gigantic", culminating in the *Panzer VII*, known as the *Maus* (Mouse, the name was deliberately ironic), which sported a

128mm gun and 200mm of frontal armour. At 188 tons there was not a single bridge in Europe it could cross and remains the heaviest tank ever built. Only two prototypes were finished before the end of the war, making it the largest monument to Hitler's obsession with heavy tanks.[72] The *Tiger II*, at a mere 68 tons, was at least a more practical vehicle, though hardly less of a reminder of Hitler's technical folly.

In February of 1943, Krupp received the contract to build the long 88mm gun Hitler had so long desired. The 88mm shared the performance of the Rheinmetall *Flak 41*, with both guns being capable of penetrating 148mm of armour at 1,500 meters but nothing else. Krupp's gun was shorter, at 62.98cm, than the Rheinmetall 65.48cm gun. The two guns were further differentiated by Krupp's inclusion of a muzzle brake to assist with recoil.[73] With a gun finally ready to be fitted, it was now down to Henschel to finish designing the tank. The *VK45.03*, was approved by the army in January of 1944. The new tank was then christened the *Tiger II*. Hitler finally had the heavily armoured tank with a long 88mm gun that he had wanted since 1941.[74]

One final *Tiger* variant, based on the chassis of the *Tiger II* remains to be examined, the *Jagdtiger*. This tank destroyer, unlike the other members of the *Tiger* family, was not created to satisfy the wishes of Adolf Hitler but came from soldiers serving in the East. They wanted a "heavy assault gun with 128mm cannon" to be able to support infantry and engage both unarmoured and armoured targets at up to 3,000 meters.[75] This view was supported by OKH, which put in an official request to Krupp to fit a 128mm gun to the *Tiger II* chassis. This decision was made despite the fact that at this point, in early in 1943, there was no enemy tank in service that required a gun of this size to destroy it, nor would there ever be a similar Allied tank. Its development was therefore based less on countering a current or anticipated threat but was instead built to preserve German technical superiority regardless of practical need. Thus, on the 5th of February 1943, development began despite the fact that there was no compelling operational reason to do so. The new vehicle was based on the chassis of *VK 45.03*, which was lengthened by 26 cm to accommodate Krupp's 128mm gun. Due to the size and weight of the gun, the *Jagdtiger*, like the *Ferdinand* was designed as a casemate tank destroyer, which was the only way to transport the gun. The vehicle also featured 250mm of frontal armour, angled at 75 degrees. These features made the *Jagdtiger* the best protected and most powerfully armed vehicle fielded by the Germans during the war, as well as being the heaviest, at 75 tons.[76]

As with most of the members of the *Tiger* family *Jagdtiger* development was marred by political interference. In January of 1944, Ferdinand Porsche made his final foray into tank design, convincing Hitler to accept his plan for the suspension of the new tank destroyer. Rather than keeping the interleaved road wheels and transverse torsion bar suspension from the *Tiger II*, Porsche's suspension featured pairs of road wheels in wheel trucks, suspended from longitudinal torsion bars, a system similar to that found on Porsche's earlier designs. Porsche's name and influence were far from the only things that made this new system attractive. His suspension also cut 1,200 kg from the vehicle's weight, 450 work hours, and 80 cm of ground clearance. Best of all, it offered a cost savings of 404,000 Reichsmarks.[77] Unfortunately, Porsche's bad luck with tanks would continue. His running gear had many advantages but when two prototypes were tested in May 1944, one with the Porsche running gear and the other with the Henschel, things did not go well for the carmaker. The *Jagdtiger* fitted with the Porsche running gear caused an "almost unbearable" shaking in the suspension and so the traditional Henschel running gear won out.[78] In spite of this failure, the Porsche suspension was still fitted to the first nine production vehicles to use up the supply of parts and ensure timely delivery of vehicles. With the first *Jagdtiger* coming off the production line at Nibelungenwerk in July of 1944, the story of the *Tiger* development was finally at an end.[79]

The development of the *Tiger* series of vehicles from 1935 to 1944 exposed a number of problems. Not only was the development of these vehicles complex and subject to delays as necessary technologies proved ineffective in their intended roles (as seen with the engines on Porsche's *VK45.02* and the *Jagdtiger* running gear), but it was also heavily influenced by not only traditional motivating factors like organizational needs, but also individual whims, most of them Hitler's. The indecision of both the army and its *Waffenamt* over the role of a heavy tank led to seven years without a design being selected, despite numerous prototypes being developed and discarded. Only Hitler's personal intervention finally created a concrete set of design parameters. Unfortunately, Hitler's continued interference in the design process led to the great weight of the *Tiger I* and would create the *Tiger II*, even though there was no evidence that the performance of the *Tiger I* was poor enough to warrant a new vehicle.

A perception that German vehicles needed to be bigger and incontrovertibly superior to all possible Allied foes led to the development of the *Sturmtiger* and the *Jagdtiger*, despite the fact that neither vehicle allowed the army to fulfill some pressing operational need. Only the *Ferdinand* could be said to be filling an urgent need as there was a desperate need for any kind of armoured vehicle that German industry could supply in 1943. The tank destroyers proved to be highly effective in the defensive war the army was fighting from that point onward (whether the *Ferdinand* was truly effective in this role was another matter, discussed fully in Chapter 9).

This long process paints a picture of a vehicle selection and development system that was deeply dysfunctional, one lacking clear vision, wasting resources on projects of dubious value and highly susceptible to political interference. It was a testament to the designers of these vehicles that despite the dysfunction that surrounded them, they were nevertheless able to create functional vehicles. The question of how these new vehicles would be used operationally was another matter entirely.

PANZER DOCTRINE

y the time the design parameters for the *Tiger I* were finalized by Hitler on the 26th of May 1941, finally creating a clear vision for Germany's heavy tanks, the *Panzerwaffe* (Armoured Force) had a well-established and battle-tested doctrine. Ironically, this doctrine had no real need for a heavy tank like the *Tiger*. The emphasis was on speed and maneuver. Thus, the incorporation of the *Tiger* into the army did not reflect the filling of a necessary doctrinal void. Instead, it represented a sort of "covering of the bases," to counter enemy heavy tanks and fulfill a breakthrough role, which the doctrine's emphasis on maneuver made largely redundant in the circumstances of the time. In the early years of the war, neither side was constructing anti-armour defences in sufficient depth to make a breakthrough tank necessary. By 1943, when defences were arranged in sufficient depth to give heavy tanks more of a role, Germany was firmly on the defensive, leaving the *Tiger* with few opportunities to perform its designated role.

Panzer doctrine, like all German doctrine of the time, was the fusion of centuries-old Prussian doctrine with modern technology. Created after 1919 by the *Heeres Amt* (Army Office), the emphasis was on speed, maneuver, and surprise. These three key elements were reflected in both of the tanks of the interwar period, the *Panzer III* and *IV*, which were to become the mainstays of the *Panzerwaffe*, as well as the army's teachings.

The tanks and their associated doctrine would be vindicated in spectacular fashion during the French Campaign of 1940. The Germans were able to outflank the main Allied armies and the vaunted Maginot Line with a surprise attack through the Ardennes Forest. Then the ability of the tanks to outmaneuver and surprise their foes allowed them to smash through Allied positions, driving to the English Channel and winning one of the greatest German victories of the Second World War.[80] Paradoxically, by 1941 Germany was ready to begin building a heavy tank that was incompatible with their successful doctrine. A doctrine which had demonstrated that there was no compelling need for a heavy tank.

The basis of Prusso-German doctrine was summed up well by one of Germany's best Second World War generals, *General der Panzertruppe* (General of Armoured Troops) Hermann Balck:

> *The German ideas about war were derived from the geographical position of Prussia and Germany, which faced superior enemies all around and unsecured borders. In order to survive they had to be faster than their enemies, stay ahead of them, and hit them decisively at a vulnerable point with locally superior forces.*[81]

The doctrine was known as *Bewegungskrieg* or war of movement. Commanders used maneuver to strike at an enemy's most vulnerable point. The doctrine also embraced the century-old concept of *Auftragstaktik* or what NATO now calls Mission Command. This Prussian concept expected junior leaders to exercise a great deal of initiative and aggression to attain their objectives without detailed instructions from more senior leaders or higher headquarters.[82]

These concepts had served the Prussians well and continued to serve their German successors until 1914, when the First World War forced them to adapt them to suit the new realities of twentieth century warfare. The descent of the Western Front into a *Stellungskrieg* or positional war demanded new solutions to overcome the devastating effects of machine guns and modern artillery. One solution adopted by the Germans was *Stoßtruppen* or storm troopers, elite soldiers that would lead the breakthrough of Allied positions combining hand grenades and sub machine guns with the aggression, speed, and the initiative of the traditional German system.[83]

Another solution, embraced by both sides, was the tank. The British were the first to adopt them and deployed tanks for the first time on September 15, 1916, at Flers-Courcelette, France during the Battle of the Somme.[84] The first German tank, the *A7V* followed in May of 1917.[85] In Denis Showalter's assessment, it remains a "clear front runner for the title of 'ugliest tank ever built' and a strong contender in the 'most dysfunctional' category." [86] These less than glowing remarks reflect its high box like profile. It was a formidable weapon with one 57mm gun and six machine guns, but the eighteen-man crew proved almost impossible to manage.[87] The tank's performance was further hampered by vulnerability to artillery due to its slow speed and frequent breakdowns.[88]

The German Army's Chief of Staff, Erich Ludendorff found little to encourage greater production at the expense of other, more proven weapons. Despite Ludendorff's skepticism, there were those within the army who believed that the tank had potential. *Generalleutnant* (Lieutenant General) Wilhelm Balck, [89] who commanded the 51st Division, described the tank as being "at first a grossly underestimated weapon" that became "an extremely potent attack weapon."[90]

The Eastern Front saw no clashes of armour during the First World War but offered a different kind of fighting from the Western Front. Since operations were conducted in the great open spaces of Russia, there were numerous opportunities for a traditional war of maneuver. One of the best examples of this mobile war was in November of 1916. After Romania entered the war on the Allied side, Germany launched an invasion of Romania. Pushing through the Transylvanian Mountains, the Germans ran into a strong Romanian position in the Iron Gate region of the Danube Delta. To overcome this position, *General der Infanterie* Erich von Falkenhayn assembled a combined arms battle group under *Hauptmann* (Captain) Alfred Picht. Picht's battlegroup had simple instructions: "Open the Iron Gate."[91] Picht brought his forces up to the Romanian positions at night, drove through a weak sector and positioned himself in the enemy's rear. After fending off a number of counterattacks and with German reinforcements arriving, the Romanians were forced to withdraw.[92] *Hauptmann* Picht's penetration of the Romanian lines suggested that with lower-level initiative there was scope for infiltration and exploitation even when faced with seemingly significant defences.

After the war, the *Reichswehr*, under the guidance of its new Chief of Staff, *Generaloberst* Hans von Seeckt, set about to institutionalize the lessons learned from the experiences of the First World War. Von Seeckt was an Eastern Front veteran and firmly believed that the traditional system could still be successful in a mechanized world. From von Seeckt's perspective, the mass armies of the Great War were too large and vulnerable to the enormously destructive power of artillery and machine guns. Thus, the *Reichswehr* needed only to be large enough to survive a surprise attack. Then its superior ability to maneuver would allow it to destroy any attacker. He wrote that "mass becomes immobile, it cannot maneuver and therefore cannot win victories, it can only crush through sheer weight."[93]

The *Reichswehr* quickly adopted von Seeckt's beliefs, not just out of conviction but also because the Treaty of Versailles limited it to 100,000 men, leaving few alternatives other than innovation as a means to overcome quantitative inferiority. German military leadership became firmly committed to maneuver and combined arms as the keys to victory. After a short time, the tank was added to this traditional doctrine – even though the Treaty of Versailles banned them. In 1924, training maneuvers featured no actual tanks, merely wooden mockups on bicycles, but their presence was still important. For these maneuvers a blue infantry division and a cavalry division were tasked with countering a red force that was crossing the Oder River. Blue was ordered to envelop Red's left (southern) wing as it crossed the Oder. Meanwhile Red enveloped Blue's right (northern) wing as they crossed the river. As both forces worked to envelop the other's flank a Blue cavalry regiment was able to charge at the flank of two Red artillery batteries. Before they could complete this potentially devastating maneuver, a new Red force, including a number of tanks, flanked the Blue cavalry. Blue's position was only salvaged by a renewed cavalry thrust that outflanked Red's advance guard and penetrated into the enemy's rear.[94] This exercise demonstrated the value of tanks in a supporting role while also re-emphasizing the premium that the *Reichswehr* placed on maneuver.

The 1928 maneuvers represented the Germany's nascent armoured corps in transition. In these maneuvers, the tanks were divided into three waves. The first two broke through the enemy line, driving deep into the rear to strike at enemy artillery. Meanwhile, the third wave remained with the infantry. Once the exercise was over, the Exercise Director, Otto von Stülpnagel, Chief of Motorized Troops, drew an important conclusion: The infantry must be kept with the first wave of tanks so that their weapons could support the tanks and prevent enemy infantry from simply waiting for the tanks to pass them before engaging the oncoming infantry. The necessity of close co-operation between infantry and tanks had been confirmed, but working towards fully independent armoured units with organic infantry components was not yet something the *Reichswehr* was ready for.[95]

In 1929, the army gained access to a tremendous new resource, the Kazan Tank School. Here, deep in the Soviet Union and far from the prying eyes of Allied inspectors, the Germans began to test actual tanks. The school was the result of negotiations between the two governments, trading German technical expertise for Soviet space to develop technologies made illegal under the Treaty of Versailles. Only at Kazan could the secretly built tanks, referred to as "tractors" to fool Allied inspectors, be tested.[96] Von Stülpnagel wrote glowingly about Kazan and its potential:

> *[Kazan] is at the present time the only place where really positive work on the area of tanks can be achieved. Clear insight into the true worth of the tank, the effect of its weapons, the possibilities of its employment, the tactics*

to follow etc., can only be acquired there, with the actual material. The most detailed study of foreign literature, the best theoretical reflections, and well-prepared experimental exercises with tank mock-up units, can only yield an approximate value.[97]

Von Stülpnagel was quite correct. The writings of British theorists like J.F.C. Fuller and B.H. Liddell Hart were important but remained theoretical. Various tank mock-ups, which had been serving the army for a decade were likewise of great use in visualizing this forbidden technology. However, since they were only mock-ups, their speed, size and capabilities were always wildly different from those of actual tanks.[98]

It was here that the *Grosstraktor* and *Leichtetraktor,* discussed in the previous chapter, were tested. The 16-ton *Grosstraktor* with a 75mm gun was designed as an infantry support tank while the *Leichtetraktor* weighing 8.9 tons and mounting a 37mm gun was intended to be a tank killer.[99] This separation of roles was in line with conventional thinking in the late 1920s. Tanks were still viewed as being primarily for infantry support with the heavy tanks acting in the same way as their First War counterparts, breaking through enemy defences. Then, the light tanks would support and exploit the breakthrough.[100]

With their first tanks in production and the beginnings of a doctrine, the practical birth of the panzer division soon followed. This birth came in a series of exercises overseen by *Generalmajor* Oswald Lutz, the Inspector of Motor Transport Troops in 1931 and 1932. In these exercises, a full battalion of tanks was created, alongside supporting motorized infantry. Emphasis was placed on the importance of massing tanks for the greatest effect. The exercise resulted in some novel conclusions. Lutz and his chief of staff, Heinz Guderian, concluded that not only speed but also surprise and constant movement were needed to facilitate and sustain breakthroughs. They also stressed the importance of ensuring that the infantry was moving at the speed of the tank to maintain the momentum of the attack and to allow for full exploitation of the breakthrough. Based on these maneuvers, Lutz and Guderian developed the modus operandi of the panzer division in 1932, embracing the traditional German emphasis on aggression and combined-arms operations, and combing these with fully mechanized and motorized units to create an extraordinarily powerful tool for *Bewegungskrieg*.[101] The new tank doctrine was summarized in Guderian's oft repeated mantra of *Klotzen, nicht kleckern*.[102]

On the 30th of January 1933 Adolf Hitler became Chancellor of Germany. Soon after, Guderian had an opportunity to showcase a platoon of *Panzer I* tanks, then in the prototype stage. Guderian recorded, "Hitler was much impressed by the speed and precision of movement of our units and said repeatedly: 'That's what I need! That's what I want to have!'"[103] Hitler's endorsement was certainly a boost to the development of tanks and in 1935, the 1st, 2nd and 3rd Panzer Divisions were created. These new divisions were exceptionally well equipped. Each division contained two tank regiments, and each regiment contained two *Panzer Abteilungen* (battalions). Each battalion was divided into four *Panzer Kompanien* (companies) divided into three *leichte Panzer Kompanien*, (light companies) with tanks designed to combat enemy tanks and a *mittlere Panzer Kompanie* (medium company), tasked with providing infantry support.[104] All told, each division had a staggering 561 tanks and also contained a motorized infantry regiment, also of two battalions, a motorized artillery regiment, a motorcycle battalion, a motorized reconnaissance battalion, a motorized pioneer battalion and a motorized anti-tank battalion. In the words of Richard Ogorkiewicz, a panzer division was a "self-contained combined arms team in which tanks were backed by other arms brought up, as far as possible, to the tank's standard of mobility."[105]

To outfit the divisions properly, three new tanks were in development throughout the 1930s. These were in addition to a training tank, the 5.4-ton *Panzer I*.[106] The *Panzer II*, a 7.6-ton vehicle with a 20mm cannon acted as the *Panzeraufklärung* or divisional reconnaissance vehicle.[107] The 15.4-ton *Panzer III* filled the light companies, using its 37mm gun to combat enemy tanks while the 17-ton *Panzer IV* was assigned to the medium companies, employing its 75mm gun in an infantry support role.[108] In combat, the light companies would be employed first, piercing the enemy line with the motorized infantry, engaging any enemy tanks and thereafter striking into "the heart of the enemy battle zone."[109] The medium companies would follow, using their firepower to reduce enemy strongpoints and to facilitate the advance of the light companies and the infantry, all the while protecting the flanks of the advancing units.[110] As conceived in the mid 1930s, the *Panzer Abteilung* or tank battalion was a powerful force, with a good mixture of vehicles. They were equipped fulfill an offensive role, with a capacity to both engage enemy tanks and facilitate an infantry breakthrough. While the division's anti-tank battalion was certainly part of the former category, the prominence of the light tank companies indicated that a high premium was placed on the ability of the tanks to combat other tanks, rather than relying on anti-tank guns, which were to be used in a purely defensive role.[111]

This system was not one that had an explicit need for anything heavier than a *Panzer IV*. That said, the concept of a heavy tank had not been neglected. As described in the previous chapter, the *Neubaufahrzeug* had been in development since 1929, to offer the Germans a heavy breakthrough tank. While the project was canceled in 1934 as impractical, it nevertheless demonstrated that the idea of a heavy tank was something that had been under consideration for some time, though not without a considerable amount of confusion over the specifics of its role.[112]

The *Waffenamt* initial proposal from 1935 envisioned a heavy tank specifically designed to counter the French *Char 2C*, changing the emphasis of the vehicle to being a heavy tank killer, a role not completely out of line with German doctrine.[113] The *VK 30.01*, following in 1937, returned to the breakthrough role as the tank's primary purpose.[114] This shift in priority was not absolute, as the *VK 30.01* could still act as a counter to enemy heavy tanks. But it does indicate that the *Waffenamt* was embracing the conventional view of heavy tanks in the period. Both the British and the French saw their heavy tanks of the late 1930s, the *Matilda* and the *Char B1*, as breakthrough vehicles to aid the infantry and lighter tanks.[115] This shift in priority was not absolute however, as the new tank was still expected to act as a direct counter to enemy heavy tanks as well.

During the Invasion of Poland in September of 1939, the panzer divisions performed well, breaking though Polish lines, and doing a great deal to aid in the German victory. Despite their central role, the fact remained that the Poles had been forced to defend a great deal of territory with comparatively few forces, making it easier to create breakthroughs in their lines. It was not clear in 1939, whether the panzers would perform as well as against the British and French which possessed much larger armies arranged in greater depth across a smaller area (relatively speaking). They also had larger and much better equipped armoured forces. It would be against these more formidable foes that the panzers would have their greatest test and it would be in France that the need for a heavy tank could be more accurately assessed. [116]

There were a number of battles during the French Campaign where the presence of a German heavy tank would have been useful as a means to counter Allied heavy tanks. The French counterattacks against the German bridgeheads over the Meuse from the 15th to the 17th of May were very good examples. During this time, the fighting was concentrated on the village of Stonne which changed hands 17 times as the 10th Panzer Division and Infanterie Regiment Großdeutschland battled the French for control of the vital bridgeheads. The principal French unit was the 3rd Armoured Division, which possessed four battalions of tanks. Two were equipped with the *Hotchkiss H39*, an 11-ton tank with a 37mm gun roughly comparable to the 10th Panzer's *Panzer III* and *IV*. The other two battalions were equipped with the vastly superior *Char B1*. This French heavy tank had 60mm of frontal armour (twice the frontal armour of the *Panzer III*) and sported a higher velocity 47mm gun in its turret, as well as a 75mm howitzer in the front of the hull.[117]

General Jean-Adolphe Flavigny, the French divisional commander and his inexperienced staff found it impossible to deploy the division as a cohesive whole, instead deploying it piecemeal. Nevertheless, the *Char B1* proved to be a formidable vehicle. One *Char B1* took 140 hits, none of which penetrated and was able to destroy 12 German tanks. Another caught a column of German infantry in the open and literally ran them down.[118]

The only way to halt this assault was for the *Pak 36* crews to wait for the tanks to close in before striking their more thinly armoured sides and rear. This was a "near ultimate exercise in nerve and discipline" for the Germans but in this way, they were able to destroy or at least discourage enough of the *Char B1s* to allow the tide to turn in the Germans' favor.[119] By the end of the day on the 17th, the Germans retained the village and their bridgeheads. The cost had been high with over 50 tanks, both French and German, filling Stonne.[120]

At Stonne and Arras, the latter mentioned briefly in the previous chapter, the inadequacy of current German panzers and anti-tank guns in the face of Allied heavy tanks was amply demonstrated.[121] This inferiority suggested that the Germans required a heavy tank of their own if tanks involved in a breakthrough were to survive. The *Char B1* and the *Matilda* represented a minority of Allied tanks. The majority, like the *H39* and the British *A13 Cruiser* were roughly comparable to their German counterparts.[122] Consequently, when German and Allied tanks met in combat, German victory owed less to the vehicles and more to their superior handling. The Germans fought as part of a combined arms team, using infantry, tanks, anti-tank guns, and aircraft in close cooperation, all unified by the radio, which every tank, aircraft and platoon carried. By contrast the French rarely coordinated their operations between units and even individual tanks often failed to support each other in the heat of battle. They also lacked radios, with one company commander reduced to running between his tanks while under fire in an effort to coordinate their movement.[123] In these circumstances, training and organization were key advantages that demonstrated the superiority of the German panzer division concept as a means to win battles. Tanks like the *Char B1* could certainly increase the cost the Germans would pay for victory, but without strong doctrine, emphasizing a combined arms approach to their use and effective command and control, the French could not prevent German victories. In such battles having a heavy tank was not necessary as the maneuverability, coordination and co-operation of the Germans was more than enough to compensate for any qualitative inferiority their tanks may have suffered.

In the end then, the battle for France was a resounding German victory and one that did not seem to call for a heavy tank. The panzer division concept had been proven in astonishing fashion, playing a key role in defeating one of the dominant military powers in Europe in just six weeks. Since the campaign had been decided by rapid maneuver, which specifically avoided the sort of defences that the heavy tank was designed to overcome, there seemed to be little need for them. But the presence of the *Char B1* and the *Matilda* loomed large over the men of the *Waffenamt*, especially since those tanks had put German infantrymen to rout. Avoiding such embarrassments in the future became vitally important.

The simplest solution was to improve German weapons and that was pursued quickly after the end of the campaign. New 50mm anti-tank guns were in production, and the *Panzer III* was also outfitted with a new 50mm gun of its own, though the *Panzer IV*, due to its status as an infantry support tank, did not receive a new gun at this point, with a longer barreled 75mm gun only being fitted in 1942.[124] Upgrading the German arsenal was not only a straightforward solution but also preserved the doctrine that proven so successful in France.

Integrating a heavy tank into this doctrine as a way to counter enemy heavy tanks had the potential to completely upend panzer doctrine by adding a slow vehicle, the use of which demanded methodical planning. Its needs made it hard to reconcile with a system that was at its best when it was fast and unpredictable. Nevertheless, the desire to have a heavy tank to counter to any similar Allied vehicle and serve as a breakthrough vehicle, against stronger defences, overrode those considerations, especially given Hitler's desire for a heavy tank. So, after the end of the Battle of France the *Waffenamt* asked Henschel to mount a 105mm gun on their heavy tank, creating *VK 36.01* and Porsche also put the 88mm gun on their *Type 100*.[125] With the *Waffenamt* and Hitler on board, Germany would get a heavy tank, regardless of its need for one. The only question that remained as the *Tiger* entered service in September 1942, was how best to use and integrate them with their faster and more agile brethren.

TIGER TANKS IN GERMANY'S WARTIME ECONOMY

etween 1942 and 1945, 2,021 *Tiger* tanks and variants were constructed. The *Tiger I* and *II* were constructed by Henschel in Kassel, the *Ferdinand* and *Jagdtiger* were built at Nibelungenwerk in Austria, and the *Sturmtiger* by Alkett in Berlin. Production of these vehicles embodied many of the strengths and weaknesses of the German wartime economy. They were technically complex and expensive vehicles, which led to slow and limited production. Fabrication was further delayed by Allied strategic bombing, which also destroyed a number of vehicles under construction.. Despite this damage, the *Tiger* was still produced in quantities that the army requested for much of their production run. Relative success with the *Tiger* family was not, however, indicative of wider economic success, and undoubtedly detracted from it. While the German economy was successful in the production of individual vehicles and weapons, the economy at large was very inefficient.

Throughout the war the economy remained badly managed by Western standards as a vast array of ministries, offices, and organizations, many with overlapping economic mandates all competed for Germany's resources, which while substantial, were nevertheless dwarfed by those of her enemies. Efforts by Fritz Todt and Albert Speer to centralize and streamline the economy failed to transform it. Full centralization proved impossible and the armaments ministry itself, especially under Speer, grew to be a vast byzantine organization, unequal to the task of effectively harnessing the German economy for the war. Allied bombing just made the job that much more difficult.

The production of *Tiger* vehicles was a disproportionately heavy burden on German industry and the decision to produce them in an effort to overcome the Allies' quantitative advantage had dire consequences. Attempting to overcome quantity with quality meant that Germany increasingly fielded far fewer tanks than its opponents. Even in those instances where superior German command-and-control measures created local concentrations of German armour, the quality versus quantity argument failed. German reliance on the qualitative superiority of the *Tiger* was a questionable strategy given their poor mechanical reliability, which ensured that the Germans were never able to field them in the numbers intended and certainly not in quantities that might have helped to turn the tide of the war in their favor.

Tiger Production

Production of the *Tiger I* was slated to begin in June of 1942 but didn't start until August. This two-month delay was the result of ongoing problems with the transmission, steering gear and brakes. The delay was sufficient to rectify the issues in the steering gear and brakes and while the transmission would be brought up to a satisfactory production standard, it nevertheless remained a point of weakness owing to the great strain of moving a 56-ton vehicle.[126] Only eight vehicles were finished by August of 1942.[127]

As inauspicious as this start was, *Tiger* production then became much smoother. By October of 1942, Henschel was able to exceed its monthly production goals, finishing 25 tanks, not the 18 that was prescribed. By September of 1943, the goal was 75 tanks for that month and Henschel produced 85.[128] This relatively smooth production was a testament not only to the engineers and workers at Henschel but also the success of the many firms that contributed parts to the *Tiger*.

Henschel was the principal manufacturer, but it was just one of many firms building key components. Krupp supplied the guns and also the armour plate, though due to Krupp's other commitments, many of these components were not manufactured at the company's famed Gusstahlfabrik but instead by other companies. Dortmund Hoerder Hutten Verein (DHHV) was the most prominent, producing a significant quantity of armour plate and being one of two companies responsible for the production of the 88mm gun, along with Wolf Buchau. Maybach developed and produced the engines at its factory in Friedrichshafen.[129] These parts, manufactured across the Ruhr Valley, the industrial heart of Germany, were then shipped to Henschel for final assembly. This decentralized system allowed specialty manufacturers to contribute high quality products using Germany's vast rail network to ship them to a central location in order to assemble a high-quality machine. In December of 1943 and throughout 1944, the vulnerabilities of this system were exposed as many of the factories and the rail network that connected them were targeted by the Allied Combined Bomber Offensive.

Royal Air Force (RAF) Bomber Command began bombing Germany on the 4th of September 1939, the day after Britain declared war.[130] Their goal, as summarized by Tami Davis Biddle was to "create a general level of destruction which ...[would] overwhelm the enemy's war economy and especially his will to fight."[131] This effort initially met with little success as a lack of navigational aids made it extremely difficult to find blacked out cities at night, to say nothing of bombing them. In this first act of the bomber offensive, which lasted until March of 1942, the factories that were to be integral parts of *Tiger* production were largely safe. Essen was the first city involved in the production to be targeted on the night of the 8th of March 1942, although this early raid and others in the same period caused little damage.[132]

The massive RAF bombing campaign was supported by another carried out by the United States Army Air Force's (USAAF) 8th and 15th Air Forces during the day. The operations of the two air forces, bombing Germany day and night, had a decidedly mixed effect. The cities where the key *Tiger* factories were located all suffered under Allied bombing, with Essen and Kassel being targeted regularly as they sat in the Ruhr Valley, Germany's industrial heartland. By the war's end, each city had suffered over twenty raids. While Essen itself was devastated by Allied bombing, the Krupp works there remained functional for most of the war and in 1943 only lost 7.6 percent of its planned output despite repeated attacks designed specifically to destroy the famous arms maker's factory.[133] Consequently, Krupp and DHHV were able to complete production of armour plate by June 1944, without lasting interruptions, completing enough to finish the *Tiger I* production run of

1,346 vehicles. DHHV also produced the 88mm gun along with Wolf Buchau. Between them 1,514 guns were produced by July of 1944, with minimal disruptions.[134]

The Henschel factory in Kassel was not as fortunate as Krupp's Gusstahlfabrik. On the night of the 22nd of October 1943, the city suffered a fire storm. An estimated 6,000 people were killed, and 59 percent of the city was destroyed. The Henschel works were badly damaged, and 79 *Tiger* were lost. This loss was the equivalent of almost two complete tank battalions. As devastating as this short-term loss was, the factory was quickly rebuilt and in January, just three months later, the factory was once again meeting its production targets, with 93 tanks completed. This recovery was mirrored by the rest of the city, as by January the Kassel's industrial output reached 90 of its pre-raid level.[135]

The rapid recovery of Kassel after the devastating bombings of 1943 was the result of two factors. As numerous photographs of shattered German cities attested, the bombing was exceptionally good at destroying buildings. But the heavy machinery often survived the bombing. Thus, the roof and many of the walls of Germany's vital factories were often blasted apart but the machinery that was at their hearts was more often than not largely intact.[136] For Henschel, it took three months for production to fully recover, but by the third week of November they were able to finish 22 tanks, indicating that much of the essential production equipment had either survived the RAF bombs completely intact or at the very least suffered only minor damage.[137]

The second factor that enabled the rapid restoration of German industry was a vast and ruthless mobilization of labour to restore key industries. Like all other wartime powers, the Germans were forced to try to balance the needs of industry with the insatiable demands of the *Wehrmacht*. In May of 1939, the German workforce consisted of 39.4 million people, 24.5 million men and 14.6 million women, with an additional 300,000 foreigners. In 1940, the workforce demographics had already changed significantly. There were now 20.5 million men and 14.4 million women employed. The gap created by the expansion of the *Wehrmacht* was filled not by women, as the majority were already working on farms. There was no pool of surplus female labour to draw upon. Instead, the lost men were replaced by 350,000 Prisoners of War (POW) and 800,000 foreigners.[138] The use of foreign slave labour and concentration camp inmates who joined the work force in 1942, as well as POWs, increased as the war went on until by 1944 they represented one in every three workers in the Reich.[139] It was this labour force, which worked to not only keep the factories running but also restored them after they had been attacked by Allied bombers. Without this army of slave labour, the German economy would not have proven so resilient.

Returning to *Tiger* production, the Maybach factory in Friedrichshafen was also badly affected by Allied bombing, though not until 1944. While only 153 engines were completed in 1942, 4,346 were finished in 1943. From January to April of 1944, an estimated 1,785 engines were produced before a raid on the city in late April so devastated the plant that it could not be returned to service until October. To fill this gap in production, Autounion's Siegmar-Werk in Chemnitz was commissioned to take over production. From April of 1944 to April of 1945, the company produced a further 4,366 engines.[140] The use of the Siegmar-Werk was an example of the Germans' use of alternate producers and dispersion of vulnerable production deeper into the Reich, out of the reach of Allied bombers. Substitution and relocation provided the economy with much greater flexibility in the face of Allied bombing than had been anticipated prior to the war. Thus, production could be maintained even in the face of increasingly heavy strategic bombing.[141]

The next *Tiger* variant to enter production was the *Ferdinand*. Converting the Porsche *Tiger* into the *Ferdinand* tank destroyer required the work of four firms. Design of the vehicle was undertaken by Alkett. This firm had extensive experience with tank destroyers and assault guns, having been the primary manufacturer of the *StuG III* since 1940.[142] While the vehicles were being designed in Berlin, the Nibelungenwerk in Austria continued to fulfill part of the original Porsche contract, completing the vehicle hulls and running gears. The finished hulls were then sent to Eisenwerk Oberdonau, a steel works in Linz, near the Nibelungenwerk. Eisenwerk Oberdonau was responsible for reconfiguring the hulls, moving the fighting compartment from the front to the rear of the vehicle and moving the engines from the rear to the middle. Once the hulls had been modified, they were initially to be sent to Alkett for final assembly, but Speer ordered them to be returned to Nibelungenwerk in February of 1943 to simplify production and limit the time the hulls would spend travelling from Austria to Berlin.[143]

St. Valentin was outside the range of Allied bombers in 1943, so Nibelungenwerk was able to complete its work fairly quickly, though not without some delay. Production began in November of 1942, but a shortage of running gears, which had earlier afflicted production of the Porsche *Tiger*, continued to impede *Ferdinand* production.[144] Consequently, the first hulls were not finished until February and Krupp began to deliver the armoured fighting compartments designed by Alkett in March. Given that the *Ferdinand* vehicles were to be completed in time for the upcoming summer offensive, these delays were problematic. Nevertheless, the first 30 were delivered in April, with the last 60 finished in May, allowing the complete production run to be used in Operation Zitadelle in July.[145] Production of the *Ferdinand* may have had some initial delays, but their rapid production did display the speed and efficiency of German industry when unaffected by Allied bombers.

The *Sturmtiger* was the only *Tiger* variant that had straightforward production. In April of 1944, Hitler ordered production of the vehicle to begin. Alkett was given 18 *Tiger I* hulls from Henschel for the project. These were recycled hulls, remnants of tanks that were so badly damaged that they had be returned to Germany for repair or scrapping. This decision was not an effort at recycling per se, but was done at the behest of the army, which was extremely reluctant to give up any *Tiger* production for the project. Alkett designed a superstructure to put atop them. This structure was built by the Brandenburgische Eisenwerke in Kirchmöser, just west of Brandenburg. Alkett then finished assembly. All 18 hulls were converted into *Sturmtiger* by the end of September of 1944.

The *Sturmtiger* saw limited production and even more limited use – they first saw service in the Warsaw Uprising and then in the defence of Germany in 1945. Despite this limited production, the *Sturmtiger* nevertheless remained a good example of resources sunk into a vehicle of dubious value. In the defensive war the Germans found themselves waging in 1944, there was little need for assault vehicles like the *Sturmtiger*, and while another 18 *Tiger* tanks would not have shifted the balance of the war, they certainly would have had far more battlefield utility than the reconfigured *Sturmtiger*.[146]

The *Tiger II* production history followed many of the themes established by the production of the *Tiger I*, though strategic bombing had a greater effect upon its production. In Kassel, Henschel produced the steering and suspension themselves and handled the final assembly. Krupp's Gusstahlfabrik in Essen manufactured the majority of the armour, with plates for 444 hulls and 385 turrets finished by the end of February of 1945. Dortmund's DHHV produced comparatively little, with plates for only 157 hulls and turrets completed by war's end. The Skoda works, in Mlada Boleslav, Czechoslovakia also produced armour plate for the *Tiger II*, but only enough for 35 vehicles. As with the *Tiger I*, Maybach and Autounion produced the engines. The 88mm gun was designed by Krupp but all 802 of them were built by DHHV. Final assembly of the guns was dispersed, with 55 percent finished by firms in Frankfurt and 45 percent in DHHV's home city of Dortmund.[147]

Tiger II production began in October of 1943, with just one vehicle produced that month. Production remained slow until May of 1944. By that point only 38 tanks had been completed, a far cry from the anticipated 191. The slow start to production was blamed on start-up problems for the new production line. Over the summer of 1944, production finally began to meet and then exceed production targets, with 94 finished in August, 14 more than the original production goal.[148]

September and October saw a number of heavy bomber raids on Kassel, with the express purpose of destroying the Henschel works. The raids began on the 22nd of September 1944, with subsequent raids on the 27th and 28th of September as well as the 2nd and 7th of October. Over the course of these five raids, 2,906 tons of high explosive and 1,792 tons of incendiaries were dropped. This quantity of ordnance, guided by the many navigational and targeting aids available by 1944, was able to destroy 95 percent of the Henschel plant. Subsequent raids on the city on the night of the 27th of October, another raid on the

Henschel works on the 15th of December and additional raids on the city on 30th December and January 1st, caused more damage and imposed even more delays on the plant's recovery. From September 1944 to January 1945, only 211 of a planned 380 *Tiger II* were completed.[149]

The bombing of the Henschel works in the fall of 1944 was part of an intensification of Allied bombing that had begun in September of that year. By then Bomber Command and the USAAF possessed over a thousand bombers each. They had developed a reliable and accurate set of navigational aids, as well as having obtained effective air superiority over Germany. In combination, this allowed the bombing campaign to reach its height. From September of 1944 to the war's end, three quarters of all the bombs used against Germany were dropped. In that same period, an estimated half of all German bombing-related fatalities occurred.[150] The devastation wrought upon the Henschel works was part of this intense period of bombardment.

Autounion's Siegmar-Werk in Chemnitz was also heavily damaged in a raid on 11th of September reducing the factory's output from 800 engines a month to just 198. Since Maybach was still restoring its own factory after the raids of April 1944, an effort which was not completed until October, there was a shortage of engines. This shortage was exacerbated by the bombing of the Henschel factories later in the month, which prevented the installation of any available engines. It also signaled that dispersal was no longer an effective strategy.. At this stage in the war, the Allied bombers had the range to hit targets anywhere in Germany. Even Chemnitz, far from the Ruhr, was no longer immune.[151]

A report to Speer's ministry from the *Hauptausschuss Panzerkampfwagen* (Main Committee for Armoured Fighting

Vehicles), which oversaw the production of tanks, written in January of 1945 summarized the issues faced by the tank producers. "While during 1943 the influence of hostile air attacks was not yet very noticeable in the tank industry ... in 1944 there was no single tank producing plant which did not suffer directly and above all indirectly to a considerable extent."[152]

One major indirect source of damage was the increased disruption of transportation networks. Part of this disruption was the inevitable result of damage to German cities but in the final phase of the war, increased emphasis was placed on destroying the Ruhr's transportation links. Key losses included the draining of the Dortmund-Ems Canal by the Allied bombers at the end of September of 1944, and the destruction of the Köln-Mulheim bridge on the 14th of October.[153] These large-scale attacks and numerous smaller ones served to isolate the Ruhr. The loss of rail infrastructure further negated the advantage of dispersion, as even undamaged factories found it difficult to transport their products to their customers. This created additional friction for German industries, already badly battered by the direct effects of strategic bombing. It was this combination of direct and indirect damage that led to low production of the *Tiger II* even after the Henschel works were repaired in early 1945. This included the completion of just 30 tanks in March 1945, meaning the company could not meet its revised goal of 45 tanks in that month, to say nothing of the 150 originally planned for production prior to the intensification of Allied bombing.[154]

Damage to Germany's rail system was problematic not only in terms of finished products lost but also in terms of lost coal. Over 90 percent of Germany's industries were powered by Ruhr coal. Almost 20,000 railcars full of it left the Ruhr every day in August of 1944 to fuel German industry. By

October, only 7,000 cars were leaving the Ruhr daily. With so little coal leaving the Ruhr, Speer reported to Hitler on the 5th of October that German industry could only be fueled for another eight to twelve weeks.[155] Re resolve this crisis required a vast army of labourers. Thankfully for the Germans, the past several years had made them masters of mobilizing labour. But the traditional solution of relying on slave labour was no longer effective. The occupied territories the Germans had so ruthlessly pillaged had largely been liberated and with the collapse of the Reich in sight, the remaining foreign labourers were no longer considered politically reliable enough for many tasks, especially for the restoration of Germany's vital infrastructure. So, 2,000,000 German workers were pulled from their factories to rebuild the shattered rail lines. Another 350,000 were sent to repair damage to the oil industry and a further 300,000 were drawn to restore the chemical industry. These new manpower demands, added to previous losses of skilled German labourers to the *Wehrmacht*, made it increasingly difficult for firms to produce even the simplest items, to say nothing of complex weapons like the *Tiger*.[156] Faced with all of this direct and indirect damage, the *Hauptausschuss Panzerkampfwagen* report concluded, "At this moment one can no longer speak of planned production at all." [157]

The report also described the last-ditch effort of German industry in the war's final months. "The extraordinary extent of the stoppages throughout the whole of the armaments industry caused all external assistance in overcoming these difficulties to diminish more and more, and firms were largely dependent on helping themselves."[158] Despite this pessimistic appraisal of the situation, it was still believed in January of 1945 that Henschel could draw upon sufficient resources to return to the production of 125 *Tiger II* a month by August of 1945. This was hopelessly optimistic and in February, the *Panzer Notprogramm* (Emergency Tank Production Program) was issued by Speer's ministry. This program aimed to wind down the production of advanced vehicles like the *Tiger II* in favor of simpler models like the *StuG* and other casemate tank destroyers. These lighter and simpler vehicles were better suited to not only the production situation at the end of the war but also the nature of the defensive fighting that the Germans were undertaking in the final defence of the Reich.[159] This plan envisioned sharing production between the Henschel plant in Kassel and the Nibelungenwerk (which was already producing the *Jagdtiger*). Production of *Tiger II* between the two plants would be halted once 350 vehicles had been completed, a milestone that was expected to be reached in October 1945. Then both plants would be converted to production of other, simpler vehicles. This plan proved useless, as Nibelungenwerk never produced a single *Tiger II* and Kassel fell to the Allies at the end of March. By that point, 492 *Tiger II* had left Henschel but Allied bombing had prevented the construction of a further 657 from 1943 to 1945.[160]

The consequences of this lost production were keenly felt. Of the 14 heavy tank battalions created between 1942 and 1944, only nine received a full complement of *Tiger II*, the rest continued to use the *Tiger I* until the war's end. The second company of 508 was particularly short charged. The *Kompanie* left Italy in September of 1944, moving to the training grounds at Paderborn to be trained on the *Tiger II*. With the heavy damage to the Henschel works that month, they were left without vehicles to train on and so they waited – for five months. Finally, on the 30th of March 1945, they were given new orders. The company's veteran *Tiger* crews were re-roled as infantry to counter the approaching American army.[161]

It was a strange way for tank veterans to end the war, but it illustrated the dire straits in which Germany found itself as both its production lines and its front lines collapsed in the war's waning months.

The *Jagdtiger* was subject to the same late war production pressures that had such an impact on the *Tiger II*. Henschel designed the *Jagdtiger,* but they lacked the capacity to build them, so Nibelungenwerk was given the contract instead. As with the *Ferdinand*, the nearby Eisenwerke Oberdonau handled the production of the hulls while the 128mm gun was provided by Krupp's Bertha Werk in Breslau.[162]

The first *Jagdtiger* was supposed to be finished in December of 1943, but Nibelungenwerk was ramping up its production of *Panzer IV* to 300 vehicles a month and so the first *Jagdtiger* was not ready until February of 1944. The initial vehicles were used for testing, and production did not begin in earnest until July with three *Jagdtiger* completed. By September, Nibelungenwerk was turning out eight per month with production expected to continue to increase.[163]

It was not to be. Increased production was delayed significantly by a bombing raid on the factory on the 16th of October 1944. The vulnerability of factories deep inside Austria at this stage in the war reflected not only the long range of Allied bombers based in England but also the growing number of bombers based in Italy. Between the two air fleets, no corner of the Reich was immune. Vulnerable though Nibelungenwerk was, the October raid caused little lasting damage. While only nine *Jagdtiger* were completed that month, by December the plant was producing 20, which would be the monthly production record for the vehicle.[164]

Just a few days before the bombing raid on Nibelungenwerk, on the 12th of October the decision was made to produce only 150 *Jagdtiger* and then convert the production line to the *Panther*. On the 3rd of January Hitler overrode this decision, ordering that under no circumstances was production of the *Jagdtiger* to be halted. Instead, production was to be increased, with 100 vehicles to be finished by April of 1945. Then, without delay Nibelungenwerk was to convert its assembly lines to producing *Tiger II*, with 25 to be finished in May. *Jagdtiger* production would be transferred to the Jung firm in Jungenthal, which was expected to begin production without delay.[165]

Of course, Hitler's plan never came to fruition. Instead, the February *Panzer Notprogramm* superseded it, calling for an end to production in April 1945, with 150 *Jagdtiger* finished. This plan was more rational but, like the plans for the *Tiger II*, overtaken by events. Nibelungenwerk was bombed again on the 23rd of March 1945, ensuring that the plant could finish only three vehicles that month. Despite these setbacks, the Nibelungenwerk was still committed to manufacturing *Jagdtiger* when it was occupied by the Red Army at war's end on the 9th of May. Through the chaos and confusion of late war production, only 79 *Jagdtiger* were completed, representing a considerable expenditure of effort for so few vehicles.[166] The production of the *Jagdtiger* provides further evidence of the effect of Allied bombing on production, though the capacity of the plant to recover and continue manufacturing until the last days of the war is a testament to the restorative capabilities of German industry even at the very end of the war.

The production of the *Tiger* variants from 1942 to 1945 illustrates several key aspects of the German war economy. First and foremost, production was reasonably effective, as vehicles were still produced in quantity despite Allied bombing. While the dispersed nature of production created additional hurdles late in the war as the Allies increasingly targeted Germany's transportation network, it nevertheless proved to be a system that could, until the fall of 1944, provide the army with the number of tanks it requested. The Combined Bomber Offensive had little impact on *Tiger* production until late 1944, when the bombing reached its height. Even then, when the Allies sent vast fleets of heavy bombers over Germany day and night, the damage they inflicted was never enough to halt production. As the Nibelungenwerk proved, the Germans were still able to marshal the resources and labour necessary to repair damaged factories right up to the end of the war. Thus, strategic bombing was unable to prevent the production of the *Tiger*, only hamper it.

The Economic Burden of Tiger Production

Impressive as German *Tiger* production was, the question of whether this effort was worthwhile remains. One way to answer this question is to examine what might have been produced instead. *Tiger* production represented an effort to overcome Germany's quantitative weakness through superior quality. This effort was compromised by the inherent inefficiency of the German economy, which prevented even the greatly expanded wartime economy from closing the quantitative gap between Germany and her foes. It was further compromised by the nature of the *Tiger* vehicles. While they embodied Germany's pursuit of quality over quantity, their unreliability and lack of replacement vehicles owing to their expense did not allow the Germans to field enough of them to even begin to overcome the Allies' quantitative advantage. Had the Germans focused on producing fewer types of less complex vehicles, more of them could have been produced, and the quantitative gap could have been narrowed, even if it could never be closed. The efforts by Speer to create more efficient production programs, including the *Panzer Notprogramm* of February 1945, came far too late to have any real impact.

The complexity of the broad range of *Tiger* variant production was in many ways representative of the complexities and failings of the wider German economy. Long before the first *Tiger* left the Henschel works in Kassel in August of 1942, the German economy had been poorly managed and was incapable of meeting the demands of war with the world's great industrial powers. It may not have appeared that way to the outside world but that was the result of propaganda, not reality.

When the Nazis came to power in 1933, German rearmament began in earnest. The popular image of German rearmament is of vast industrial concerns moving from clandestine to open military production, quickly and efficiently arming the *Wehrmacht* that would overwhelm Europe. This story was first told by the Nazis themselves and repeated often in the decades that followed. Georg Baur, a Krupp director in the 1920, said of the Gusstahlfabrik, "Germany's past is buried here... and Germany's future lurks here likewise, in these old furnaces."[167] Alfried Krupp boasted in 1942 that the principles of the *Wehrmacht* weapons his firm was producing had been designed in the 1920s, under the noses of Allied inspectors attempting to enforce the treaty of Versailles.[168] In works like William Shirer's *Rise and Fall of the Third Reich* an unbroken line is drawn between these clandestine efforts and the rapid rearmament of Germany, which was conducted on such a scale that by 1934 it could no longer be hidden. This rapid mobilization of German industry gave Hitler a "monstrous mechanized juggernaut such as the earth had never seen" with which to conquer Europe.[169] The truth was far less straightforward.

Germany's "cluster of world-beating industrial companies", the likes of Krupp, Siemens and IG Farben may have had a great portion of Germany's future lurking within them, especially regarding German rearmament, but Hitler's new Reich was not the industrial powerhouse that it was popularly portrayed to be.[170] Instead, over 15 million people still worked either as peasants or in traditional handicrafts. In 1939, even after the acquisition of Austria and Czechoslovakia, Germany, along with Italy and its empire, had a combined gross domestic product, which Britain and France and their vast empires exceeded by sixty percent.[171] As Germany rearmed, the pressing question was how to build in short order an industrial machine that could defeat these larger powers.

To prepare for and ultimately wage war, all of the major powers centralized their economies. The Germans were no exception, at least in theory. In practice, while more and more control of the economy was given to government bodies, it was not handed over to one or two central organizations with clear mandates, but instead to many organizations with overlapping mandates. In peacetime, the Economic Ministry and the Reichsbank managed the economy, but their central positions were challenged first in 1935. The *Wehrgesetz* of 21st of May 1935, established the post of *Generalbevollmächtiger für die Kriegswirtschaft* (GBK: General Plenipotentiary for the War Economy), who was tasked with marshaling all of Germany's resources in wartime, superseding the pre-existing civilian bodies. But the GBK soon found that his mandate clashed with OKW economics staffs as well as the economic and procurement staffs of each of the armed forces.[172] Matters were further complicated in 1936 when German rearmament was made a major priority, with the aim of creating a military ready to go to war within four years. To meet this goal, Herman

Göring created and chaired the *Büro des Vierjahresplans* (Office of the Four-Year Plan). Like most Nazi organisms, the various offices of this plan had overlapping areas of responsibility with all of the other pre-existing organizations.[173]

The consequences of this confused state of affairs was felt acutely by the nascent *Panzerwaffe*. All told, each tank division were supposed to have 561 tanks of various types. Initial plans for a force of three panzer divisions in 1935, which would have required 1,683 tanks, were quickly abandoned as rearmament accelerated. By 1939, the *Reichsheer* possessed seven panzer divisions, and four light divisions. This force required 5,051 tanks to equip, to say nothing of replacements and training vehicles.[174] Unfortunately, there was not enough steel to make them in the numbers the army required. As the Four-Year Plan began in 1936, demand for steel far outstripped supply and new plants designed to alleviate this shortage were not slated to come on-line until 1938. The first short term solution, to preserve dangerously low stocks of iron ore and scrap was a 15 percent production cut, later increased to 25 percent. Exports could not be cut, since they were one of the few things standing between the Reich and total financial ruin, and as rearmament was largely debt financed. So further cuts fell on production for the domestic market. At that point 1.725 million tons of steel were produced monthly, with 1.325 million tons available for domestic use.

After the 25 percent cut was imposed in November of 1936, only 1.070 million tons were available for the internal use.[175] But the army required 270,000 tons of steel a month just for its own expansion and with the new production cuts, and the rationing that followed in 1937, they were rationed to just 195,000 tons a month. With that reduction they estimated that ammunition production would not reach planned levels until 1942 and the planned series of border fortifications would not be ready until 1948.[176]

As rearmament increased in size and scope, the broad array of economic agencies made it difficult to set priorities and allocate resources like steel. For 1939, the *Wehrmacht* steel ration was cut from 530,000 tons to just 300,000 tons. This blow hit both the *Reichsheer* and the *Luftwaffe* particularly hard. In the area of tank production, the 1,200 *Panzer III* and *Panzer IV* that were to be produced from October of 1939 to October of 1940 was cut in half as a result.[177] This final pre-war cut to their steel allocation combined with the shortages from previous years, led to a badly diminished panzer force to attack Poland.

For the invasion of Poland, only the 1st Panzer and 1st Light Division were able to field medium companies at all, and their light companies were made up mostly of *Panzer I* and *Panzer II*. While the latter tank had a 20mm main gun, the *Panzer I* was a training tank armed only with a pair of machine guns. In total 1,445 *Panzer I* and 1,223 *Panzer II* would participate in the invasion of Poland, while only 98 *Panzer III* and 211 *Panzer IV* saw service in the campaign. Another 280 Czech tanks designated as *Panzer 35(t)* and *38(t)* also saw service.[178]

It's important to note that a shortage of steel was far from the only problem effecting production since both the *Panzer III* and *IV* were still in the early stages of production when the war broke out. The *Panzer III* went through a number of iterations to prefect its suspension and running gear while the *Panzer IV* underwent a number of changes to its chassis.[179] Nevertheless, the heavy reliance on training and reconnaissance tanks for want of sufficient medium tanks spoke to the fact that the army, and especially the armoured force, was poorly prepared for war as a result of economic mismanagement.

The chaotic nature of Germany's initial rearmament reflected an astute assessment of Germany's position vis a vis its opponents. It was an admission of Germany's economic inferiority, which could only be addressed by a rapid rearmament, followed by a short war, which would minimize the long-term economic advantage possessed by Britain and France. Luckily for Hitler, Germany's military had a long history of fighting short wars specifically to negate the greater resources their enemies could bring to bear in long wars. This tradition was especially fortunate since rearmament had been a shambles. What saved Germany was that it encountered foes in 1939 and 1940 who were even less-well prepared than they were.[180]

There was, as ever, a great deal of blame to be divided up for the state of the German economy as the war began. At the heart of the economic confusion was the man who was at the very heart of the Nazi state, Adolf Hitler. Hitler managed the Reich using the *Führerprinzip*, which positioned him as the final arbiter in all decision-making. His will became law and in lieu of direct instructions from Hitler it fell to the senior leadership of the state to act in accordance with their interpretation of his will.[181] This system was further complicated because each element of the government bureaucracy had a mandate that overlapped with other organizations' mandates. In the economy this was reflected in the overlying authorities of the Ministry of Economic Affairs, the Reichsbank, OKW, GBK and the Office of the Four-Year Plan. When inevitable conflicts emerged over the conflicting mandates and varying interpretations of Hitler's will, only he could provide guidance and impose order upon the chaos, if only temporarily. This was a system which worked very well for Hitler. It ensured that his inner circle was too busy warring with itself to ever consider overthrowing him, and by placing himself above such intrigues as the sole arbitrator, he became indispensable.[182]

Such a system was rife with problems, and from the standpoint of economics ensured that the disparate organizations that ran the economy would not, and could not cooperate, creating fierce competition for scarce resources. Hitler's personality made things worse. He had an "inability to meditate between the contestants, to weigh arguments and proposals, to harmonize actual constraints with political and ideological premises."[183] These tendencies were not helped by his fleeting interests in the day-to-day operation of the state. Once a problem was brought to his attention, he would resolve it and promptly lose interest. When all of these elements were combined, the German economy was in the hands of a man who encouraged conflict but lacked the willingness to resolve it and failed to retain interest in any decision once it was made.[184]

The conflicts among the various economic agencies was one of the two most important results of Hitler's practice. The second was a lack of prioritization. Indeed, in Denis Showalter's words, the Reich was a "regime that considered prioritization something of a swear word."[185] This had already played out with the cuts in steel production, where first it was the civilian market that was affected, then the *Reichswehr*, then the *Reichsheer* and the *Luftwaffe*, in a series of decisions made over the course of three years. It became worse once the war began. Beginning in March 1940, production priorities were altered four times. First it was munitions, then *U-Boote* and aircraft, followed by panzers and finally other military equipment. Then after the Battle of France in June 1940, the *Kriegsmarine* and the *Luftwaffe* received the priority to blockade and subjugate

England. When the Battle of Britain ended, priority returned to the army and preparations for Operation Barbarossa, with the intent of returning production priority to the other two services for the final destruction of England once the Soviets had been defeated.[186]

These constant shifts, coming month after month, created continual problems as finite work forces and resources were routinely shifted to accommodate new priorities. Krupp estimated that its workers lost 305,250 working hours from October of 1942 to June of 1944 as a result of priorities being constantly altered.[187]

Hitler recognized that the preparations for war had been haphazard, and that management of the economy was poor. So, in March of 1940, a new ministry was created to better handle the enormous task of armaments production. This ministry was christened the *Reichsministerium für Bewaffnung und Munition* (Armaments and Munitions). At its head was Dr. Fritz Todt. Speer described his predecessor as a kindred spirit, a nature-loving technocrat "one of the very few modest, unassertive personalities in government ... who steered clear of all the intrigues. With his combination of sensitivity and matter of factness... he fitted rather poorly into the governing class of the National Socialist state."[188] This was a very flattering portrayal of Todt, but it was not an entirely accurate one. Todt was technician with a PhD in engineering, but he was far from apolitical. Instead, he was an *alte Kampfer*, an old brawler, who had become a National Socialist in 1922. His unwavering loyalty to Hitler and his vision for the Autobahn made him the *Generalinspektor für das deutsche Straßenwesen* (General Inspector for Roads) in June of 1933. In this position he was outside of the authority of any government ministry and reported directly to Hitler. In the years that followed, he occupied a number of other high level technical posts, most notably creating in 1938, the eponymous Organisation Todt.[189]

Organisation Todt would be the test bed for the structure that Todt later applied to the armaments ministry. It merged state and private interests under his watchful eye to fulfill Hitler's wishes. Todt brought together technical experts from private industry and state mobilized labour, in this case from the *Reichsarbeitsdienst* (Reich Labour Service) to carry out military building projects. The first was the Westwall, better known in the west as the Siegfried Line. The success of this project demonstrated that the "initiative of the politically committed engineer, harnessing the energies of private business, could deliver what the lumbering military bureaucracy apparently could not."[190]

The new Armaments Ministry that was expected to boost Germany's flagging armaments industry had a new and radical organizational logic, which Todt had brought with him from his previous endeavors. However, while the fusion of state and private interests was a novel solution, the ministry itself embraced a traditional Nazi structure. It lacked the carefully designated powers of a traditional ministry. Instead, it was a "managerial organization, led by a charismatic figure whose executive power was not restrained by bureaucratic practice or legal norms, but depended on his ability to enforce his decisions by decrees from Hitler and his skill in outwitting his rivals within the hierarchy."[191] As a consequence, while Todt's new ministry did reorder the German economy, it did not change its fundamental nature.

Initially, the ministry was only responsible for overseeing the army's armaments directly. But its influence over vital raw materials and Todt's ready access to Hitler gave it a great deal of power over the production of armaments for the other services and other parts of the economy. To boost production in these areas, Todt began heavy investment in the procurement of vital raw materials, worked to rationalize and streamline production, and perhaps most importantly began to reorganize the economy in an effort to reduce competition and restore order.[192]

Todt recognized quickly that procurement was a major weakness of the economy and sought to rectify this weakness by undercutting OKW and OKH economic staffs. This was done by decentralizing the procurement of ammunition. In each region defined by *Wehrmacht* armament inspectorates, businesses formed their own working groups of producers for each caliber of ammunition. These working groups were coordinated by regional ammunition committees. In order to receive their ammunition, the army's procurement offices had to send their orders to these committees, rather than through their own offices. Then industry specialists assigned contracts to the best available producers. In May of 1940 these regional committees were consolidated into a national main committee, which had sub committees for each ammunition type. By November of 1940, five of these main committees existed: ammunition, tanks, weapons, general military equipment, and machinery.[193]

The *Hauptausschuss Panzerkampfwagen* was the second of the five committees established in the autumn of 1940. It was chaired until 1943 by Walter "Panzer" Rohland, who ran the specialty steelwork Deutsche Edelstahlwerke. Edelstahlwerke was a major supplier of armoured plate, giving Rohland a vested interest in the success of tank production. Rohland gained his nickname because he had joined the 11th Panzer Regiment as a captain in the Reserves back in 1935.[194] His interests in tank production, both personal and financial ensured that the panzers had a strong advocate willing to compete for scarce resources against all comers. This was a deliberate feature fostered by Todt to boost production in his main committees, which increased his own power and influence. The downside was that it did little to curtail competition among the committees and the other organizations with economic responsibilities.[195]

In 1943, Rohland left the committee to become the head of Vereinigte Stahlwerke, one of the largest steel manufactures in Germany. His replacement was Dr. Stiele von Heydekampf, the General Manager of Henschel.[196] Von Heydekampf ran the committee until the war's end, continuing Rohland's work in good fashion but in many respects while the two chairmen of the committee were important, the true power lay in their deputy, Karl Otto Saur who remained with the committee throughout its existence. Saur was Todt's and later Speer's deputy. He would earn a reputation as one of the war's "most fanatical slave drivers."[197] His drive and close connection with the minister himself ensured that while panzers were not always the first production priority, their production would also never languish.

Examining the production numbers suggests that Todt's committees worked. German tank production nearly doubled from 1939 to 1940 from 787 to 1,779.[198] Todt and his ministry took full credit for this production increase, but the main committees contributed very little to this upsurge. Instead, the increases were the result of massive increases to the army steel and copper allocations in September of 1939 that resulted in increased production beginning in February 1940. As General Friedrich Fromm, the head of army supply remarked, "Todt's bed had been made for him."[199] Nevertheless Todt's concept of industry-driven production, under the supervision of the state had worked, at least on paper.

The *Hauptausschuss Panzerkampfwagen* was not the only major change to tank production instituted by Todt to have dubious value. In 1940, he also created a *Panzer Kommission* to oversee the selection of future tank designs. This new commission didn't completely supersede the *Waffenamt* but nevertheless constituted an organization with considerable power, especially under its first chairman, Ferdinand Porsche. Porsche's close relationship with Hitler gave the commission significant authority and ensured that the selection of future tank designs would be more heavily politicized and no longer based purely on the expressed needs of the army. In the case of the *Tiger*, the influence of the commission was limited. *Tiger* designs owed more to Hitler's views than to those of the commission, or even the *Waffenamt*. That said, Porsche was "always urging Hitler and Speer [as well as Todt] to allow him to build an even bigger tank with an even bigger gun."[200] With Porsche's views reinforcing Hitler's own, it was almost impossible to reverse the trend of heavier panzers entering production. This trend was ironic since German doctrine continued to place a greater premium on mobility, than it did on armour and armament. Admittedly, it is difficult to see a commission that shared Guderian's views being able to change Hitler's mind on the designs of future panzers. Porsche's influence made it virtually impossible.[201]

Porsche's emphasis on size was in line with Hitler's thinking but his love of exotic designs which were often unreliable, didn't lend themselves to mass production. This focus led to his dismissal in 1943. Stiele von Heydekampf replaced him but while von Heydekampf lacked Porsche's love for the exotic, Porsche's precedent of favoring heavier vehicles could not be realistically changed. Porsche had embraced

Hitler's preferences. Consequently, under von Heydekampf, vehicles like the *Jagdtiger* and the *Maus* were approved.[202]

The effect of the *Kommission* on tank production cemented the primacy of heavier and more costly vehicles at the expense of their lighter counterparts, creating an emphasis on "technical virtuosity for its own sake."[203] Rather than producing the *Panzer IV*, at a unit cost of 125,000 Reichsmarks (RM),[204] it emphasized the costlier 176,000 RM *Panther* and 321,000 RM *Tiger II*.[205] For the cost of one *Tiger II*, 2.6 *Panzer IV* could be built. Thus, 1,279 *Panzer IV* could have been built for the cost of the 492 *Tiger II*.

By 1944, the panzer divisions had been reorganized several times and lacked the large number of tanks they had boasted in 1939. Now they had one tank regiment, each consisting of two battalions, one with 79 *Panthers* and the other with 81 *Panzer IV*. So, almost 16 battalions equipped with *Panzer IV* could have been created for the cost of the *Tiger II* total production.[206] These additional *Panzer IV* would not have changed the outcome of the war, as the consequences of German mistakes and Allied numerical superiority ensured that victory could not be determined by a relatively small number of vehicles. However, the extra tanks certainly would have been welcome additions to the panzer divisions, especially late in the war as the Allies closed in on the Reich. Arguably, it was in this regard that Hitler had the biggest influence on tank production. While his emphasis on heavy, expensive, vehicles didn't cost Germany the war, it did make it more difficult to close the quantitative gap between Germany and her enemies.

Todt was unable to reap the full benefits of his successes with increases in production. However, his untimely death on the 8th of February 1942, when the plane he was travelling in exploded, spared him any blame for his failures.[207] Hitler quickly replaced him with Albert Speer. At first glance, Speer seemed to be an unlikely choice for armaments minister. He was an architect by profession. But a closer look at his resume suggests a man well-suited for the position by the standards that the Nazis used. He joined the Nazi Party in 1931, after its first electoral success but before its accession to power in 1933. That made him a member with longstanding loyalty to the party. This loyalty was rewarded with a number of important positions. It was Speer who crafted the dramatic scenes of the annual Nuremberg Rallies, with the use of spotlights shining into the night air, creating what Sir Neville Henderson called "a cathedral of ice" as well as much of the spectacle of the 1936 Olympics.[208]

His visions for the rebuilding of central Berlin, with the massive *Volkshalle* as a centerpiece, made him Hitler's favorite architect and Speer was appointed *Generalbauinspektor für die Reichshauptstadt* (Inspector General of Reich Capital) in 1937, to realize his dreams for the new capital.[209] In this role, and his other work with the party, Speer demonstrated several key personality characteristics, which helped his rise to prominence. He had "ruthless determination, boundless enthusiasm and total disregard for established practice."[210] These traits were common amongst the highest echelons of the Nazi Party and helped him cultivate relationships with many key figures including Fritz Todt and Henrich Himmler. But his most important relationship was with Hitler, and it was because Hitler trusted Speer that he was entrusted with Todt's job.[211] Thus, the ministry was handed over to another man, who may not have had many conventional qualifications for the job but whose loyalty to Hitler and political savvy made him eminently well-suited.

Speer took up his post at a critical time. The winter of 1941 had been a disaster for the *Wehrmacht*. The only way to ensure victory was to organize a great increase in production that could make good the tremendous losses incurred in the Soviet Union. Only then could the *Wehrmacht* deliver a decisive blow to the Soviets before the full industrial might of the United States could be brought to bear.[212] To achieve this awesome objective Speer operated along the lines that Todt had laid out. He first added two new main committees, for Locomotives and Ships.[213] Then he began a series of more ambitious efforts to further centralize control of the economy under his ministry in the pursuit of greater production.

When he became minister, Speer's domain was relatively small. All of the army's production was under his control but only in ammunition did he have authority over the air force and navy. These two services were, at least in February 1942, out of his reach but to better coordinate the three services, Speer created yet another new agency, *Zentrale Planung*. As the name implied this was a centralized economic organization and while it was certainly not the first organization to claim this mandate, it was one of the few to actually achieve it. It functioned effectively as a partnership between Speer and *Generalfeldmarschall* Erhard Milch, who oversaw the production of aircraft. After July 1943, when Speer absorbed *Kriegsmarine* production into his ministry the two men controlled 90 percent of Germany's economy between them.[214]

While the partnership between Speer and Milch was revolutionary enough, what truly differentiated *Zentrale Planung* from all of its predecessors was the necessary longevity of cooperation. Between the 27th of April 1942, and the war's end, *Zentrale Planung* met 62 times. It met 52 times between April 1942 and December 1943, an average of one meeting every ten days. It was in these meetings that the German economy finally received a measure of centralized coordination and control.[215]

This unprecedented consolidation of economic control was only one part of Speer's additions to the ministry. The other great change was an expansion of Todt's industry-advised, government-supervised model to an even greater portion of the economy. Main rings were formed for whole groups of products, overseen by relevant experts. These included iron ore products, steel processing, metals, production plants and electro-technical products. These main rings were linked to the main committees created by Todt and to an ever-growing set of committees and sub-committees that oversaw production of parts. Under this system, processors of raw materials became intimately linked with the producers of finished products.[216]

The new rings and committees were an improvement but not in the sense that the new institutions were a more efficient ordering of the economy. Improvement came from the fact that the new system led to "consistent enforcement of rules and forms of cooperation among all those involved."[217] Now industry was able to better coordinate and cooperate, with output of armaments being the unifying goal. By recruiting growing numbers of technical experts from German industry into his ministry, Speer facilitated the transfer of some of their loyalty from their firms to himself. Barriers between firms began to fall. This cleared a number of bottlenecks created by longstanding cartel agreements and quotas designed to increase profit. Now industry leaders had the authority to remove these arrangements and focus on armaments production.[218]

These changes laid the foundation for the "armaments miracle" of 1942. By August of that year Speer reported significant increases in production across every part of his domain. Production of guns was up 27 percent and ammunition was up by 97 percent. During, those months, production of Germany's foremost AFVs, the *StuG III*, *Panzer III* and *Panzer IV* increased from 314 vehicles in February to 395 vehicles in August, with 2,282 of the 6,094 AFVs produced that year leaving the factories during this "miraculous" period.[219] In total, productivity was up 59.6 percent and Speer declared "obviously we had mobilized resources that had hitherto lain fallow."[220]

In 1942, Speer used this success to cement his position as an economic mastermind and it provided him with the clout to later absorb the *Kriegsmarine* and *Luftwaffe* production by the spring of 1944. The increase was real but did need to come with some caveats. These numbers were not a miracle owed to Speer's singular genius. He didn't extract previously unknown production out of the economy. Instead, there were many perfectly mundane factors. His efforts were not unimportant, especially in terms of expanding the ministry and creating *Zentrale Planung*, but there were many other contributors, whom Speer declined to credit in his memoirs. These included increases that were the result of the reorganization and rationalization efforts started by Todt, the results of long-term investments bearing fruit and the ruthless mobilization of labour.

So, while the increases were very real, Speer had not found a magical formula to resolve Germany's economic woes. All of the old problems remained, and the Allies soon added a new one. Todt had been fortunate during his tenure that the Allies' strategic bomber offensive had been the in hands of the RAF, which lacked sufficient aircraft and navigational aids to pose a serious threat to the German economy. In 1942, a much better equipped Bomber Command, bolstered by an ever-growing USAAF presence brought Speer's miracle to an end. At that time, the Combined Bomber Offensive lacked the power to totally cripple the German economy, but it did place very real limits on German production for the rest of the war.[221]

It is also worth mentioning that some of Speer's innovations took some time to provide any benefit. Engine production was a good example. It was clear after Speer became minister that it was necessary to consolidate production to better use factory capacity and remove bottlenecks. Maybach, which produced the majority of tank engines and was naturally in charge of their production, was to be folded into the much larger aeroengine committee. This was something that Maybach fought strenuously, partly to avoid a loss of power, but also because aeroengines were overseen by William Werner, an executive with their long-time competitor Autounion. Speer got his way but not until April of 1943, when he used his personal relationship with Hitler to make it clear that resistance was futile. He was always willing to use this close relationship with the Fuhrer to overcome obstacles. Unsurprisingly, these interventions tended to cause competition and conflict to evaporate.

Speer's miracle did not last. The long-term problems that he had supposedly driven out of the German economy came back with a vengeance. His system of committees and sub committees quickly ballooned. By the end of 1942, there were 249 committees and sub committees within the ministry.[222] This number grew as the war went on and the ministry continued to absorb its rivals, not just the aforementioned military production but also responsibility for raw materials. This acquisition resulted in a ministerial name change, to *Reichsministerium für Rüstung und Kriegsproduktion* (Ministry of Armaments and War Production).[223] These acquisitions increased Speer's power and prestige, making him

"Europe's economic dictator" in the words of the *Kriegsmarine* Commander-in-Chief, *Großadmiral* Karl Dönitz.[224] The great downside of these changes was that the growth of the ministry multiplied the size of the bureaucracy. By 1944, there were 21 main committees and the Weapons Committee alone had 60 sub committees, one for each caliber of weapon in use by the military.[225] Rather than having to compete with external agencies, now the various elements of the German economy found themselves competing with the hundreds of other entities within the ministry. Thus, the entire apparatus that controlled the German economy was "barely comprehensible and virtually unmanageable."[226]

Economic consolidation did little to address the problem of economic prioritization. On the 22nd of January 1943, to bolster enthusiasm after another dismal winter, the Adolf Hitler Panzer Programme was announced. When Speer and "Panzer" Rohland first discussed an increase in tank production the aim was for 1,400 vehicles a month by the spring of 1944. That number was to be a mix of 600 *Panther*, 50 *Tiger*, and 150 lighter tanks including the *Panzer IV*. As well, they envisioned another 600 assault guns and tank destroyers.[227] Hitler, ever ambitious, had grander plans. He wanted 900 tanks, including 475 *Panther*, 50 *Tiger*, and 245 *Panzer IV* as well as 2,000 assault guns and tank destroyers each month by the end of 1944.[228] To achieve this lofty goal, the announcement of the program decreed that achieving an "immediate increase in tank production [was] of such decisive importance for the outcome of the war, that all civilian and military agencies [were] to support this production drive with all available resources."[229] It was admitted that this program would temporarily disadvantage other areas of production, but the priority had been set.

An examination of the projected costs of the program gives a sense of its scale. Many key factories were to be upgraded. DHHV was to receive five million RM, Krupp's Gusstahlfabrik would get 16 million RM, Maybach 11.7 million RM and Henschel 4.9 million RM. In total the plan was to cost 294,163,000 RM.[230] These costs were already sufficient to bring the fiscally parsimonious to tears, but the economic dislocation caused by the new priority given to tank production meant that they had ample company in their misery.

The *Luftwaffe* found it virtually impossible to acquire crankshafts for aeroengines because Maybach enjoyed priority for their tank engines. Further delays occurred as the Panzer Programme took up an ever-increasing share of Germany's rail transport. All of these delays became so acute that Milch and his staff resorted to the absurd as a solution. They claimed Panzer Priority for their aircraft. This interesting interpretation of priority, combined with *Luftwaffe* control of 40 percent of the German economy, meant that while May of 1943 saw an impressive 1,270 tanks produced, Milch was able to produce 2,220 aircraft in that same month.[231] Milch's intervention also demonstrated that while *Zentrale Planung* provided an unprecedented level of economic coordination, it did not guarantee cooperation. At the end of the day only one's own area of responsibility really mattered. In spite of Milch's diversions of resources, May of 1943 was still a good month for tank production; but it came at the end of the Panzer Programme. In April, Hitler had ordered the priority switched to the *Kriegsmarine*.[232] In spite of the economy's greater centralization under Speer, competition and constantly shifting priorities had not been banished.

The Adolf Hitler Panzer Programme was undermined not just by the traditional structural problems afflicting the

German economy but also by the growing effectiveness of Allied bombing. In March of 1943, as the Programme was in full swing, Bomber Command launched the Battle of Ruhr. The Ruhr was the heart of German heavy industry. with steelworks, armaments factories and synthetic fuel plants. The RAF attacked over two dozen targets including the Krupp works in Essen, and Henschel's factory in Kassel.

Among the direst impacts of the bombing was damage to steel production. To accommodate the new burst of tank construction and increases in other key armaments *Zentrale Planung* anticipated that monthly steel output would reach 2.7 million tons by March of 1943 but the British deprived them of 400,000 tons before the end of the year. What followed was economic stagnation. Ammunition production had doubled in 1942 but increased by only twenty percent in 1943. Aircraft production would not rise until March 1944.[233] Tank production underwent a number of expansions and contractions. In October 1943, 328 *Panzer IV* were produced but November saw only 238 finished and production did not stabilize at 300 vehicles or more until March of 1944.[234]

Strategic bombing's ability to damage factories and limit the already inadequate supply of raw materials created additional hurdles in an economy that already had more than its fair share. Nevertheless, the fact that production stabilized by March of 1944, and began to increase once again, was a testament to the German economy's restorative capabilities. Indeed, 1944 was Germany's best year when it came to tank production, with 17, 737 produced, which was more than had been produced in the previous two years combined.[235] This was impressive growth, especially since it took place under unrelenting Allied assault, but there was a serious problem. The increase was not indicative of a healthy system. Instead it was more like "the final sprint of a marathon runner at the end of his strength."[236]

During six years of war, German industry had furnished the *Wehrmacht* with 44,688 AFVs. Of those, 2,021 were *Tiger*, or its variants. These numbers were quite impressive, given that in 1939 only 787 AFVs had been manufactured.[237] But as impressive as these figures were, they paled in comparison to those of the Allies. While the Germans exceeded the 33,356 AFVs produced by the British and the Commonwealth, the Soviets alone produced 107,359 AFVs and the Americans another 99,035.[238]

The vast gulf between German and Allied AFV production, which was emblematic of the gap that existed across the economies themselves, was the result of several factors. Unlike the Allies, the Germans were unable to maintain a long-term, high-volume bombing campaign. They lacked long-range heavy bombers to strike either the British Midlands or the Soviet factories relocated beyond the Urals, to say nothing of the United States, which was all but immune to air attack.[239] The Allies possessed a much greater pool of resources to draw upon. In steel for example, by 1944, the Allies had produced 110 million tons. By contrast the Germans had produced only 28.1 million tons.[240] Allied economies also benefited from better management, especially in terms of efficient centralization. While centralization took different forms in different countries, they arrived at similar results.

The Americans initially found that production was hindered by multiple, competing agencies but by May of 1943 they had consolidated much of their economy under the Office of War Mobilization. While this office had a considerable bureaucratic footprint, it nevertheless lacked the overwhelming array of committees and sub committees that turned Speer's ministry into a bureaucratic hell. Thus, the Americans were able to reduce infighting, allowing for more effective prioritization overall. They were then able to produce more than twice the number of AFVs produced by the Germans.[241] Richard Overy summed things up well, noting that the "huge disparity in weapons was due not only to American rearmament and Soviet revival, but also to the inability of their enemies to make the most of the resources they had."[242]

Allied production also benefited from a radically different overall design philosophy. Recognizing their superior resources and manufacturing capabilities, the Allies focused on weapons to win a war of long duration, including the vast bomber forces that inflicted great damage upon the German economy. By contrast, the Germans focused on a "maximization of specific kinds of short-term military power," be it fighters and bombers in the summer of 1940 or tanks in the winter and spring of 1943.[243] This German philosophy suited a military used to fighting short wars but it robbed the economy of stable long-term prioritization that proved so effective for the Allies.[244]

These philosophies were also present in tank design. The *Panzer III* and *Panzer IV* were comparable in quality to their Allied counterparts (at least until 1941) and were designed for mass production. But late war German tanks were not. The *Panther* and the *Tiger* were designed to be qualitatively superior to their Allied counterparts. As seen with the *Tiger*, this element of their design was partly a reflection of Hitler's personal views on tank design, and partly a quest to create the best tanks available. It also reflected a realistic appraisal of Germany's industrial position. Despite the best efforts of Todt and Speer, the Allies, with their focus on building a large number of simpler, though by no means less-effective tanks, were out-producing them. So, prioritization of quality in the hopes of mitigating the Allies quantitative advantage seemed to make sense. After all, quality had trumped quantity in France and in the Soviet Union early in the war. However, there were a number of problems with this idea.[245]

The great cost of producing the *Tiger* meant that even before a single *Tiger* fired a shot in anger, there were never going to be enough of them. It also ensured that the *Tiger* losses would be much more difficult to replace. One example came from Operation Goodwood, on the 18th of July 1944. Goodwood was one of the many efforts by the British 21st Army Group to breakout of the Normandy bridgehead. In this instance, three British Armoured Divisions, the 7th, 11th and Guards Armoured, ran afoul of the Germans defences, among them being the tanks of Panzerbataillon 503. After three days, the German defenders had destroyed over 400 British tanks. It was a devastating loss.[246] But as shocking as these losses were, the British quickly made them good. The Guards Armoured Division and the 7th Armoured were both back at full strength and ready for Operation Spring on the 25th, less than a week after the debacle of Goodwood. By contrast, Panzerbataillon 503 lost 13 of its *Tiger* tanks, effectively an entire tank company. These losses were not made good until the end of the Normandy Campaign when the unit returned to Germany.[247] It was a stark contrast.

Indeed, the Normandy Campaign demonstrated well the dangers of building the expensive *Tiger*: By virtue of its complex production, it prevented easy replacement of losses. Three heavy tank battalions served in Normandy, SS Panzer 101 and 102, and the army's Panzerbataillon 503. A total of 135 *Tiger I* and 45 *Tiger II* saw service in that campaign. Only three of them survived the entire campaign. Reinforcements were few, with only the 28 *Tiger II* arriving after the fighting began. Thus, the majority of the 175 *Tiger* that participated in the campaign from the start were lost and not to be replaced until the remnants of the decimated units returned to Germany. The expense and complexity of the vehicles led to their low production numbers, and this had very real, and devastating, effects on operational success, especially as various campaigns dragged on.

Another issue that impacted operational effectiveness throughout the war was the supply of spare parts. Part of the problem was logistical, as the Germans' far flung military operations put enormous strain on their supply lines. For example, in September of 1943, Panzerbataillon 503 lamented that urgently needed spare parts took six weeks to reach them. For units engaged in near constant combat, this was an eternity.[248] The other problem, and by far the larger one, had to do with production. The manufacture of spare parts was, at best, conducted at a ratio of one to one. Thus, for each finished tank, one engine, one transmission, etc. would also be produced as spares. This ratio was woefully inadequate, especially for items like engines and transmissions, which needed to be replaced more frequently. Todt and Speer recognized that production of spare parts was important and by 1943, their rationalization efforts ensured that between 25 and 30 percent of components produced were reserved for spare parts.[249]

This was a definite improvement, but spare parts remained inadequate. As with many other things in the Third Reich some of the blame fell upon Hitler. Guderian impressed upon Speer the importance of spare parts as a means to cheaply maintain large tank forces, at a fraction of the cost required to complete finished vehicles. Hitler was not convinced and remained fixated on the production of finished vehicles, especially since the increase in spare parts production that

Guderian wanted could be obtained only with a 20 percent cut in new AFV production.[250] Since Hitler's will had been clearly expressed in favour of finished vehicle production, there was little room to increase the manufacture of spare parts.

As Allied bombing intensified, this preference for finished vehicles made the spare part situation even worse. Shortages were exacerbated not only by damage to factories where needed components were manufactured, but also because shortfalls in production were made up by cutting into the supply of spare parts. In the summer of 1944, Maybach had cut its allotment of spare engines to 15 percent and by autumn it was down to just eight percent.[251]

The effect of the shortage of spare parts on the heavy tank battalions was significant even before Allied bombing began to seriously impact production in 1944. From the 5th of July to the 21st of September of 1943, Panzerbataillon 503 recorded 240 *Tiger* tanks going to the unit repair facility. Given that the unit had an allotted strength of 45 tanks, that meant that each *Tiger* was sent back for refit at least five times. During this period 275, 919 kilograms of spare parts were used by the battalion, most of which were not readily available to the unit. This included 25 replacement engines and 30 new gearboxes. What was worse was that the unit was still awaiting delivery of another 28 engines and 38 gearboxes when the report was filed on the 10th of October 1943. At this point the unit was still waiting on parts to refurbish 39 tanks – the majority of the battalion. In view of this situation, it was hardly surprising that the battalion found that its average daily strength was a mere ten tanks.[252]

The shortage of spare parts was further exacerbated by another major problem directly related to AFV design. The tank's complexity made the vehicles highly unreliable. Many of these problems could be traced to the drivetrain. Basically, whether it was the 56-ton *Tiger I* or the 75-ton *Jagdtiger*, the engine and transmission were not sufficiently robust enough to support these vehicles, Alfred Rubbel, a *Tiger* commander from Panzerbataillon 503wrote:

> *The engine did not take well to overloading. Its longevity in service was limited. Assuring availability for operations demanded a great deal of technical understanding and hard work from our drivers. The maintenance sections and the workshop were constantly in demand. I remember how I always kept one ear free to listen to the engine when road marching as a tank commander.*[253]

Failure to carefully manage these engines often resulted in disaster. The best example of the calamities that could befall a *Tiger* unit that failed to keep the weaknesses of their engines and transmissions in mind came from the Italian Front. On the 23rd of May 1944, a company of Panzerbataillon 508 was ordered to deploy around the town of Cisterna south of Rome to halt the Allied drive on the city, which had begun the day before. The *Kompanie* had 16 *Tiger*, two more than its allotted strength. They formed up behind the railway embankment between the Mussolini Canal and the railroad crossing. They fired on the Americans with high explosive rounds and then crossed the embankment. Three tanks were disabled in the attempt, one with gearbox trouble and two more with tracks riding onto the sprocket teeth (this was a common problem which left the track stretched taunt and incapable of moving). The 13 remaining crews then spent several hours in the open cleaning out the gun barrels because they had dug into the ground while trying to descend the steep embankment. Once their guns were cleared, they successfully engaged the advancing American forces again, driving them back three kilometers and claiming to destroying fifteen *Shermans*. During this action another *Tiger* suffered artillery fire to the left radiator and limped back to the assembly area at Cori.[254]

The next morning, May 24th, the 12 surviving tanks became 11 as one tank was struck on the final drive by an anti-tank gun and the crew later destroyed the tank. Allied advances to the north towards Cisterna led to new orders to withdraw the *Kompanie*. The commander then split his force. Five tanks were to serve as a rear guard while the other six worked to recover the three tanks the unit had left on the embankment the day before. This recovery operation proved disastrous with four of the six tanks experiencing transmission problems while trying to tow the original three deadheads away. In an effort to limit his losses, the company commander ordered the original three disabled tanks to be destroyed, while pulling two tanks out of the rearguard to help tow the newly disabled vehicles. These eight tanks were able to reach Cori. Of the four tanks left in the rearguard one was hit by anti-tank fire and two others suffered transmission troubles. Their crews then destroyed all three.[255]

In light of the deteriorating tactical position, the company commander deemed it impossible to recover the tanks in the assembly area in Cori and so he ordered nine more *Tiger* destroyed by their crews the next day. The last tank was able to escape destruction at Cori but broke down on its way to Rome. Fortunately for the battalion, the recovery platoon was able to tow it back into the city.[256] Certainly, not every loss was due entirely to a mechanical issue, but had the *Tiger* been more reliable, many the company's losses would not have occurred.

To compound the disaster, which befell the company, the battalion lost a further seven tanks. The battalion commander then reported to Hitler's headquarters where he was relieved of command for losing nearly half of his battalion in less than a week.[257] Hitler may have blamed the battalion commander, but a British analysis of the event, based in part on the interrogation of captured members of the doomed *Kompanie,* placed the blame on the company commander. His decision to recover the first *Tiger* to become disabled started the vicious cycle. Risking and losing virtually his entire command in the process, he would have been wiser to cut his losses. In that way, he would have been able to return with an almost full-strength company. His action was considered to be a case of being "penny wise and pound foolish."[258] It is also clear that he lacked sufficient knowledge of the vehicles' weaknesses in its engine and transmission that led more experienced commanders like Rubbel to use the tank more conservatively to preserve these all too-fragile components. So, in a matter of days *Tiger* unreliability had cost Panzerbataillon 508 its commander as well as an entire tank company. These losses would be bad enough in normal circumstances, but at that time the battalion was the only *Tiger* unit serving in Italy.[259]

The *Tiger I* and *Tiger II* which shared its predecessors' strengths and weaknesses were individually more than a match for the American *M4 Sherman* and the Soviet *T-34,* but the high cost of *Tiger,* its low production numbers, and its unreliability ensured that the heavy tank battalions rarely had sufficient tanks to fill their companies. Even if the units could have been maintained at a high rate of operational readiness, as Operation Goodwood showed, the Allies' ability to replace their losses far outstripped the Germans' ability to inflict them. In total 48,900 *Shermans* and 55,660 *T-34* were produced before the war's end. The tactical superiority of the *Tiger* was not sufficient to overcome such a numerical disadvantage.[260]

The warring powers may have only devoted an average of seven percent of their industrial might to AFVs, but Germany's seven percent allowed her to produce only 44,688 of them, while the Allies produced 239,750 with theirs.[261] Given this disparity, it was clear that Todt and Speer had failed utterly in the task of producing the means to defeat the Allies. *Tiger* production showed this failure well. While the production of the various members of the *Tiger* family was reasonably effective, it was hampered both from without and within. Allied bombing, destroying both the vehicles and the resources to make new ones ensured that many of the superior tanks never reached the army. In broader economic terms, Todt's and Speer's efforts at rationalization, consolidation, and centralization exacerbated, rather than diminished the infighting that had hampered the German economy before the war. Further, the lack of clear and consistent priorities created ever more problems as production lines were constantly reorganized to meet new demands. In many respects, the increases in production that the Germans were able to achieve were not the result of any kind of managerial brilliance from Todt or Speer but instead were the result of greater production of raw materials and the ruthless exploitation of a vast army of forced labour.

The idea of quality over quantity, which drove the production of the *Tiger* also proved to have little positive effect. The high cost of the vehicles and their unreliability ensured that there would never be enough of them to bring to bear upon Allies, even if the production of Allied tanks had not been so high as to render German efforts to counter them virtually useless. The German semi-official history of the war sums things up best. The economic dysfunction of the Reich, in both organization and production decisions was a "logical consequence of its own policy" and was like the "efforts of a man struggling to lift himself by his own bootstraps out of a swamp into which he had jumped of his own free will and in full knowledge of its depth."[262]

EARLY BATTLEFIELD
DEPLOYMENTS

In September of 1942, Panzerbataillon 502 of Army Group North became the first unit to use the *Tiger* in combat. In January of 1943, Panzerbataillon 503 saw its first combat with Army Group Don as it retreated towards the Donets River to escape oncoming Soviet forces eager to deal further blows to the Germans after the encirclement of the 6th Army at Stalingrad. In North Africa, Panzerbataillon 501 saw its first combat against the western Allies in December of 1942. The actions of these three battalions seemed to vindicate the *Tiger* design, especially to the converted. Individually, *Tiger* armour and the 88mm gun more than proved themselves against Allied weapons, but their overall deployments were far less successful.

The 502 deployed its tanks in marshy terrain where a number were lost, including one captured intact by the

Soviets. With a *Tiger* of their own, the surprise and shock value of these new tanks was to some extent lost, with little to show for it. In January, the 503's operations with Army Group Don were tactical successes but vehicles' mechanical failings undermined them. In just two weeks of fighting the 503 found itself able to only field a handful of tanks, an early sign of the toll that repeated combat, a lack of regular maintenance, and the vehicle's unreliability would have on the unit's fighting strength. The successes of the new *Tiger* were overshadowed by the older, more mobile *Panzer III* and *IV* of Herman Balck's 11th Panzer Division, which ultimately saved Army Group Don from being cut off and destroyed.

Balck's success demonstrated that for all of the vaunted combat power of the *Tiger*, tactical success was more dependent on employment than on which vehicle was being used. It was the traditional doctrinal of placing emphasis on speed, surprise, and aggression that was truly decisive. Elsewhere, in North Africa, the tanks of the 501 and the 504 were similarly affected by the vehicle's poor reliability and proved incapable of turning the tide in favor of the Germans.

Initial Tiger Operations in the Soviet Union

As the first *Tiger* tanks came off the assembly line at Henschel in the summer of 1942 they had to be organized for combat. During the 26th of May 1941 meeting, which had outlined Hitler's requirements for Germany's heavy tanks, he described the intended deployment of these new vehicles. He envisioned each panzer division having 20 of these new tanks to act in a spearhead role.[263] The first two heavy tank companies, formed in February of 1942, were designed to fulfill Hitler's wishes but by the spring of 1942 the plan had changed dramatically.[264] It became clear that with production of the *Tiger* being delayed until the end of the summer, there was no way to make Hitler's direction a reality. Equipping each of the 20 panzer divisions in the army in 1941 with a heavy tank company would have required 400 of the new tanks. Given the tank's actual production would have meant that every division could only be fully equipped in July 1943.[265] This number left no room for training tanks or the replacement of losses, to say nothing of further expansion of the *Panzerwaffe*.

The revised plan was to form the *Tiger* into heavy tank battalions to make the best use of these scarce vehicles. The battalions would be assigned by OKH to whichever army or corps required them the most. As a result, the limited number of new tanks could be deployed at crucial points to either fulfill their original breakthrough role or reinforce the defence of a particularly embattled area. The *Tiger* would thereby shift rapidly from being a general force multiplier that any panzer division could call upon to being a more elite unit, employed only in the most crucial of circumstances.[266]

Importantly, while the centerpiece of each heavy battalion was undeniably the *Tiger*, the initial units were not pure *Tiger* units. Each *Kompanie* had nine *Tiger* and ten *Panzer III*. The theory behind this organization was that the *Panzer III* would operate as close support for the *Tiger*, destroying anti-tank guns and defending against infantry, while the *Tiger* focused on destroying enemy tanks and fortifications.[267] This arrangement meant that the *Tiger* early deployments would not only test the vehicles themselves but also their new organization.

As the first tank battalions were being created in the summer of 1942, Hitler became increasingly anxious to employ new heavy tanks and demonstrate the correctness of his design philosophy. Speer recalled: "He regaled us with vivid descriptions of how the Soviet 7.7 centimeter antitank guns which penetrated our *Panzer IV* frontal armour even at sizable distances, would fire shot after shot in vain, and how finally the *Tiger* would roll over the antitank gun nests."[268] In September of 1942, when 502's first *Tiger* company was ready, it was sent to Army Group North to support operations around Leningrad. It was accompanied by the *Panzerbataillon* headquarters and the *Panzerwerkstatt Kompanie* (repair company). This plan was subject to a great deal of criticism by many generals, especially Heinz Guderian. Much of their criticism stemmed from the marshy terrain in which operations were to be conducted. In such conditions, the heavy *Tiger* would be confined to roads to avoid bogging down. Confined to roads, the *Tiger* would be an easy target for Soviet antitank guns and Guderian didn't share Hitler's faith in the tank's invulnerability. Guderian also criticized the limited deployment of these new machines. "A lesson learned from the First World War had taught us that it is necessary to be patient about committing new weapons and that they must be held back until they are being produced in such quantities as to allow their employment in mass."[269]

Despite Guderian's well-known and vocal criticisms of the early deployment of the *Tiger*, Hitler ordered it anyway. The first combat deployment on the 16th of September 1942 with four of the heavy tanks (all that had arrived up to that point) was a success. The tanks were able to defeat dug in infantry and artillery, with the 88mm gun performing well. The armour on the *Tiger* did not succumb to any Soviet anti-tank fire. So, a larger attack was ordered for the 22nd. This attack, supported by a *Panzer III* platoon and the men of the 170th Infantry Division did not go as well. One *Panzer III* was lost, three of the four *Tiger* tanks suffered damage to their gun barrels and the leading *Tiger* burned out and had to be abandoned. Three days later it was destroyed after efforts to recover it failed.[270]

Worse was to yet come. On the 18th of January 1943, while breaking out of Schlüsselberg to avoid being encircled by Soviet forces, one *Tiger* was fired on and the inexperienced driver attempted to turn around to get away. His efforts sent the tank off the road and into a swamp. The crew was then killed trying to escape the bogged down vehicle. Afterwards, the Soviets were able to recover the *Tiger* and by May, the Soviets had completed their analysis of the tank. They identified the weakest points. There was a "shell trap" between the turret and the hull, the gun itself was not shielded, and if the drivetrain were hit, it would destroy the brakes and multiple road wheels.[271]

The Soviets' analysis identified their own 85mm anti-aircraft gun, as well as the 122mm and 152mm howitzers as weapons capable of penetrating the new German tank. Plans were made to fit these weapons in AFVs. These efforts would not bear fruit until February 1943 with the introduction of the *SU-152*, followed by the *SU-122* [272] and the *T-34/85*.[273] Even before more powerful weapons were available, information on the *Tiger* was rapidly circulated within the Red Army. While it would take the Soviets several months to fully uncover the secrets of the new German tank, Guderian was vindicated. "The results were not only heavy, unnecessary casualties, but also the loss of secrecy and of the element of surprise for future operations."[274]

The initial *Tiger* operations around Leningrad had not been very successful. It fell to the vehicles deployed with Army Group Don at the end of 1942 to better demonstrate the new tank's capabilities. These *Tiger* were part of an effort to protect the remnants of the German southern flank after the encirclement of the 6th Army at Stalingrad. They had to protect the vital transportation hub at Rostov by shoring up the

German position long enough for Army Group A to withdraw from the Caucuses.[275] By the time Panzerbataillon 503 arrived in the Rostov area in January of 1943 the situation had become very fluid. The Germans occupied little more than a series of strongpoints and blocking positions in an effort to stall the Soviet advance. In this situation the battalion was employed primarily as a counterattack force. While this was not the offensive breakthrough role the *Tiger* was intended for, the heavy armour and powerful gun, made them useful additions, destroying key defensive positions and enemy tanks.[276]

The most important operation by the battalion came on the 9th of January. It assisted the 2nd Battalion of Panzergrenadier Regiment 128 in its attack on the village of Vessely. Only 11 *Tiger* and 12 *Panzer III* were available, a far cry from the 17 heavy tanks that had been available just three days earlier.[277] The absent vehicles had not been destroyed. They were simply down for maintenance. While this fact was of some comfort for the unit in the future, it did little for the immediate situation and spoke to the underlying mechanical unreliability of the *Tiger*. Vessely's defenders were determined and well supported. They repulsed three German assaults and while the 503 destroyed eight *T-34s,* it was poor compensation for their own losses. A *Panzer III* and two *Tiger* were lost and only one of the surviving *Tiger* was still fully operational at the end of the day. Two of them were so badly damaged that they were sent back to Germany, after they each suffered over two hundred hits.[278]

This heavy damage reflected a Soviet tactic of firing all available weapons at a *Tiger*. It was a tendency borne not out of desperation but an understanding that while many light weapons, including the 45mm *M1937* anti-tank gun could not penetrate the *Tiger* armour, these weapons could still damage sensitive components including vision blocks and running gear, ideally disabling the vehicle, and making it easier to destroy with heavier weapons.[279] Surviving such heavy fire was an ordeal and one commander's account of the damage to his *Tiger* in this period is a testament to its armour and an interesting look inside the vehicle in the midst of heavy enemy fire:

> *At the beginning of the attack, my Tiger was hit on the front of the superstructure by a 7.62cm anti-tank gun. The track links, which had been fastened to the superstructure front plate by a steel bar, were shot away. We heard a dull clang and felt a slight jolt inside the Tiger. At the same time, we observed many near misses striking the ground to the front and the side of the Tiger.*
>
> *Shortly thereafter, I received a hit on the commander's cupola from a 4.5cm anti-tank gun. The brackets holding the glass vision block flew off. The block became welded tight but visibility was eliminated by the impact of the shell fragments. A second hit on the cupola knocked brackets loose from the turret celling. At the same time, a wave of heat and a cloud of acrid smoke enveloped the crew. Two hits from 4.5cm anti-tank shells and 15 hits from anti-tank rounds were counted on the cupola after the battle.*
>
> *The loaders hatch, somewhat stuck and therefore about half open, received several hits from anti-tank rifles, which knocked some brackets off. Other rounds striking the hatch jammed the hinges so it could only be opened with the aid of a wrecking bar after the battle.*
>
> *The enemy bathed the Tiger with machine gun fire on both days. The smoke dischargers mounted on the turret side were riddled, setting them off. This smoke filtering into the crew compartment became so thick and strong that for a short time the crew could not function.*
>
> *The closer the Tiger approached the collective farm, the greater the intensity of the enemy defensive fire. Each hit on the Tiger was accompanied by a sharp clang, a slight jolt, acrid clouds of smoke, a shimmering yellow flash, and a detonation.*

> *The nerves of the crew were stretched thin. We paid no attention to hunger, thirst, or time. Even though the attack lasted over six hours, at the time the crew thought that only a short time had elapsed.*
>
> *After another 7.62cm anti-tank shell struck the gun mantle, the brackets holding the gun snapped, the recoil cylinder began losing fluid, and the gun remained at full recoil. The shaking caused by additional hits damaged the radio, a gas tube, and the gear lever by the driver. The engine caught fire when the shield protecting the exhaust muffler was shot away, but the fire was rapidly extinguished.*
>
> *An explosive charge thrown on top of the Tiger from the side was sensed as a dull explosion accompanied by heat and smoke enveloping the Tiger and the crew.*
>
> *We counted 227 hits from anti-tank rounds, 14 hits from 5.7cm and 4.5cm anti-tank guns, and 11 hits from 7.62cm anti-tank guns. The right track and suspension were heavily damaged. Several road wheels and their suspension arms were perforated. The idler wheel had worked out of its mount. In spite of all this damage, the Tiger still managed to cover an additional 60 kilometers under its own power...*
>
> *In conclusion it can be said that the armour on the Tiger can withstand the most intense punishment that the enemy can deliver. The crew can head into combat secure in the knowledge that they are surrounded by sufficient armour to keep out the most determined anti-tank round.*[280]

The Soviets gave the German armour a thorough testing, and its survivability was loudly trumpeted in the tank's user manual, the *Tigerfibel*. It declared "[The *Tiger*] will withstand anything!"[281] Thus was the legend of *Tiger* invincibility born. This statement ignored the fact that Soviet fire had been sufficient to halt the attack.[282] So while its armour was vindicated, it was also clear that the Soviets had found ways to negate the effectiveness of the few *Tiger* tanks available, even if their ability to reliably dispatch them was still limited.

On the 17th of January Panzerbataillon 503 began to withdrawal towards Rostov. The Soviet advance had made the positions they had fought for earlier in the month untenable. As it made its way back towards the Don River, the Soviets were set to destroy the still retreating Army Group A and deal a severe blow to Army Group Don. The Red Army's plan was to create a bridgehead on the western bank of the Manych River at Manychskaya near the Manych's junction with the Don. From there it was just 40 kilometers to the main bridgehead over the Don at Bataisk, Army Group A's main escape route. On the 22nd, the Soviets gained their desired bridgehead. At that point Battalion 503, with the most powerful tanks in the world, could do absolutely nothing. Two weeks of hard fighting and constant movement had prevented much of the necessary routine maintenance that each *Tiger* required, and only two out of 24 were still battle-worthy. Even if every tank had been ready for action, Rostov was too distant for the slow, heavy tanks to be sent roaring across the steppe to the rescue.[283]

Thus, the task of saving Army Group A fell not to the new wonder weapons, but to the old workhorses, the *Panzer III* and *IV* of *Generalleutnant* Herman Balck's 11th Panzer Division. Balck and his division were well-accustomed to this role. They had spent the previous month holding a line along the Chir River against the Soviet 5th Tank Army. Balck's division was a "fire brigade" for the XLVIII Panzer Corps in what Denis Showalter described as "an example of staff work, willpower, and tactical skill still legitimately cited as among the greatest divisional battles ever fought."[284] In these battles, Balck inevitably came "tearing down on the enemy with the whole weight of his armour in accordance with the old maxim, *Nicht kleckern, sondern klotzen.*"[285]

Balck applied the same principles to the Soviet bridgehead at Manychskaya, even though by this point his division could only muster 30 tanks at best. On the 23rd, Balck pushed back the leading elements of 3rd Guards Tank Brigade into Manychskaya itself. Three attacks launched by the Germans were repulsed. By the next day, he had a new plan to defeat the Soviets. As before, the Germans began by bombarding the northeastern part of the town, then assaulting it with armoured cars and halftracks. But this was only a feint. Once the Soviet brigade's tanks had left their positions in the south of town to counter the German attack, the artillery shifted to the south of Manychskaya, Balck's true target. The tanks roared in, striking the Soviets in the rear. Outmaneuvered and badly battered in the bargain, 3rd Guards withdrew back over the Manych. The Guards lost 20 tanks, and the brigade suffered between 500-600 casualties. 11th Panzer, by contrast, suffered only one man killed and 14 wounded. Balck's excellent attack pushed the Soviets off balance, convincing them that a full-strength panzer division lay before them, not Balck's badly depleted force. With the Soviets reverting to the defensive, Army Group A was able to complete its withdrawal on the 31st as the last units of 1st Panzer Army reached safety.[286]

Balck's victory at Manychskaya was a triumph that further cemented his reputation as a "born leader of armour", but in a larger sense it was also a further vindication of the traditional German doctrine.[287] Even when badly outnumbered, the traditional elements of speed, surprise, and aggression could win the day, provided the tanks were used aggressively and well led. By contrast, while the *Tiger* tanks of the 503 had performed well, with the unit claiming to have destroyed at least 39 Soviet tanks, with only two *Tiger* lost outright, their overall impact had been limited and fleeting.[288] The *Tiger* tanks were a powerful force multiplier for counterattacks but lacked the speed and reliability that had allowed the *Panzer III* and *IV* to have a decisive impact on the campaign.[289]

Operations of the *Tiger* in North Africa lacked the dramatic contrast seen above between the new heavy tank and the older mediums in Army Group Don. Nevertheless, in Tunisia from December of 1942 to May of 1943 the employment of the *Tiger* reflected the same strengths and weaknesses seen in the Soviet Union. Panzerbataillon 501 was the first of two heavy battalions sent to reinforce the German-Italian Armoured Army in November of 1942. When the formation arrived, the situation was particularly perilous. Earlier, the Axis had suffered two devastating blows in quick succession. In the east, on the 4th of November 1942, they had lost the 2nd Battle of El Alamein to Lieutenant General Bernard Montgomery's 8th Army and in the west, on the 8th, Operation Torch, the first major successful Allied amphibious landing of the war saw a combined British and American force invade Algeria and Morocco.[290] The battalion was now to support part of Rommel's effort to restore the situation in North Africa, halting the Allies two-pronged convergence on Tunisia.

The first elements of the 501 arrived in Tunis on the 23rd of November 1942 and the battalion saw piecemeal deployments until the new year. This was the result of both the strained logistical situation faced by the Axis, especially as Allied aircraft and submarines took a heavy toll on the ships needed to sustain the *Panzerarmee*, as well as the precarious tactical position of the army. The unit's first action came on the 1st of December with just three *Tiger* and four *Panzer III*. This initial fighting was part of *General der Panzertruppe* Walter Nehring's efforts to protect the vital port of Tunis from the Allies in the Tebourba area, just 32 kilometers from the city.

Nehring's plan was to employ four *Kampfgruppen*[291]
These were KG Koch, KG Lüder, KG Hudel and KG Djedeida,
which would attack from three directions. While Koch fixed
the Allies' attention from the south, Lüder and Hudel struck
from the north. The fourth Kampfgruppe, Djedeida, launched
attacks from the east. The three Tiger tanks were split between
Lüder and Djedeida for the initial attack, with Lüder receiving
one and Djedeida the remaining two. The initial attack met
with a great deal of success. Lüder and Hudel successfully
attacked from the north driving back the American units
in front of them. They also repulsed a counterattack by two
British armoured battalions, the 17th Lancers and 21st Lancers,
with five *Crusader* tanks destroyed, though it was unclear who
accounted for any of these kills.[292] *Crusaders* were not the only
victims. The two *Tiger* tanks with Djedeida engaged a group of
General Lee tanks (American tanks supplied to the British) at
100 meters. At this range the British tanks couldn't penetrate
the *Tiger* side armour, but the Germans had no trouble
penetrating the Allied tanks. Once two of the *General Lees*
were destroyed, the rest withdrew.[293]

This initial attack in North Africa was far more
auspicious than the first *Tiger* action in the Soviet Union back
in September, although one *Tiger* was taken out of the fight
by engine failure. Nevertheless, the tank's armour and gun had
more than proven their value against the western Allies. But
overall, German the effort was less successful. The attack by
KG Lüder and KG Hudel had stalled between the Tebourba
Gap and Tebourba and while the *Tiger* had bested both the
General Lee and *Crusader*, the British held their line – for the
moment. By the 3rd of December Tebourba had fallen and
while the *Tiger* tanks were deployed only in small numbers,

they were nevertheless welcome force multipliers for the German attacks.[294]

After a number of other small-scale engagements in December, January saw the first major deployment of the Panzerbataillon 501 in Operation Eilbote I (Courier). Eilbote was conducted by part of *Generaloberst* Hans-Jürgen von Arnim's 5th *Panzer* Army. It was designed to protect the lines of communication between Tunis and Rommel's Afrika Korps, by attacking Allied forces between Enfidaville and Sousse. This operation was the first major deployment of the battalion, but it did not represent a deployment of *Tiger* tanks en masse. Only nine of the 19 in theatre were available. The rest were either awaiting repairs or were still being unloaded at Tunis.

Tanks awaiting repair proved to be especially problematic for the battalion. The unit's repair company yet to arrive, leaving reparations in the hands of the smaller and less well equipped *Panzerwerkstatt Zug* (repair platoon) attached to each *Kompanie*. Repairs were also hampered by an especially acute shortage of spare parts caused by the Allied interdiction of Axis supplies.[295] Four *Tiger* tanks were assigned to Kampfgruppe Weber, assigned to handle the initial break in of the Allied line, allowing Kampfgruppe Lüder, with five *Tiger* and ten *Panzer III* to exploit the initial attack.[296]

Kampfgruppe Weber's initial attack was successful. But it came at a heavy cost. Previous attacks had struck Allied positions that were often poorly prepared to repulse tank attacks. This time, the Allies had had ample time to prepare their ground and had seeded the area with large quantities of landmines. While the attack was a success, with the attached armoured engineers clearing over 100 mines, the mines still exacted a high price on the understrength unit. One *Tiger* suffered transmission damage and another *Tiger*, as well as three *Panzer III* were disabled by the mines.[297] Reinforcing success, Kampfgruppe Lüder continued its attack, the next day capturing its objective, the crossroads outside El Glib. Unfortunately for the panzerbataillon, Allied mines continued to take their toll, with two more *Tiger* tanks disabled.[298] Kampfgruppe Lüder may have gained its objective, but again, it came at a high price. British 6-pounder (57mm) anti-tank guns engaged at ranges varying between 900 to 576 meters. The guns made short work of six *Panzer III* and two *Tiger* tanks.[299]

German reports corroborate much of this account, describing both *Tiger* tanks as having burst into flames after being hit, though they recorded the loss of only four *Panzer III*.[300] The Germans were subsequently able to recover the second *Tiger* after nightfall but the first tank remained in place until destroyed by British engineers who feared its recapture. While the vehicle was destroyed before a thorough examination could be completed, examining the wreck and especially the hull armour, which was intact, allowed the British to develop a good assessment of the effectiveness of their anti-tank weapons against the new German tank.

They concluded that the 6-pounder could not penetrate the *Tiger* from the front. Firing two rounds at the front plate at 300 yards (274 meters) failed to penetrate the 100mm frontal armour. Thus, the *Tiger* had to be engaged, as they were in this instance, from the flanks. This conclusion was proven by the Germans, as analysis of the second, recovered *Tiger*, showed 24 hits by 6-pounder rounds. Of those, only five penetrated the armour – all from the sides of the vehicle. None of the rounds that struck the front of the tank penetrated.[301] It was this series of tests, and examination of another *Tiger*, captured in March of 1943, that spurred the British to develop the

17-pounder (76.2mm) anti-tank gun, which would be capable of penetrating the *Tiger* from the front.[302]

While the British got the better of the engagement on the 20th, both in terms of vehicles destroyed and knowledge gained, the overall German attack by Kampfgruppe Lüder had been successful and the *Tiger* remained in the area until the 25th, to secure their gains. Nevertheless, the 501 found, as had the 503 before it, and every heavy tank battalion would find subsequently, that repeated use had a rapid and debilitating effect on the vehicles. The unit's after-action report recorded an average of just three functional heavy tanks per day during this operation and by the 25th "the fact that only one *Tiger* out of nine was still fully operational and two or three others were conditionally operational at the end ... should not be disregarded."[303] After five months in combat, the *Tiger* had established its reputation as mechanically unreliable.

These combat actions demonstrated that the Allies were beginning to develop effective counters to the *Tiger*. The heavy Allied use of minefields was the most prominent example, and while the 501 proved that a sufficient number of tanks could simply "bull through" a minefield, their ability to wear down *Tiger* formations continued to make minefields useful throughout the war. It is also worth noting that unlike the Allies, who invested heavily in mine clearance tanks, using either rollers or flail drums, the Germans continued to rely either on highly vulnerable combat engineer units or simply charging through until the war's end, especially as efforts to clear mines with remote controlled explosive carriers at Kursk were not particularly successful on a large scale.[304]

It was also clear that Allied anti-tank guns like the 6-pounder didn't have sufficient power to overcome the tank's formidable frontal armour, but the tactic of using flanking shots allowed these guns to be used effectively against the vehicle's thinner side armour. Accordingly, like the Soviets, whatever initial shock value the *Tiger* had was quickly dissipated and even though the Allies lacked a definite "Tiger Killer" at this point, they had nevertheless rapidly adapted available weapons to defeat the new German heavy tank.

The story of the 501 in North Africa closed on 17th of March 1943, with the 11 remaining *Tiger* tanks being transferred to the newly arrived Panzerbataillon 504.[305] The 504 had even less success in Tunisia than had the 501, participating in a number of small-scale actions as Axis forces retreated towards Tunis, with the final elements of the battalion surrendering on the 12th of May along with the rest of the Axis forces in North Africa. One incident is worth discussing however, the capture of *Tiger* 131. On the 19th of April, two *Tiger* were attached to the 3rd Battalion, Fallschirmjäger (Paratroop) Regiment 5 for an attack on Djebel Djaffa. The operation was codenamed Fliederblüte (Lilac Bloom). The attack met with little success and the tanks found themselves in combat with the *Churchills* of the 48th Royal Tank Regiment (RTR).

These British heavy tanks actually had more frontal armour than the *Tiger*, with 152mm thick vertical front plates, but the 6-pounder gun mounted on the 48th RTR's *Churchill Mk. IV* was ineffective against the *Tiger*, especially when compared to its 88mm gun. Nevertheless, B Squadron's *Churchills*, advancing in support of the defending battalion from the East Surry Regiment were surprised to find the 504's two *Tiger* behind a ridge. A close-quarters battle fought at just 183 meters ensued. Two *Churchills* were quickly knocked out, one of them providing ample evidence of the superiority of the Germans 88mm gun as a round entered the hull machine gun position and ended up embedded in the engine. This was hardly a glowing endorsement of the *Churchill's* armour. Nevertheless, the British attack clearly caught the Germans by surprise, causing the crews of two *Panzer III*, one *Panzer IV* and *Tiger* 131 to abandon their vehicles, despite none taking serious damage.[306] Like the 502 *Tiger* that the Soviets had recovered from the swamps around Leningrad in January, *Tiger* 131 provided the Allies with invaluable insights into the new German tank and was instrumental in understanding the vehicle's vulnerabilities. This knowledge combined with the 17-pounder gun proved essential in Allied successes against the *Tiger*, especially in Normandy in the summer of 1944.[307]

The early engagements of the *Tiger* from September 1942 to May 1943 had been generally poor in operational terms and with infrequent tactical successes. The 502 had been unable to positively impact the Germans position around Leningrad and neither the 501 nor the 504 could tip the balance back in favor of the Axis in North Africa. Their failures were due partly to the shortage of *Tiger* tanks, with none of three units being able to field a full battalion during this period owning to low production numbers and poor transport capability. Tactically, the *Tiger* performed well, with early engagements establishing the legendary reputation of both its gun and its armour. But these engagements also established the tank's reputation for unreliability. Both the Soviets and the British rapidly adapted their tactics to counter the new German heavy tank, and more importantly, in the longer term each captured *Tiger* spurred the development of more powerful weapons to combat these tanks.

Indeed, the only thing that had not been sufficiently tested regarding the *Tiger*, was its ability to carry out its intended breakthrough role. Even in its offensive uses in North Africa, the heavy battalions were considerably understrength and were not operating at their full potential. The true test of the *Tiger* in its intended role would come later. In July of 1943 at the famed Battle of Kursk, the *Tiger* would finally be tested on the offensive, with the full might of the *Wehrmacht* to support it.

OPERATION ZITADELLE

he initial employment of the *Tiger*, both in the Soviet Union and in North Africa, demonstrated its value in both the counterattack role, and in offensive actions of limited scope. But overall, German forces were too weak and the *Tiger* fleet too small to allow for the tank's use in its intended breakthrough role. That changed in the summer of 1943. On the 5th of July the *Tiger* finally got the opportunity to perform in this role with the launching of Operation Zitadelle, more widely known as the Battle of Kursk.

Zitadelle was designed to be the answer to the German strategic dilemma in the East in 1943. After two years of heavy fighting, the *Wehrmacht* no longer had the strength to launch an offensive on the scale of the previous year's Operation Blue, to say nothing of another operation the size of Barbarossa. Nevertheless, Germany still needed to stage some kind of eastern offensive in 1943 to convince its wavering allies of the continued supremacy of German arms, and to buy time. Destroying the Kursk Salient would, if all went according to plan, cause enough damage to the Red Army that its inevitable summer offensives would have to be delayed.[308]

This operation proved to be the only opportunity to use the *Tiger* tanks en masse in their intended role. The results were decidedly mixed. While *Tiger* tanks were able to facilitate some German breaches in the Soviet lines, especially when units were operating at close to full strength, the rapid accumulation of losses meant that their overall effectiveness declined rapidly. In a broader sense, the *Tiger* was also hampered by the Soviet numerical superiority, along with the depth of their defenses, which made it difficult to exploit whatever successes the *Tiger* tanks were able to create. Not only had the Allies been able to learn how to deal with the *Tiger*, but they had also learned how to deal with German armoured tactics more broadly, which doubly hampered their performance during the operation. Ultimately, the rapidly diminishing strength of the *Tiger* units and the general German weakness in the summer of 1943 limited their effectiveness during *Zitadelle*.

The *Tiger* played an important role in the offensive, with five such units taking part. Starting in the north, there was Heavy Tank Battalion 505 which was attached to XLVII Panzer Corps, the spearhead of *Generaloberst* Walter Model's attack along the northern side of the salient. The battalion had only been activated in February and Zitadelle was its first major engagement.. Unlike the rest of the *Tiger* units, 505 started the operation understrength, the 3rd Company not arriving until the 8th of July.[309] In the south, *Generaloberst* Herman Hoth's 4th Panzer Army contained the largest *Tiger* concentration with four heavy tank companies. One company was attached to the Großdeutschland Panzergrenadier Division, which was assigned to XLVIII Panzer Corps. The other three were attached to the three panzergrenadier divisions of the SS II Panzer Corps: the Leibstandarte Adolf Hitler, Das Reich, and the Totenkopf.[310]

The independent companies attached to these elite divisions reflected partly their status but also the last vestiges of Hitler's initial concept for the use of the tanks. As discussed, Hitler intended for each panzer division to have a heavy tank company and while production realities made this plan unworkable, these divisions were still permitted to test the theory.[311] All of these companies had been activated at the beginning of the year and had been employed in the recapture of Kharkov in March of 1943, the culmination of *Generalfeldmarschall* Erich von Manstein's "backhand blow."[312]

While the heavy tank companies operating with 4th Panzer Army had some experience, none had as much as the final unit to see combat during Zitadelle, Panzerbataillon 503. Unlike the other *Tiger* units, the 503 was not assigned to one of the principal assaulting corps. Instead, it. was attached to III Panzer Corps in *Armee-Abteilung* Kempf (Army Detachment, an ad hoc formation that was larger than a corps but smaller than an army). Armee Abteilung Kempf was tasked with keeping pace with SS II Panzer Corps on its left to protect the right flank of the SS divisions as they advanced. The veterans of 503 attached to bolster the forces engaged in this upcoming task.[313]

Before discussing the operation, one final organizational note should be mentioned. Recall that the heavy tank battalions had been organized with mixed companies comprising both *Panzer III* and *Tiger*. By May of 1943, the experiences of the units serving on the Eastern Front and in North Africa had sparked considerable debate. The commanders of 501 and 502 continued to view the mixed composition as being essential.

They argued that this mix gave the units greater flexibility because the lighter *Panzer III*, could conduct reconnaissance or escort the heavy *Tiger*.[314] The commanders of 503 and 13th Company, Großdeutschland believed that the units should instead be "purebred", consisting only of *Tiger* tanks. This conviction was based partly on the logistical burden created by having to procure two sets of spare parts. But it was also based on the Soviet tendency to target the *Panzer III*, rather than the more difficult to destroy *Tiger*.[315] This debate was ultimately settled by Guderian in his role as *Generalinspektor der Panzertruppe*. He sided with the 503 and Großdeutschland, calling for the removal of the *Panzer III*.[316] The new purebred companies saw service during Zitadelle and right through to the war's end.

The 5th of July 1943, the opening day of Operation Zitadelle, was a day of mixed results for the *Tiger*. Panzerbataillon 505, attached to XLVII Panzer Corps, led Model's attack, acting as the spearhead for the 6th Infantry Division. During the initial advance to the Oka River, they encountered the Soviet first line of defense. Among its defenders was Lieutenant Vasiliy Krysov's battery of *SU-122* assault guns. His unit, the 1454th Self Propelled Artillery Regiment was part of the Red Army's growing arsenal of anti-tank weapons capable of taking on the *Tiger*. As discussed in the previous chapter, the 122mm *M1938* (M-30) howitzer had been identified as one of the few weapons in the Soviet arsenal capable of effectively engaging the *Tiger*. To improve its mobility, it was mounted on a *T-34* chassis to create an effective assault gun.[317]

The effectiveness of the *SU-122* and all that the Soviets had learned about the *Tiger* were demonstrated by Krysov's battery. He saw the *Tiger* tanks, supported by *Panzer IV* of the 20th Panzer Division approaching his well-camouflaged position. His men waited for the *Tiger* tanks to close to within 500 meters, whence they could reliably penetrate the *Tiger* frontal armour. At that point the battery opened fire [318]. One *Tiger* was knocked out, but a second tank began to move ahead and was engaged by Krysov's own vehicle. As he recalled in his memoir, *Panzer Destroyer: Memoirs of a Red Army Tank Commander*:

> 'Valeriy! At the second [tank] from the left! Fire!' I ordered the gunlayer. The shell exploded on the upper part of the turret. However, the tank not only kept advancing, but it also continued to fire...I gave Korolev [the gunner] a new aiming point: 'At the tracks! Fire!' The heavy shell smashed a track! The tank swerved to the left, exposing its right side. Vasily Tsybin, the experienced gunlayer on Gorshov's crew, who hadn't fired prior to this, had been waiting for just such an opportunity- in an instant he sent a shell into the side of the enemy tank and set it ablaze![319]

These vehicles disabled two *Tiger* tanks and while the Germans recovered both, the action was a testament to the effectiveness of new Soviet anti-tank weapons and the dissemination of information across the Red Army regarding the tank's weaknesses. Gunners had learned to disable the vehicle before striking its thinner side armour.[320]

The Soviets may have been better prepared to face the *Tiger* in 1943, but the heavy tank battalions continued to demonstrate their effectiveness. Once they had driven off Krysov's *SU-122* battery with artillery and crossed the Oka River, the division was attacked by waves of *T-34*. Here the *Tiger* proved its worth. The waves of *T-34* were broken up by highly accurate 88mm fire. An astounding 42 of the *T-34s* were lost, and the division's subsequent advance caused the collapse of the Soviet 15th Rifle Division. With the rifle division's collapse, a hole was opened on the right flank of the 70th Army.

Unfortunately for the Germans, the 2nd Panzer Division was not slated to begin its attack until the next day and was not ready to exploit this opportunity.[321] Nevertheless, 505 had been very successful. The Soviet's front had been breached, 42 Soviet tanks had been destroyed and not a single *Tiger* lost.[322]

The next day, on the 6th, *Tiger* tanks were instrumental in defeating a Soviet counterattack. The Soviet 107th Tank Brigade had the extreme misfortune of driving right into them, losing 46 of their 63 tanks in less than 15 minutes.[323] With the Soviet counterattack destroyed, the German tanks moved towards the Olkhovatka Heights in the northern part of the Kursk Salient, the key terrain feature in the northern part of the Kursk Salient. Once this high ground was in German hands, the tanks broke onto the open plains on the way to Kursk.

The initial German assault was unsuccessful, and 18 *Tiger* tanks were damaged in the effort.[324] Repeated attempts over the coming days not only failed but also exacted a heavy toll on the 505. By the 8th, only three tanks remained operational, leading to their withdrawal into XLVII Panzer Corps reserve until the 10th.[325] This two-day reprieve allowed 12 tanks to rejoin the unit, a testament to the skills of the maintenance company. They were also joined by the newly arrived tanks of the 3rd Company 505. With these new tanks, 505 was ready to fight when Model renewed his advance.[326] Despite this boost to the unit's fighting power, the attack failed and the 505 lost another 15 tanks. While all of them were recovered and repairable, the unit was reduced to only 11 vehicles, too few for even a single tank company.[327]

Model tried one more time the following day but failed once again. To make matters worse, the Soviets had launched Operation Kutuzov, a counteroffensive thrust towards the city of Orel, north of the salient. If Orel fell, then the 9th Army would be cut off and likely destroyed. So, the northern attack of Zitadelle came to an end. As Model withdrew his battered panzer divisions to meet this new Soviet threat the *Tiger* tanks of the 505 remained on the defensive until the 18th because they were too slow to go fend off the new Soviet offensive and were needed to hold the Germans gains, such as they were.[328]

Turning to Army Group South's actions the discussion will focus on the heavy tank companies, primarily 13th Company, Leibstandarte SS Adolf Hitler (13. LSSAH). 13. LSSAH's performance reflected the successes and limitations of practically all these units and that of the *Tiger* units throughout the battle, irrespective of which division they belonged to.

On July 5th, the three SS panzergrenadier divisions, led by their heavy tank companies, made good progress, though two tanks in Leibstandarte were disabled by mines. One of these was *SS Untersturmführer* (Lieutenant) Michael Wittmann's *Tiger*. Wittmann was an experienced tanker, having commanded a *StuG* since 1941, but his actions at Kursk, and later in Normandy turned him into a legendary panzer commander, closely associated with the *Tiger*. Prior to the disabling of his *Tiger*, Wittmann and his crew had destroyed eight *T-34s* and had run over several anti-tank guns. (This may seem like rash bravado, but *Tiger* crews were encouraged to save ammunition by simply crushing anti-tank guns if possible).[329] The 13. LSSAH had one other *Tiger* disabled, which was struck in the rear by an anti-tank gun. Das Reich had two of its tanks disabled by mines as well, and Totenkopf suffered the most, losing five.[330]

By the 8th, the SS divisions had made good progress northwards, and then began to pivot northwest towards the railway junction at Prokhorovka, which would allow the Germans to seize the rail junction and avoid crossing the

Psel River, instead breaking out onto the open plain to link up with Model's 9th Army.[331] As the SS divisions advanced, one remarkable story came out of 13. LSSAH. While the rest of the unit advanced, *Tiger* 1322[332], commanded by *SS Unterscharführer* (Corporal) Franz Staudegger was moving his damaged vehicle back to the division's rear when he encountered 50-60 Soviet tanks. He and his crew destroyed 17 of them in the initial engagement and Staudegger accounted for five more when they attacked again. After being thoroughly mauled by the lone German tank, the surviving Soviets beat a hasty retreat.[333] He was subsequently awarded the Knight's Cross for this action.[334]

On the eve of the 12th, the LSSAH arrived at Prokhorovka, the Panzergrenadier divisions were badly worn out, with most of their heavy tank companies in particularly poor shape. Totenkopf, holding the Corps' left flank over the Psel River was in the best condition, with 11 tanks still operational, which reflected a particularly efficient tank maintenance platoon, given that on the 9th, only one *Tiger* had been operational.[335] In the center, the Leibstandarte had only four operating tanks left.[336] On the right, Das Reich had not a single *Tiger*, having had one tank destroyed the previous day and the rest being disabled by mines and enemy fire.[337] On the 12th, the Soviets launched a massive counterattack, which struck the SS Panzer Corps dead center, on the frontline of the Leibstandarte, outside Prokhorovka.[338]

The battle that followed the Soviet counterattack, spearheaded by Lieutenant General Pavel Rotmistrov's 5th Guards Tank Army, has gone down in history as one of the greatest tank battles of all time with Soviet and German armour meeting in a close-quarters death match: Commander of the

5ᵗʰ Guards Tank Army Lieutenant General Pavel Rotmistrov gave this account:

> *The intensity of the battle grew with incredible fury and force. Because of the fire, smoke and dust it became increasingly difficult to make out where own were and where the other sides [were]...Tanks were circling as if caught in a giant whirlpool. The T-34 crews, maneuvering, turning were firing at Tigers and Panthers, but they themselves, coming under the direct fire of the enemy heavy tanks and self-propelled guns, were stopping, burning, dying.*[339]

At the end of this dramatic battle the price to the Soviets had been high with over 200 tanks lost, but the Germans had suffered a serious defeat, with 400 German tanks destroyed, including 70 *Tiger* tanks, at least according to Rotmistrov.[340] His account, which would become the definitive Soviet narrative of the battle was almost entirely incorrect. As stated earlier, the Leibstandarte had only four operational *Tiger* and it must be said that there were only 56 *Tiger* tanks in the 4ᵗʰ Panzer Army when the operation began. The entire story was a cover up, a very effective attempt to hide Rotmistrov's failures.[341]

Rather than an epic clash of armour on the steppe, Prokhorovka instead resembled a twentieth-century Charge of the Light Brigade. The counterattack had been hastily planned and the emphasis that the Soviets had placed on secrecy meant that Rotmistrov and his staff had lacked accurate maps of the area. Consequently, the majority of his tanks were left to drive across an open plain towards a massive anti-tank ditch, over which there was just one bridge. Racing towards the bridge, the Soviet tanks came under the fire from every available tank and anti-tank gun. Under this fire few of Rotmistrov's tanks even reached the bridge.[342] At this time the *Tiger* units were employed on the division's left flank. Wittman's troop of four tanks, covered the October State Farm. Arrayed against them were 100 Soviet tanks. At long range, the 88mm guns made short work of the Soviets, but they pressed on regardless and the fight became a close-range melee.[343] Wittmann's tank was struck twice but suffered no lasting damage.[344]

One of Wittmann's tanks was not so fortunate as Leibstandarte veteran Erwin Bartmann recalled:

> *As we advanced...we came across a trail of spent shell casing leading to the smoldering hulk of a Tiger tank. The sickening stench of hot steel and roasted flesh stuck at the back of my throat. The tank's turret, pockmarked with craters where Soviet tank shells had struck, had shrugged off dozens of hits, each one of which must have stretched the crew's nerves to snapping point. Near the base of the turret was a circular hole surrounded by silvery metallic globules where the Tiger's armour had melted like candle wax. A Russian shell had finally found a weak spot. In the surrounding fields, half a dozen Soviet tanks burned, each ringed by scorched grass. It appeared to me that the crew of the Tiger, tormented by the swarm of T-34s, had fought heroically until it took the fatal shot. With no sign of a massive internal explosion, it had probably run out of ammunition.[345]*

The 13. LSSAH's defence of the October State Farm became a key element of Wittmann's legacy as a great tank ace. He and his *Tiger* commanders accounted for many of the estimated 340 Soviet tanks destroyed on the 12th of July, while only losing one *Tiger*.[346] The losses for the rest of the division were similarly low, with only seven vehicles lost.[347] While the battle had been a crushing defeat for the Soviets, the intense fighting had still taken a toll on the Leibstandarte, and the loss of both men and materiel were worsened by the fact that they came after 11 days of constant combat. *Generalfeldmarschall* Erich von

Manstein, who as Commander Army Group South, oversaw 4th Panzer Army, rejoiced believing that the Soviets were nearly broken. Hoth was more cautious however, recognizing that the divisions which had been at the sharp end of the offensive were nearly spent. Also, with the ending of Model's attack in the north to counter Operation Kutuzov there was little point in continuing the advance, especially with exhausted divisions.[348]

The experiences of the independent heavy tank companies of Großdeutschland and the three Waffen SS divisions didn't provide the concept of having divisional heavy tank companies with any vindication. With only 14 *Tiger* tanks each, a company could ill afford losses, even if they were only temporary. Even minor losses had serious effects on the company's fighting power. It was this rapid accumulation of losses, combined with the logistical difficulties inherent in supplying both the unique needs of the *Tiger* and those of the rest of the tanks in a normal panzer regiment that led to the disbanding of the heavy tank companies in the months following Kursk.[349] Instead, the companies became the nuclei of several new heavy tank battalions.

Großdeutschland's tank company became the 3rd Battalion, Panzer Regiment Großdeutschland in August 1943.[350] The Leibstandarte and Das Reich companies became parts of SS Heavy Tank Battalion 101 and SS Heavy Tank Battalion 102 respectively. While many of the men from these companies helped to form these new units, in the summer of 1943 the companies themselves remained at the front until April 1944, at the end of the Soviet offensives which began after Kursk.[351] The only exception was the 9th Company, Totenkopf, which retained its *Tiger* tanks until the end of the war, though whether this was because of Henrich Himmler's particular fondness for the division, or as a final attempt to try the heavy tank company concept remains unclear.[352]

The final *Tiger* group to see combat during Zitadelle was the 503, attached to Armee Abteilung Kempf. While 505 was deployed as a complete battalion, the 503 was broken up, with each company being assigned to one of the three panzer divisions of III Panzer Corps. The 1st Company, 503 was assigned to the 6th Panzer Division, the 2nd to the 19th Panzer Division and 3rd to the 7th Panzer Division.[353] This decision ensured that each of III Panzer Corps' leading panzer divisions had its own *Tiger* force to help them breakthrough the Soviet lines. His decision was not popular with *Hauptmann* Clemens *Graf* von Kageneck, the commander of 503. He felt that this deployment of his unit violated "Guderian's maxim of *Klotzen, nicht kleckern,* which called for the massing of armour, not its dispersion.[354] His immediate superior, *General der Panzertruppe* Hermann Breith, commanding III Panzer agreed but it would be several days before the battalion was reunified, so the companies began the offensive independently.[355]

The initial employment of the 503 did not go well and was fraught with problems, which were compounded by the fact that III Panzer Corps had to cross the Donets River before it could even begin its offensive in earnest. Destroyed bridges and unmarked German minefields cost the company nine vehicles before it even began to assist the divisions of III Panzer.[356]

From the 6th to the 11th, when the companies were finally reunited, III Panzer Corps continued to advance, though its advance proved to be much slower than that of SS II Panzer Corps. This was problematic since the task of the Armee Abteilung was to protect the corps' right flank. During this time the 1st and 3rd Companies, serving with the 6th and 7th Panzer Divisions respectively, were able to effectively aid these divisions, despite their own losses, including the reduction of the 1st Company to just four operational tanks on the 8th. It is important to note that the 19th Panzer Division, which lacked the support of the 2nd Company, after its heavy losses on the 5th, did not perform markedly worse than its *Tiger* supported comrades. Part of this fairly even performance – regardless of the presence of *Tiger* – was due to the extensive Soviet defenses, which made any kind of rapid progress difficult. It also reflected the fact that a single *Tiger* Company was not a sufficient supporting element for a division in these circumstances.[357]

Richard von Rosen, a *Leutnant* with the 3rd Company 503 attached to the 7th Panzer Division, gave a good account of the intense resistance that faced the *Tiger* tanks during Zitadelle in his memoir, *Panzer Ace: The Memoirs of an Iron Cross Panzer Commander From Barbarossa to Normandy.* Operations on July 6th were typical:

> *[We] approached the wood. There was no way through it except through a glade to the right, which forced us to close up, but there was no alternative. Therefore, we drove towards the glade, to the left it was about 500m to the wood, to the right a bit more but it was also thick woodland there too. Suddenly we saw muzzle flashes, at first from the right, but not from standard anti-tank guns, whose flashes were different. Afterwards I established that they came from SU-152 self-propelled assault guns armed with a 152mm flat trajectory howitzer which we had not previously come up against [While SU-152s were employed at Kursk, the only unit equipped with them fought with the Central Front, which faced Models Ninth Army. It is more likely that these were 152mm howitzers being employed in an anti-tank role[358]]...My two Tigers of the right-hand group were in good form, engaged the enemy and shot better than the Russians. Black smoke rose up from the vehicles hit, but at the same moment the Russians opened up from the edge of the wood to the*

left-four, five, six muzzle flashes like a necklace of pearls. They seemed to be T-34's. We knocked out some of them and then felt our way cautiously forward. When we had the wood closer on both sides we received fire from the left again...My Tiger was hit, but the front armour was thick...Our initially rapid advance now developed into a tough struggle through this deep-layered Russian, defensive front...We kept going, the glade broadened out and I saw the rise before me about two kilometers ahead. I was just thinking that we were through the defensive positions when more than twenty barrels flashed from countless anti-tank guns dug in on the forward slope.[359]

Stukas cleared this hilltop position, but not long afterwards a mine disabled von Rosen's tank.[360] His experiences dealing with the depth of Soviet defenses and their concentration of firepower helped to explain why the Germans' progress was generally so poor, even with the advantages offered by the *Tiger*.

On the 11th, the 503 was able to field 22 *Tiger*, which was fortunate because III Panzer Corps desperately needed them. III Panzer was still expected to link up with SS II Panzer, now approaching Prokhorovka, to either continue the offensive, or as seemed more likely, to at least encircle and destroy a number of Soviet formations between the two corps. For the attack, *Tiger* tanks would be in the lead, assisting the 40 remaining panzers of the 6th Panzer Division. Considering the size of Operation Zitadelle, 62 tanks was not much, but the opposing Soviet 69th Army had no remaining tanks of their own, which helped to even the odds. While 6th Panzer took the lead in the center, 19th and 7th Panzer supported on the left and right flanks respectively.[361]

Here the 503 demonstrated what concentrating *Tiger* troops could do. They smashed through the Soviet front line and pressed on. The opposing 35th Guards Rifle Corps cracked, allowing the 7th Panzer and their 11 tanks to press on.

With the Soviets yielding for a change, the tanks reached the village of Olkhovatka (no relation to the Olkhovatka heights encountered by the 9th Army further north), with only minimal resistance. By nightfall, the Soviet resistance had once again stiffened, but the 6th Panzer Division and its accompanying *Tiger* unit had reached the village of Kazache, the center of 69th Army's second line of defense. The eleven-kilometer advance was the corps' best in the whole operation and demonstrated once again that Guderian was right, *Klotzen, nicht kleckern* was the best way to employ armour. With the success of their operations on the 11th, III Panzer Corps was, for the first time since Zitadelle began, poised to link up with SS II Panzer Corps and encircle the 69th Army.[362] While a daring nighttime advance by Major Franz Bäke, secured a bridgehead over the Donets, III Panzer Corps was unable to link up with the SS Panzer Corps on the 12th.[363]

For all intents and purposes, the 12th of July was the end of Zitadelle. Field Marshal Model had just ended his attack to counter Operation Kutuzov and Hoth's 4th Panzer Army lacked the strength to renew its offensive. To make matters worse, the Allies launched Operation Husky, the invasion of Sicily, on the 13th, necessitating the withdrawal of units from the east to counter this new Allied front.[364] So Zitadelle ended in defeat. Eleven days of grinding combat under the hot July sun had left the Germans with little to show for their efforts. The Kursk Salient was still present and the Soviets' 177, 847 casualties, while significant, were by no means sufficient to delay the coming Soviet offensives, despite the commitment of substantial reserves as the launching of Operation Kutuzov on the 12th showed.[365]

For the *Tiger* units, the results were mixed. Once again, the armour and armament had demonstrated their superiority, with even Staudegger's lone damaged *Tiger* proving to be more than a match for 60 Soviet tanks. It had also been a triumph for the vehicle's survivability, with only ten of the 146 employed being lost.[366] Praise must also be given to the units' mechanics for the rapid return of damaged vehicles, though the depletion of operational vehicles spoke to both the tank's underlying unreliability and the immense concentration of firepower employed by the Soviets.

In broader terms, Zitadelle allowed the *Tiger* units to perform their intended role. But they found little success in it. This lack of success can be traced back, at least in part, to the failure of the Zitadelle plan itself. The Germans did not have the numbers to break through the Soviet defenses and instead engaged in battles of attrition they simply could not win.[367] But neither had the *Tiger* fleet performed well in its intended role. The poor operational readiness of the *Tiger* resulted in units routinely operating at less than half strength, denying them the numbers necessary to effect any kind of breakthrough. Even when they had sufficient numbers, as 505 did on the 5th and 503 did on the 11th, the units that were to exploit the break in were either not yet ready or lacked sufficient numbers to conduct the rapid breakouts of years past. As a report from the 16th Panzergrenadier Division summed up the dichotomy well, "As a result of propaganda, the *Tiger* was presented as an invincible battering ram. Sadly, that is not correct."[368] The *Tiger* was not only not as powerful as had been advertised, but the Allies' anti-tank capabilities were ever improving, giving further lies to *Tiger* invincibility. While there had been few weapons available in the fall of 1942 that could reliably penetrate *Tiger* armour, especially from the front, by 1943 the Allies had identified a number of weapons that could destroy a *Tiger* and were adding ever more to their inventories.

Finally, the greater depth of Allied defenses, taken to an extreme at Kursk, provided ample opportunities to exploit the known weaknesses of the *Tiger*, such as flank attacks against its weaker side armour, further increasing casualties and reducing its overall effectiveness. The rapid decline in a *Tiger* unit's fighting power, combined with German weaknesses generally, in the context of the Allies growing anti-tank capability, and their materiel and numerical superiority, ensured that the *Tiger* could never be truly successful in its intended role. Instead, they became part of a new operational reality where "there was no position the Germans could defend, no line they could maintain, if the Red Army was willing to pay the price of taking it or breaking it."[369] In this new reality, the *Tiger* could only increase the price the Allies would pay for victory, but that price would never be high enough to tip the balance back in the Germans favor.

ON THE DEFENSIVE IN
THE EAST 1943-44

fter the failure of Zitadelle, the Germans were forced onto the defensive as the Soviets pushed them back towards the Reich. In this period of defensive fighting, the panzer divisions deployed in the East saw heavy use, both in their intended offensive role, counter attacking against Soviet penetrations, but also in defensive roles for which they were often ill-suited. The heavy tank battalions likewise found themselves torn between their traditional defensive role as force multipliers for counterattacks and a new role as *Korsettstange*. The term referred to the fact that in many areas where German defenders were stretched perilously thin, only the *Tiger* tanks held the line together. The tanks had some successes against long odds, but these were eclipsed by the fact that these actions pushed the already mechanically unreliable vehicles to their limits. Thus the *Tiger* was constantly overcommitted and proved unable to overcome the Soviets' numerical superiority.

To best analyze this tumultuous period, the initial focus will be on a series of large-scale operations involving the heavy tank units' defense of Kiev in November and December of 1943. Here, Heavy Tank Battalion 509 as well two SS heavy tank companies, the Leibstandarte's 13th Company, and 8th Company from Das Reich were committed. These actions saw an interesting mixture of good and bad employment of both tanks in general and the *Tiger* in particular, providing a valuable look at some of the pressures the Germans were operating under. These large-scale operations will be examined in conjunction with small-scale actions by Heavy Tank Battalion 502. Examining 502 in detail will expose some of their successes in their defensive role as well as providing an excellent look at their weaknesses.

Following the failure of Zitadelle in July of 1943, the Soviets launched a series of offensives all across the Eastern Front. Germany's capacity to withstand this succession of blows was poor owing to the heavy losses incurred over the previous two years. The concentration of mobile formations for Zitadelle had further weakened the German's ability to turn back Soviet advances by concentrating those forces in the Kursk Salient, rather than positioning them across the front to parry Soviet attacks across the breadth of the front. While the Soviets spared no Army Group from their attentions, they initially concentrated on the destruction of the Army Group South, and the liberation of the resources of the Ukraine. The Soviets attacked with overwhelming force and by September, the Army Group was retreating to the Dnieper River.[370]

In the midst of this chaotic period the Germans fought a series of battles in an attempt to hold Kiev. Their efforts demonstrated that the demands of defensive fighting at this stage of the war often led to the poor employment of armour. By the end of September 1943, Army Group South had stabilized its line on the western bank of the Dnieper, though the Soviets had a number of bridgeheads over the river, which negated its effectiveness as a defensive barrier. The strength of the two opposing armies offered a good look at their overall status after the events of the summer. The Soviets 1st Ukrainian Front [371] could call upon 671,000 men, supported by 650 tanks. By contrast the Germans had four understrength infantry divisions and the 8th Panzer Division, which had a grand total of 14 tanks. Despite their weakness, the Germans were able to keep the Soviets from taking the city until the 6th of November 1943. [372]

Hitler was most displeased at the loss of the Ukrainian capital and ordered *General der Panzertruppe* Erhard Raus, newly installed commander of the 4th Panzer Army, to retake the city. Initially the odds seemed to be tipping back in the Germans' favor. The newly refitted 1st Panzer Division and the Leibstandarte were rushed in. Joining them was the newly raised 25th Panzer Division and Heavy Tank Battalion 509, which had only finished its final inspection on October 17th.[373] Raus had a potent force with 588 tanks, including 172 *Panther* and 72 *Tiger*.[374]

The plan was for another "backhand blow," striking the open western flank of the 1st Ukrainian Front, enveloping its rear north of Zhitomir, ending the Soviets' offensive efforts, and allowing for the recapture of Kiev.[375] Unfortunately for Raus, the plan was undermined by friction before it could begin. The transport of the new panzer divisions was hampered by Soviet partisans which left the tanks arriving piecemeal, and often arriving at different railway stations, making it difficult to construct any coherent attacking forces. Also, the Soviets had not yet halted their operations and continued to attack throughout the first weeks of November, threating Zhitomir and threatening to overrun the Germans' assembly areas.[376]

To prevent this, Raus employed Das Reich (Unlike the Leibstandarte it had not been refitted and mustered just 33 tanks, including five *Tiger*), Kampfgruppe von Wechmar of the 25th Panzer Division and elements of heavy Tank Battalion 509 to attack the Soviets' spearheads south of Fastov on the 9th. The deployment of 509 is emblematic of the chaotic transport situation created by Soviet partisans with only the 2nd and 3rd Companies arriving in time for the attack but lacking logistical support. The companies were also split between the two attacking divisions, with the 2nd Company, 509 attached to Kampfgruppe von Wechmar and the 3rd Company, 509 attached to Das Reich.[377] The entire effort, a hastily planned attack using whatever was available, was not a recipe for success.

By the time the attack finished on the 13th, the Germans had little to show for their efforts. They claimed to have destroyed over 30 enemy tanks, but they had done little to blunt the Soviet offensive. Things were particularly bad for the *Tiger* tanks of the 509. Their attacks on the 10th, which were poorly supported by infantry, especially by Kampfgruppe Wechmar, resulted in the destruction of six of them. Two were destroyed by their own crews as being unrecoverable but the rest were lost to Soviet fire, a grim introduction for the unit to the effectiveness of Soviet anti-tank weapons at the end of 1943.[378] Das Reich's 8th Company fared better, losing only one *Tiger*. The company had been in combat almost constantly since Zitadelle began in July, and at this stage only able to field on average a reinforced *Tiger* platoon per day. Not much help for the division.[379] Wolfgang Schneider summed up the effort well, stating "This dispersed and overly hasty action [brought] the penetration to Fastov to a halt, ultimately achieving nothing!"[380]

Then things got worse. A Soviet thrust from the west captured the vital rail junction at Zhitomir on the 13th. In response, the counterattack was revised. It would no longer be a "backhand blow" against the 1st Ukrainian Front. Instead, it was to be a more modest effort to retake Zhitomir and Fastov. On the 15th the Leibstandarte attacked north towards Brusilov to cover the advance of the 1st and 7th Panzer Divisions, which was to retake Zhitomir. In the meantime, the 19th Panzer Division encircled Soviet forces in Brusilov while the 25th Panzer and Das Reich covered the German right flank. By the time the operation was completed on the 26th, the Germans had obtained a modest victory. Zhitomir had been recaptured and a tenuous encirclement had been completed at Brusilov. The Germans claimed to have killed 3,000 Soviets and destroyed 153 tanks in the pocket. But the bulk of the Soviet forces in the area were able to escape. Consequently, the Germans had achieved relatively little, especially given the enormous effort expended.[381]

The performance of the *Tiger* units in this operation mirrored that of the larger panzer divisions. The 509 had been attached to the 25th Panzer Division, guarding the German right flank. Arguably, 509 might have been better suited attached to one of the attacking divisions. But their role in this operation reflected the need to protect the formation's vulnerable flank as well as support the inexperienced, and already badly mauled 25th Panzer Division. In this role the battalion was fairly successful, supporting the capture of several villages to help stabilize the division's front from the 21st to the 24th. But these successes were overshadowed by the heavy casualties suffered by the unit. On the 21st the 509 had 17 *Tiger*, but by the 24th, only seven were still battle worthy. While none of these vehicles were total losses, it was nevertheless another example of operations where the gains in no way justified the effort expended.[382]

The SS heavy tank companies fared better than their army counterparts but not by much. Das Reich's 8th Company, which like the 509 was deployed on the right flank, had no noteworthy successes, and lost three tanks, a serious blow to the small and already understrength company.[383] The 13. LSSAH, being deployed alongside its parent division in the offensive role for which the *Tiger* was designed, fared better. Over the course of the operation, the tanks remained at the forefront of the division and were very successful, claiming the destruction of over 50 *T-34s* and a similar number of anti-tank guns with no losses of their own. While their claims are difficult to verify, it is clear that the company performed well in the thick of the fighting, a stark contrast to the units fighting on the periphery of the German effort. This contrast again raised the question of the specialized nature of the *Tiger* and whether the tank lent itself well to actions outside of its intended role.[384]

There were two more modest encirclements in December, at Radomyschyl and Meleni, but like Brusilov before it, these victories were minor and did little to disguise the fact that the Germans had failed to recapture Kiev. A renewed Soviet offensive, launched on Christmas Eve put an end to any further efforts to recapture the city. The Germans were forced to abandon everything they had fought to regain by the end of the year.[385] These operations demonstrated that while the Germans still had many tactical advantages, which enabled them to outmaneuver and encircle their foes several times, they lacked the strength to achieve their overall objectives.[386]

The operations around Kiev also demonstrated many of the ways in which tank doctrine had been compromised in this defensive fighting. These deviations were outlined well by Heinz Guderian, in his role as the *Generalinspekteur der Panzertruppe* in the first issue of the *Nachrichtenblatt der Panzertruppe* (Panzer News Bulletin), published on the 15th of July 1943. While this issue was published just after the failure of Zitadelle, its commentary remained applicable to German operations in the East throughout the next year. In Guderian's view the fundamental principles that had governed the use of the tanks were still completely sound. Concentrated use of armour, well supported by other arms, would continue to produce victory. The main issue at the tactical level was not so much German materiel weakness, though he would admit that it was a problem. Instead, the main issue on the ground was that the tanks had often been poorly used, being employed without adequate support from other arms and in too small numbers, including use as "bunkers in the front line." They had also been employed without the necessary time provided between operations for proper maintenance.[387]

Guderian's views were generally correct. Well-supported panzer divisions could still deliver victory and would do so at the tactical level until the end of the war. It was also true that poor cooperation and a lack of planning were present, especially in the Germans' initial engagements around Fastov in November, with both factors playing important roles in that operation's failure. However, he underrated the importance of Germany's materiel weakness, which rendered any victories fleeting in the face of Soviet materiel superiority. It also must be said that Guderian's complaints were not entirely applicable to the fighting around Kiev. The use of tanks in small numbers and as bunkers in the front line were not present in the battles around Kiev. Most of the units there were at full strength and were not being deployed in defensive roles. Instead, they were used in highly mobile operations, with the Germans often launching powerful counterattacks with full divisions. In the more traditional defensive operations of Battalion 502, where only small numbers of tanks could be mobilized at any given time, Guderian's complaints about the tanks' defensive deployments and the limitations of the panzers and the *Tigers* in particular were even more appropriate.

By the summer of 1943, Army Group North was a badly depleted force, especially since Zitadelle had stripped away virtually all of their mobile formations. The army group now resembled an army of 1917 more than of 1943, with its horse-drawn transport and foot-sore infantry. Only Heavy Tank Battalion 502 remained to provide the Germans with the mobile firepower that was supposed to be the hallmark of the *Reichsheer*. In the previous year the 502 had done a great deal to help hold the line, though it could not prevent the Soviets from securing a land route into the besieged city of Leningrad in January.[388] Regardless of its performance, the battalion of 45 *Tiger* tanks was a pitifully small force, given that the Germans had a 750-kilometer front to man.[389]

During the summer and fall of 1943, Bataillon 502 was repeatedly employed in small packets to beat back Soviet incursions across the army group's frontage. In this effort the *Tiger* was almost always successful, repeatedly repealing the Soviets and restoring the German front line. However, this success came at a high maintenance cost since the dispersed nature of the unit made routine care difficult. On the 10th of August, in the midst of the 3rd Battle of Lake Lagoda, the battalion was able to field 13 tanks. Ten days later only six could be called upon. In that month of fighting, the battalion had performed well. Only three tanks had been destroyed, a far cry from the over one hundred Soviet tanks the unit claimed to have destroyed. Nevertheless, the maintenance cost had been high and by the time the Soviets attacked again on the 6th of October Bataillon 502 was a little over half strength, with only 26 operational *Tiger* tanks.[390]

The scattered deployment of 502 during the summer and fall of 1943 reflected the weakness of Army Group North extremely well. While the battalion had been successful in its defensive efforts, the manner in which they had been deployed was something against which the battalion vigorously protested. In one report they issued, "Points for Panzer Employment" from 1943, they repeated Guderian's mantra of *Klotzen, nicht kleckern*, stating, "Only the massed use of tanks brings success."[391] This report was also critical of the decision to employ the *Tiger* directly on the front line, rather than retaining the tanks in the rear for use in counterattacks or to halt enemy penetrations. While the *Tiger* could and did perform this task fairly well, it also exposed them to the full weight of enemy fire. This had the effect of endangering the supporting infantry, who inevitably suffered from being near the fire-drawing tanks. It also contributed to the high maintenance losses, both as a result of enemy fire and because these deployments made it more difficult to withdraw them to complete regular upkeep tasks.[392] Heavy Tank Battalion 506, serving with Army Group South, lamented in a similar vein that "the Grenadiers were too weak, completely worn out."[393] They also declared, in a statement that most, if not all *Tiger* units would have agreed with, "It is unacceptable that the *Tiger* have to stand constantly behind the front lines as moral support."[394]

While the heavy tank battalions despised their new roles, both for being contrary to doctrine and an exceptional drain on their vehicles, other panzer units demonstrated a better understanding of the overall situation. A report from the 25th Panzer Division, "Use of Tanks in the Main Line of Resistance to Support the Infantry," made the same points as the documents from the *Tiger* battalions, with one noteworthy exception. While they implied that the poor employment of their vehicles reflected general ignorance of their intended use, the 25th Panzer Division was willing to acknowledge that while the current employment of tanks was very poor and prevented them from being used to the best of their ability, this was not the result of ignorant infantrymen, but rather a sign of the times. It freely acknowledged that the infantry had borne and were continuing to bear the brunt of the defensive fighting in the East, leaving units badly understrength. Consequently, the tanks had to be employed to fill the gaps left by infantry units that lacked the strength to fully defend their positions, regardless of their preferences.[395]

In 1944, Army Group North continued its retreat, with its frontline centered around the two towns of Luga and Narva. On February 1st, the Soviets gained several bridgeheads over the Luga River, and by the 13th, despite determined German resistance, the town of Luga fell. While this was a disaster, so long as Narva remained in German hands, the Army Group could hold on. As benefited its reputation as the army group's main defensive stalwart, the 502 was transferred to Narva.[396] The fighting around Narva in March and April 1944 took place during a period of relative quiet for Army Group North as a whole. Unbeknownst to them, the Soviets were preparing to renew their offensive in July.[397] The local fighting that occurred during this lull provided sometimes dramatic examples of the successes that small numbers of well-handled tanks could achieve. It was here also that the limitations of the *Tiger*, and the German Army in the East were most starkly revealed, even before the Germans were struck again in July of 1944.

During this period, 2nd Company 502 fought southwest of Narva, where the Soviet 59th Army had obtained a bridgehead over the Narva River near the village of Lembitu. While the Germans held the *Rollbahn* (The MSR or main supply route) that led to Narva itself, and the major north-south trail that linked to it, the Soviets dominated the areas to the east and the west of this trail. This created what became known both officially and unofficially as the west and east "sacks", on either side of the trail. These Soviet positions provided bases from which to encircle and destroy the local German defenders and drive on to Narva. In March of 1944, it fell to the tanks to play a major role in both defeating Soviet thrusts from the two sacks and reducing their threat.[398]

The nature of the Narva Sacks forced the *Tiger* back into the role of *Korsettstange*. They were once again the main force holding the German front line in the area. Their first time back in this role came on the 17th of March 1944, when the Soviets launched their first major attack from the east sack. The Soviet preliminary barrage had a devastating effect on the German defenders and the infantry were routed even before the barrage had stopped, a clear indicator of their poor morale. After the barrage lifted, Otto Carius, whose memoir *Tigers in the Mud* provides a great deal of detail about this period, and two other *Tiger* commanders alone manned the front line. While they claimed to have destroyed 16 *T-34s*, the Soviets were still able to occupy the two eastern strong points had anchored the German line.[399]

Since the captured strongpoints allowed the Soviets to dominate the far side of the railway embankment and offered a good jumping off point for an attack on the *Rollbahn*, they had to be retaken. The counterattack was to be a pre-dawn assault, but with a force of only three tanks and 16 infantrymen, it was a daunting task. Further, it was one that could not be said to be well supported by any metric. The western ruin was quickly retaken and occupied by eight men, but the eastern ruin proved to be a more formidable position. It had been reinforced with several anti-tank guns and artillery pieces. After a gunnery duel, which lasted several hours, the Soviet position remained secure and the eight-man German infantry squad had lost two dead, and two wounded. Since the four survivors were nowhere near enough to take the position, the Germans were forced to withdraw, leaving the task of retaking their front-line positions unfinished.[400] In the days that followed, the eastern strongpoint changed hands several times, until it was finally recaptured on the 21st.[401]

At this point one of Germany's most famous tank commanders entered the picture. Hyacinth *Graf* Strachwitz von Groß-Zauche und Camminetz also known as the "Panzer Graf" was Army Group North's panzer commander. Newly promoted and having just received his swords for his Knight's Cross, he returned from hospital to lead his tanks against the Narva bridgehead. On the 26th of March 1944, the Kampfgruppe Strachwitz attacked the flanks of the Soviet 109th Rifle Corps with the commander himself in the lead. By March 31st the west sack had been taken back with heavy Soviet casualties. The east sack was successfully reduced by Strachwitz in April. The 59th Army's bridgehead over the Narva remained defiantly in place.[402] Heavy Tank Battalion 502 lost three Tiger during these operations and to add insult to injury had failed to inflict serious damage on the Soviets. Retrospective Soviet reports noted that "the enemy managed only to cut off two small bridgeheads of our positions in the region", making it clear that their ability to threaten Narva had not been substantially weakened by the Strachwitz counterattacks.[403]

Once again, the *Tiger* could still act as a potent force multiplier but only when well supported. As the October 1943 *Guidelines for Employment of Panzers in Cooperation with an Infantry Division*, had stated, "It is crucial for success that the infantry hold on to the tank attack and use its paralyzing effect on the enemy."[404] This was an ideal that the increasingly depleted *Reichsheer* could not achieve. There were too few infantrymen to exploit the tanks' successes.

Whatever limited positive effects von Strachwitz's counterattacks had on the German position were erased by a subsequent Soviet offensive. On the 22nd of June 1944, the third anniversary of Operation Barbarossa, the Soviets launched Operation Bagration against Army Group Centre. This operation was an enormous success, virtually annihilating the depleted German units in front of it. By the time the offensive petered out at the beginning of August, the Germans had their backs to the gates of Warsaw.[405] This offensive not only destroyed Army Group Centre, but also unseated Army Group North. The initial collapse of Army Group Centre created a new front, the "Baltic Hole." From there, the Soviets could either strike for Vilnius with the aim of reaching the East Prussian city of Königsberg or launch a more limited attack towards Riga. Either way, Army Group North was threatened with imminent encirclement.[406]

On the 2nd of July, Heavy Tank Battalion 502 was dispatched to Dünaburg, which was situated in the midst of the "Baltic Hole," and was the target of the Soviet 6th Guards Army. Their first mission was launched on the 8th of July. To reach the area of operations the battalion was required to conduct a rapid 50-kilometer road march. The unit protested this decision, owing to the unreliability of the *Tiger* engine but was overruled. When the march began there were 22 road-worthy *Tiger*. By the time it ended, only eight were still ready to fight.[407] On the 10th of July the 3rd Company 502 supported an attack by a battalion from the 205th Infantry Division, southwest of Garniai, to relieve encircled German forces. The attack failed and two more *Tiger* were lost. Another five vehicles were lost to mechanical breakdowns, which were recovered with great difficulty on the 11th.[408]

From the 11th to the 21st of July, the *Tiger* tanks of 502 participated in a number of small-scale engagements, usually with an average of five tanks along the southern bank of the Düna River. On the 21st, the Soviets broke through German lines north of the Düna, forcing the battalion to shift northwards in three march columns to counter these new Soviet threats. As part of this shift, Carius took the 2nd Company 502 back to Dünaburg to cover the main road to the north of the city.[409] On the 22nd in the small town of Malinava, Carius and his men had their first major engagement with a new Soviet heavy tank, the *Iosef Stalin 2* or *IS-2*, as it was more commonly known (also known as the *JS-2*).

The *IS-2* was the result of Soviet disaffection with the *KV-1*'s performance by the summer of 1942. The *KV-1* lacked the mobility and reliability of the *T-34*, which made the two vehicles difficult to employ together. It was also outclassed in armour and armament by late 1942. In 1941 its 75mm frontal armour and 76.2mm gun had been among the best in the world, which allowed single tanks to stall local German advances for significant periods.[410] During the summer of 1942 however, the longer and higher velocity 50mm and 75mm guns being mounted on German tanks were allowing them to meet the *KV-1* on more equal footing, and that was to say nothing of the vast performance gap between the *KV-1* and the *Tiger*, once they appeared in September of 1942. The new Soviet heavy tank was faster, more reliable, and had armour and armaments that could match the *Tiger*. Its role was, like both the *KV-1* and the *Tiger*, a breakthrough tank.[411]

Soviet tests in the summer and fall of 1943 showed that the 85mm *M1939* anti-aircraft gun, slated to be fitted in the new version of the *T-34* would not consistently penetrate the *Tiger* armour. The *A-19* 122mm howitzer proved to have superior penetrative capabilities, with later German tests showing that the gun could penetrate the 100mm front plate of the Tiger I at 1,500 meters.[412] It was this gun that gave the *IS-2* its offensive punch, though its use of a separate charge and projectile meant that it had much slower reload time than the *Tiger* which used unified ammunition. In armour it surpassed the *Tiger*, with a maximum of 120mm of frontal armour. The effectiveness of the armour was greatly enhanced by the extensive use slopes, similar to what was seen on the *Tiger II* and by the vehicle's comparatively low profile, a definite asset on the open steppes. It was also equipped with a reliable V-12 engine, something that the *Tiger* certainly could not boast.[413] On paper, the Soviets had developed an almost ideal tank to counter the *Tiger*. Its frontal armour could only be penetrated by the tank's 88mm gun from a distance of 300 meters, whereas the *A-19* 122mm gun could do the same to the *Tiger* at 1,500 meters.[414] Unfortunately for the crews of the *IS-2* their battles with the *Tiger* did not take place on paper, but in the much more unforgiving real world.

Returning to Carius in Malinava, he observed that the town was only held by a reinforced company of tanks, an estimated thirty *IS-2*s and *T-34*s. In keeping with the aggressive initiative that was a hallmark of the German way of war, Carius, with six *Tiger*, decided to destroy the exposed Soviet position. The attack came as a complete surprise to the Soviets and in less than 25 minutes it was all over. The Germans claimed 17 *IS-2*s and five *T-34*s. Another 28 tanks were later ambushed by the company as they approached the village, unaware of their comrades' fate. This effort derailed the initial Soviet assault on Dünaburg.[415] This effort derailed the initial Soviet assault on Dünaburg.[416] Even as Heavy Tank Battalion 502 fought to defend Dünaburg, the position of Army Group North was collapsing. On July 10th, the Soviets 2nd and 3rd Baltic Fronts launched new attacks against the embattled Army Group, reaching Vilnius on the 13th and by the months end forced the Germans out of Lithuania and into Latvia.[417] So once again, the actions of the Tigers were impressive on their own but proved to have little lasting effect, as the Soviets losses around Dünaburg did nothing to stall their broader offensive.

This period also provided some interesting insights into the *IS-2*. The new Soviet heavy tank was an impressive opponent, though few of its engagements with the *Tiger* tanks of the 502 in July showcased the vehicle at its best. Surprise engagements at close range favored the faster-firing *Tiger*. Nevertheless, by the time the war ended the *IS-2* had developed a reputation as a formidable tank and one that was very much a "Tiger Killer", even if that was not its intended role. In one instance, the driver of a *Tiger* was killed by a 122mm shell that penetrated the vehicle's 100mm frontal plate, something that no other weapon then in service had achieved.[418] Events like that led *Tiger* veteran, Karl Bormann to recall, "The Iosef Stalin was without a doubt our best opponent."[419]

The *IS-2's* superiority was only really present against the *Tiger I* and its flat armour. With the end of *Tiger I* production in August 1944 and the appearance of the first *Tiger II* on the Eastern Front that same month, the *IS-2's* moment of superiority proved fleeting. The *Tiger II* was substantially better armoured, with 150mm of sloped frontal armour and was also better armed, with a higher velocity 88mm gun. These features allowed the *Tiger II* to defeat the *IS-2* at a range of 2,600 meters while the *IS-2* had to close to 1,500 meters to penetrate the armour of the *Tiger II*.[420]

One combat report from an unspecified heavy tank battalion (likely 501), which appeared in the September 1944 issue of *Nachrichtenblatt der Panzertruppe* detailed the imbalance between the two vehicles. A heavy tank company was advancing through thick woods, accompanied by an infantry battalion. With the thick trees the *Tiger II* tanks were forced to move in single file. The lead *Tiger II* saw an *IS-2* in front of it. In a short, sharp engagement fought at an incredible 35 meters a pair of *Tiger II* engaged two *IS-2*. The second *Tiger II* was hit, but the round failed to penetrate the 150mm front plate. The faster firing *Tiger II* tanks then destroyed the two Soviet tanks.[421] Again the *Tiger II's* substantial advantage in rate of fire proved decisive, especially in an engagement in which combatants were at close range where penetrating hits were likely.

The *IS-2* was not the only Allied heavy tank designed, at least in part to counter the *Tiger*. The Americans fielded the M26 *Pershing* heavy tank. It was armed with a 90mm gun and designed as a breakthrough tank, like its German and Soviet contemporaries. Only twenty of them arrived by the end of the war and saw little service, owing to an American focus on infantry creating breakthroughs with medium tank support, while tank destroyers engaged enemy tanks, a doctrine which left little room for a heavy tank until a desire to match the *Tiger* became attractive towards the end of the war.[422]

Thus, the *IS-2* was left as the only Allied tank roughly comparable to the *Tiger* in armour, armament and role to see substantial wartime service.[423] Nevertheless, both tanks demonstrated that the Allies invested considerable resources into creating tanks to compete with the *Tiger*, an outgrowth of their efforts to enhance their anti-tank capabilities. Although their general improvements were highly effective, neither country managed to create a tank that was truly equal to the *Tiger*, especially the *Tiger II*. In fairness though, they did not need to. Their materiel superiority meant that qualitative failings in their vehicles were more than compensated for by the sheer number produced.

From the summer of 1943 to the summer of 1944, the *Wehrmacht* was forced onto the defensive and began its retreat back to Germany. This move onto the defensive stretched panzer divisions and the heavy tank battalions to their breaking points, as tanks were routinely employed as *Korsettstange* to compensate for a lack of infantry. As the efforts of Heavy Tank Battalion 502 demonstrated, these efforts seriously diluted and diminished their fighting strength by parceling their vehicles in small numbers to reinforce threatened sectors, rather than massing them for operations and by denying the already mechanically unreliable vehicles opportunities for repair.

While operations as *Korsettstange* were far from ideal, the *Tiger* tanks were able to achieve some impressive successes against long odds, and in spite of the great losses suffered by the army in the East, the fundamental principles governing the use of the armour remained sound, as was seen in the battles around Kiev in November and December 1943. These victories were, however, all rendered fleeting by the Soviets' numerical and materiel superiority, which allowed them to weather any number of local defeats on their way to achieving their overall goals. Additionally, the Soviets ever-expanding arsenal of anti-tank weapons and the introduction of both the *IS-2* and the large number of assault guns and tank destroyers made it easier for the Soviets to inflict losses upon the *Tiger* forces and eroded their position of technical superiority. So, while the *Tiger* could still turn the tide in local engagements, its ability to affect the wider war had largely vanished.

TIGERS IN NORMANDY

On the 6th of June 1944, the Allied landings in Normandy opened up the long-awaited second front. After the initial success of the D-Day landings, the Allies and the Germans found themselves engaged in a slow and grinding battle of attrition until the end of July. Among the German units employed in this campaign were three heavy tank battalions: SS Heavy Tank Battalions 101 and 102, and the army's Heavy Tank Battalion 503. The operations of these units did not alter the by now familiar routine of *Tiger* engagements, where success was fleeting, and failure was all but inevitable. But in some ways, the Normandy Campaign was unique. It was in Normandy that the *Tiger* mystique was in many ways firmly established in the English language literature of the war, with many Allied accounts discussing its superiority over their own vehicles. While there was some factual evidence to support this view, it also represented an exaggeration because Allied vehicles and tactics were often better than was frequently supposed. Actions in Normandy involved both the *Tiger I* and the first combat uses of the *Tiger II*. While the vehicles could still inspire a degree of fear amongst its foes, Allied tactics and weapons had improved to the point that the combat effectiveness of the *Tiger* was severely diminished.

To best demonstrate these events, several key engagements involving the *Tiger* will be covered in this chapter. First, the counterattack by SS Heavy Tank Battalion 101 at Villers Bocage on the 13th of June 1944, in which *Tiger* commander Michael Wittmann had a starring role in a highly overrated counterattack which proved far too costly to the Germans despite spectacular British losses. Second, Operation Goodwood from the 18th to the 20th of July, where Heavy Tank Battalion 503 proved to be decisive in the repulse of a major British offensive despite heavy losses to Allied bombers. Third, Operation Totalize on the 8th of August, where Michael Wittmann was killed leading a poorly planned counterattack, but the mere presence of the *Tiger* still derailed key components of the Canadian offensive – the last time that the tank's mere presence did so.

For the Normandy campaign, the British substantially upgraded their tanks to face the *Tiger*. This action was based on the experience gained in North Africa and Italy where none of the British tanks had proven to have the firepower or armour to compete with the *Tiger*. Only the *Churchill*, with its 152mm-thick front plate compared with the *Tiger*, though the 88mm gun could still penetrate the *Churchill* frontal armour at a range of 2,500 meters.[424] In terms of guns, both the *Churchill* and the lighter *Cromwell*, were armed with the 75mm MV gun. This gun could only penetrate 76mm of steel at 450 meters. It was sufficient to penetrate the side armour of a *Tiger* but could not do so frontally.[425]

While these two British tanks saw considerable service in Normandy, many armoured units were outfitted with the American M4, known as the *Sherman*. Like its British counterparts, the *Sherman* compared poorly to the *Tiger*. Its frontal armour was only 51mm thick and could be reliably penetrated by the *Tiger* at a range of 3,000 meters. The *Sherman's* protection did have one advantage over its British counterparts. Its frontal plate was sloped, though this was not much of an advantage when facing a *Tiger* and its high velocity 88.[426] The M3 75mm gun on the *Sherman* could only penetrate 68mm of steel at 500 meters, giving it similar performance to the standard British guns of the period.[427] The inferiority of all Allied tanks to the *Tiger*, as well as the *Panther* became a great concern to their crews during the Normandy campaign, but British tank designers ensured that they would not go into battle without any kind of response to the *Tiger*.

In 1942, in recognition of the inadequacy of the 6-Pounder (57mm) tank guns being fitted to British tanks in North Africa, development began on a gun capable of penetrating any German tank at a distance of 1,300 meters. The 17-Pounder gun, previously discussed, was initially a towed anti-tank gun, but efforts to mount the gun in a tank were quickly started. Efforts to convert the new *Cromwell* to fit an even newer gun resulted in the *Challenger*. Accommodating the new gun meant lengthening the chassis and enlarging the turret ring, a process that proved too time consuming for the tanks to available for use on D-Day, with the first examples only be ready to be issued to combat units in August 1944.[428]

A plan to create a *Churchill* with a 17-Pounder began in in 1944 as well but by the time the vehicle, christened the

Black Prince, was ready for trials in September 1944, it was clear that the need for such a vehicle had passed and only six prototypes were made.[429] Efforts to create tank destroyers with the 17-Pounder were similarly delayed. Neither the *Achilles*, an American made *M10* tank destroyer with a 17-Pounder or the *Archer*, which mounted the gun on a *Valentine* tank chassis, were available in quantity until the end of the Normandy campaign.[430] Owing to these delays, emphasis was placed on a conversion of the *Sherman*, starting in October 1943. While the 17-Pounder did have to be modified so it could safely recoil in the confines of the *Sherman's* turret, the effort was a success when the vehicle was trialed in January of 1944. With the invasion only six months away, a rapid production program was ordered for the *Sherman Firefly* as it was known. By the 31st of May, 342 *Fireflies* had been completed, a testament both to the relatively straightforward conversion process and the capabilities of British industry. This quantity of *Fireflies* was sufficient to give every four-tank troop for the invasion one of the vehicles, with the other three tanks being either *Shermans* armed with 75mm guns or *Cromwells*.[431]

The *Sherman Firefly* had the same armour as its unmodified counterparts, with all the advantages and disadvantages that entailed, but its gun was markedly superior. The standard armour-piercing round could penetrate the 100mm frontal armour of a *Tiger* at 1,000 meters. But it was the British development of the APDS round (Armour Piercing Discarding Sabot) that gave the *Firefly* its fierce reputation. This ammunition featured a sub caliber shot, the sabot, inside the round. When fired, the external case fell away and the sabot was propelled forward with all the velocity of the larger round, but without the friction associated with the larger projectile. It was fundamentally a large caliber steel bullet. This increase in muzzle velocity allowed the round to strike the target with much more force, in this case allowing the round to penetrate 172mm of armour at 1000 meters, which was enough to penetrate any armour on the *Tiger I* and allowed it to penetrate most of the armour on the *Tiger II* (though in practice the front plate proved impervious to fire under combat conditions).[432] One British sergeant summed up Allied responses to the *Firefly* well when he commented, "At last a gun which one could trust to get its teeth really deep into any German tank it met."[433]

The first heavy tank battalion to arrive in Normandy was SS Heavy Tank Battalion 101. It had been training in France since the beginning of the year and in March the battalion was supplemented with the men of the 13. LSSAH including Wittmann who took command of the 2nd Company. In April, this mix of Eastern Front veterans and newly trained crews were stationed in the Pas de Calais area in anticipation of the Allied invasion.[434] Since the Allies invaded in Normandy, the battalion was forced to rush to the invasion front. It began its journey on June 7th, but extensive damage to the French rail network forced them to detrain at Versailles and conduct road marches. Allied air superiority restricted them to night moves, starting on the 9th. By that point, the unit had already taken some casualties and lost many support vehicles. As a result, the leading elements of the battalion did not arrive until the 12th.

The road march into Normandy and the constant Allied air attacks took their toll on the unit, with the 1st and 2nd Companies both arriving understrength, with eight and six tanks respectively. The 3rd Company did not arrive until the 15th. While these losses were not insignificant, it must be emphasized that despite the loss of many of its supporting vehicles SS Heavy Tank Battalion 101 was not badly hindered. Like their comrades in the East, who were not suffering under the same kind of heavy interdiction, the unit was able to field an average of 15 to 20 *Tiger* tanks. Thus, while Allied airpower was an additional source of friction, sufficient tanks remained to keep the unit in reasonably good shape, aided by its tank repair company.[435]

The arrival of the SS *Tiger* tanks came in time for Operation Perch. Perch called for an attack on the western flank of the German line by the 7th Armoured Division's 22nd Armoured Brigade with elements of the division's infantry brigade, the 131st Queen's Brigade. This attack sought to exploit a gap that had opened up between the Panzer Lehr Division and its neighbor, the 352nd Infantry Division by taking the town of Villers Bocage. Once the town was secured the Panzer Lehr Division could be effectively outflanked.[436]

By 8 AM on the 13th, the 4th County of London Yeomanry (4th CLY of the Desert Rats) had arrived at Villers Bocage and advanced east to Point 213.[437] This proved to be a fateful mistake. Six *Tiger* tanks from Wittmann's 2nd Company were concealed in a defile between the town and Point 213. Watching the vast column of British vehicles which ran from Point 213 through Villers Bocage, Wittmann assumed that the British would continue on to Caen without pause, so he elected to attack. Unfortunately for him, the defile was only wide enough for a single *Tiger*, and he felt that there was no time to organize his five functioning tanks for an attack. Instead, he attacked alone.[438] In his after-action report written later that day, Wittmann described the battle:

> *I had no time to assemble my company; instead, I had to act quickly, as I had to assume that the enemy had already spotted me and would destroy me where I stood. I set off with one tank and passed the order to the others not to retreat a single step but to hold their ground. [I] Drove up to the column, surprised the English as much as they*

had me. I first knocked out two tanks from the right of the column, then one from the left and attacked the armoured troop carrier battalion [A Company, 1ˢᵗ Battalion of the Rifle Brigade] in the middle of the armoured regiment. I drove toward the rear half of the column on the same road, knocking out every tank that came towards me as I went. The enemy was thrown into total confusion. I then drove straight into the town of Villers, got to approximately the center of town where I was hit by an anti-tank gun [which destroyed a portion of his running gear]. My tank was disabled. Without further ado, I fired at and destroyed everything around me that I could reach.[439]

Wittmann and his crew then abandoned his tank and returned to the German lines. In the course of his one-tank attack he destroyed a total of 12 tanks, 13 halftracks and universal carriers as well as two anti-tank guns.[440] This action earned Wittmann the Knight's Cross from Hitler and decades of adulation since.[441] It is here that many accounts of the battle end, with Carlo D'Este saying of Wittmann, "Almost single-handedly, this one audacious and brilliant German tank commander had crushed the British advance around Villers Bocage and forced the 7ᵗʰ Armoured on to the defensive."[442]

The truth of the matter is rather more complicated and involved several more attacks on the embattled 4ᵗʰ CLY. After Wittmann launched his attack, the other tanks of the 2ⁿᵈ Company, reduced to three functional vehicles by mechanical failures, launched their own attack towards Point 213, destroying an additional five tanks and capturing 230 prisoners. In spite of this impressive result, the unsupported *Tiger* tanks were unable to make any impression on the British defenders of Point 213.[443]

In the afternoon, the 1ˢᵗ Company stationed to the north, under the command of *SS Hauptsturmführer* Rudolf Möbius launched its own attack on Point 213, with support from some

Panzer IV from the Panzer Lehr Division. They were able to defeat the elements of the 4th CLY holding the position, which had been isolated by Wittmann's earlier attack. This force then turned its attention to Villers Bocage. While the Germans had been retaking Point 213, B and C Squadrons of the 4th CLY and the infantry of the 1st and 7th Battalions Queens Royal Regiment had reoccupied the town and prepared an ambush. Driving through the town, two *Tiger* and one *Panzer IV* were destroyed by a *Sherman Firefly*, penetrating their thinner rear armour. Three other *Tiger* also ran afoul of British anti-tank guns in the town.[444] Despite this victory, the British withdrew to their starting positions, after the losses they had suffered, which were all the more galling given the elite reputation that the Desert Rats had earned in the North African campaign.[445]

In this more complete telling of the fighting in and around Villers Bocage on the 13th of June 1944, it is clear that the battle was not just a tale of Michael Wittmann's skill and courage. Instead, it was more a story of British blunders and German luck. In the first place Operation Perch had been delayed for several days as XXX Corps and 2nd British Army exhausted other alternatives. While starting the operation on June 10th or 11th would not have guaranteed its success, attacking before the *Tiger* tanks of SS heavy tank battalion arrived would have certainly been beneficial to the 7th Armoured Division. It was also undeniable that an attack by a reduced armoured brigade, with limited infantry support was not a good idea either, especially since the plan involved an ambitious end run around stout German defenses. Consequently, the chances of success for Perch were slim from the outset even without the intervention of Wittman and his *Tiger* company. Their involvement only compounded the failure and ensured that it would loom large in the legacy of the campaign.[446]

While Operation Perch was certainly not the Desert Rats' finest hour, it is difficult to argue that it was the finest hour for Wittmann or his battalion either. In his book, *Tigers in Normandy*, Wolfgang Schneider, himself a former German tank commander in the post war West German Army gave Wittmann credit for his courage but little else. His one tank assault violated many key tenets of armoured warfare, not least of which that tanks must be concentrated for action in line with Guderian's *Klotzen* maxim.[447] Had Wittmann positioned his vehicles better and been willing to wait, its likely that he would have achieved greater results with more firepower and mutual support. As it was, Wittmann was fortunate that the British were so unprepared. Engaging the *Cromwells* at close range would have allowed them to penetrate the *Tiger* armour, negating one of the vehicle's greatest advantages.[448]

His ultimate mistake, which could have been fatal, was ending his attack inside Villers Bocage. He sacrificed his mobility and created ideal circumstances for an ambush. Wittmann's after action report did not provide any reasoning for this decision. Neither did the unit report submitted subsequently with a recommendation for his Knight's Cross.[449] It remains unknown if this decision was the result of simple hubris or if Wittmann had some other complex plan to perform his own end run through the British column to return to the company assembly area. The subsequent counterattack by his brother company commander and Panzer Lehr also cannot be considered a particularly good use of armour. They made the same mistake as Wittmann and advanced into a built-up area without infantry support, resulting in substantial losses.[450]

Despite these many German tactical failings, the balance sheet still favored them. Seven *Tiger* had been lost but 7th Armoured Division had been repulsed and had lost over 40 vehicles over the course of a single day. This positive assessment may have been true in the short term but not in the long term. By the 16th of June, the 4th CLY had totally replaced its losses. SS Heavy Tank Battalion 101 was not so lucky. It received no replacements for its lost vehicles during the campaign, meaning that the unit had lost half of a company, with little to show for it, save Wittmann's Knight's Cross.[451]

Villers Bocage was far from a good example of *Tiger* employment, but the appearance of the *Tiger* there and the damage that Wittmann was able to inflict had serious psychological effects on Allied servicemen in Normandy. While the *Firefly* was a great boost to the firepower of the armoured units of 21st Army Group, it by no means provided much solace to the men crewing other tanks which lacked the 17-Pounder's ability to destroy the *Tiger*, especially after Villers Bocage, which convinced Allied tankers of their inferiority. Steve and Tom Dyson of the 34th Tank Brigade noted that, "We also learned to our dismay, of the devastating effects of the German 88mm...anti-tank guns, and *Tiger* tanks. The shells apparently went through our *Shermans* like a knife through butter."[452]

This quality of Allied armour plate was shared by the *Cromwell* and the *Churchill*, but it was the *Sherman* in particular that came to dominate these conversations due to its prominent role in the campaign. One report submitted by Brigadier Harold Pyman to Major General Robert Erskine, General Officer Commanding 7th Armoured Division, described the problem. "The result is that while 75mm shot has been failing to penetrate the front face of Tigers and Panthers at ranges down to 30 yards, they can knock Shermans and Cromwells out at ranges up to 1500 yards with ease."[453] Pyman was not wrong, the *Sherman* and the *Cromwell* could not penetrate the frontal armour of the *Tiger*, but they were not completely impotent either.

The *Sherman's* maligned 75mm gun was more than capable of penetrating the side armour of a *Tiger* at 900 meters.[454] Defeating a *Tiger* was difficult, but courage and good tactics did offer a reasonable chance of success. One of the best examples of this came not from Normandy, but from the Eastern Front. Dmitry Loza, who commanded a *Sherman* in the Soviet 223rd Tank Brigade stated that the best way of dealing with a *Tiger* in the open was to assign each *Tiger* to two *Shermans*. The first would open fire at 400-500 meters, the best range to knock the tracks off. Once the *Tiger* was immobilized the other *Sherman* could either drive around or wait for the undamaged track to turn the *Tiger* ninety degrees, exposing its more vulnerable rear. This maneuver was extremely risky, especially given the close range that the *Sherman* had to fire from to achieve the best results, but it is a testament to how tactical skill, coordination and a good helping of courage could compensate for the *Sherman's* weaknesses.[455]

Good tactics did allow for success against *Tiger*, but they did nothing to dispel the aura of invincibility that surrounded not only the *Tiger*, but also the *Panther*, which as Pyman's report indicated, was a similarly formidable vehicle. Soldiers were convinced that every tree and hedgerow in Normandy concealed a *Tiger*.[456] This *Tiger* phobia was discussed in many post war memoirs, including George Blackburn's *Guns of Normandy* where the *Sherman* was described as "grossly inferior" to the *Tiger*.[457] Nonetheless, despite this prominence in the memoir literature, in many encounters between a *Tiger* and Allied vehicles, the actions were marked not by panic and fear but instead cool heads and good tactics. This trend was already evident at Villers Bocage, where B and C Squadrons

of the 4th CLY and the infantry of the 1st and 7th Battalions
Queens Royal Regiment had overcome their initial shock
and effectively dispatched the counterattack which followed
Wittmann's foolhardy attack, to say nothing of the anti-
tank gun crew that had disabled his tank in the first place.
Consequently, it is clear that *Tiger* phobia was present, but
mostly had the effect of overinflating the number of *Tiger*
tanks reported in Normandy, rather than affecting the Allies'
ability to destroy them.[458]

After Villers Bocage, the *Tiger* returned to prominence
during Operation Goodwood on the 18th of July. After little
over a month in Normandy, the Allies had yet to achieve a
decisive breakthrough. Operation Goodwood was intended
to be the breakthrough they had been looking for, allowing
the thrust to Germany to begin at last. Facing them were the
Tiger tanks of 503.[459]

Heavy Tank Battalion 503 had been the last of the three
heavy tank battalions to be deployed to Normandy. It left
the Eastern Front on the 25th of May 1944 after two years of
hard fighting. During its reconstitution in June of 1944, the
unit was issued with twelve *Tiger II* tanks, some of the first
issued. All were assigned to the 1st Company. Once the unit
was fully equipped it was transported by rail to the Paris area
between June 29th and July 5th. From there, like Bataillon 101
it conducted road marches into Normandy. Unlike the SS, by
moving at night 503 was able to avoid losses to Allied aircraft.
It was not, however, carried out without incident. On the
6th of July, while crossing a bridge near the village of Canon,
a *Tiger* commanded by *Feldwebel* Seidel crashed through it.
Seidel and his crew were injured but survived the event. Their
Tiger did not.[460] After this less than auspicious start, they were
involved in a number of small actions on the eastern flank of

the invasion front, but Goodwood was to be their first large scale engagement of the campaign.

The companies of 503 were dispersed behind the German front line. The 3rd company had its assembly area outside Manneville. This proved to be an unfortunate placement. It was one the areas targeted by the RAF. *Leutnant* Richard *Freiherr* von Rosen, the acting company commander experienced the bombing first-hand, feeling as "helpless as a drowning man tossed into raging seas."[461] When the bombardment finally ended "of the once so beautiful parkland nothing remained but shredded trees, churned meadows and giant bomb craters so numerous that they overlapped – a gray, repulsive moonscape."[462] In the midst of this moonscape sat the remnants of his company. The bombs had decimated it. One tank took a direct hit and "looked like a giant opened sardine tin."[463] Another lay on its turret, the force of the blasts overturning the 56-ton vehicle. Even the surviving tanks were not in fine fighting trim, having been covered in dirt up to their turrets, covered in fallen trees and many having broken tracks.[464] Moving on foot, von Rosen was able to establish contact with the battalion. He was ordered to ready as many tanks as he could and proceed to occupy positions between Manneville and Cagny, on what was correctly suspected to be the left flank of the British attack.[465]

Of the 13 *Tiger* tanks the company had at the beginning of the day, only six were still roadworthy, but two of them were forced to travel slowly on account of engine fires. There was one additional problem. The blasts had de-calibrated their guns, meaning that they needed three shots to hit targets they could normally hit with one.[466] Nevertheless, they were able to reach their position between Manneville and Cagny. At this point two tanks were destroyed by rounds that penetrated their frontal armour. This came as something of a shock to the men of the 3rd Company, who had not previously encountered a British weapon that could penetrate their frontal armour, a belief that suggests they had not been informed of, or had forgotten in the heat of the moment, about the *Firefly* and its 17-Pounder.

Ironically, it was not a British weapon that had destroyed the two tanks, but a battery of 88mm Flak guns defending the Cagny airfield which *Oberst* Hans von Luck of the 21st Panzer Division had ordered into action to hold the flank. [467] In the confusion, the nervous *Luftwaffe* gunners had mistaken the lead *Tiger* for an Allied tank.[468] Despite this setback the Flak guns and von Rosen's *Tiger* troop were ideally situated to attack the 11th Armoured Division's leading brigade, the 29th Armoured. Its leading regiment, the 3rd Royal Tank Regiment was able to avoid the worst of the German fire, but the following unit, the 2nd Fife and Forfar Yeomanry, which was supposed to have masked Cagny, took the full brunt of the German crossfire. With the Yeomanry being battered by the Germans, the following units from both the 11th Armoured and the Guards Armoured divisions were delayed and began taking fire.[469]

After the battle, von Luck observed an estimated 40 British tanks destroyed in the fields between the Flak battery at Cagny and von Rosen's tanks. This victory was a deadly testament to the long-range firepower of the "damned 88s", but it was not the only operation conducted by Heavy Tank Battalion 503 on the 18th July.[470] The 1st Company had also been hit by the Allied bombing but four of its *Tiger II* were still fully functional, though one *Tiger* slipped into a bomb crater and could not be recovered. These *Tiger II* alongside the *Tiger I* of the 2nd Company, which had escaped the bombing were key components in a pair of counterattacks in the afternoon.

That afternoon, the *Tiger II*, alongside eight *Panzer IV* of the 21st Panzer Division attacked Démouville. The attack was repulsed with heavy losses. Two of the *Tiger II* were destroyed outright by Allied fire, giving them the dubious distinction being the first *Tiger II* destroyed by direct enemy fire.[471] While details were limited, it was clear that the dug-in British defenders of Démouville and the *Shermans* of the Irish Guards were more than a match for the small German counterattacking force, especially since the Germans lacked the infantry support that might have helped to neutralize the town's defenders. Given that not even the 17-Pounder could penetrate the 150mm frontal armour of the *Tiger II*, it is likely that the tanks were either destroyed by well concealed anti-tank guns, striking the thinner side and rear armour or by outflanking *Shermans* targeting the same weaknesses.[472] In this first engagement of the new *Tiger* variant, they had proven to be no match for the well prepared British defenders, which demonstrated not only that *Tiger* phobia was by no means ubiquitous but also that the western Allies, like the Soviets by 1944, had developed a number of weapons and tactics to destroy the *Tiger* and not even the much improved protection of the *Tiger II* was protection against them.

While the 1st Company was giving its *Tiger II* a bloody baptism of fire, 2nd Company's *Tiger I* fleet was engaged in its own counterattack. They, alongside the training battalion of the 16th Luftwaffe Field Division, which had already been decimated by the bombing and Anti-Tank Battalion von Obstfelder of the 346th Infantry Division, attacked northwest of Toran. This effort proved much more successful than the attack of the 1st Company, protecting the open hole left by the badly mauled 16th Luftwaffe on the German right flank.[473]

By evening, the survivors of the battalion including the 3rd Company, which had been reduced to only one operational tank – the others succumbing to the damage inflicted by the RAF earlier in the day – were withdrawn to the Frenouville area to defend the Cagny-Vimont Road. There they stopped a further attack to the southeast from Cagny, which had fallen earlier that afternoon.[474] During this action, a *Tiger II*, was destroyed in a highly unconventional manner. In the midst of engaging *Shermans* from the Irish Guards the inexperienced *Tiger* commander ordered it to reverse straight through a hedge where it promptly ran into a British *Sherman*. The tank's gunner, *Gefreiter* Thaysen recalled what happened next:

> *There was a jolt, and we were hung up with an Englishman. There was no way that we intended to ram the enemy, all the more so since we ran into him with the rear of the tank, and I was still at twelve o'clock, busy with the Tommy who was firing at us. We had barely hit the Englishman when, an anti-tank gun- probably as 75mm Pak- firing at the Englishman hit us instead. It hit us in the left between the track and the running gear. The round penetrated and sliced the seat right out from under my backside...At the same time, the round tore open a shell casing and the propellant charge ignited in a jet of flame. There was nothing for us to do but bail out, and quick.[475]*

This encounter left both crews with "the war story of a lifetime" and brought 503's day to an end, but there was still more to do.[476] SS Heavy Tank Battalion 101, along with the *Panther* of the Leibstandarte were part of the SS I Panzer Corps reserve. These forces, assisted by one of the Leibstandarte panzergrenadier battalions, launched a counterattack in the afternoon towards Bourgebus to protect the Bourgebus Ridge. A formidable, combined arms force of infantry and tanks, including 19 *Tiger I* tanks, halted the final attacks of the 7th Armoured Division.[477]

Operation Goodwood lasted until the 20th of July, but the debacle on the first day had taken its toll on the attacking divisions and little additional progress was made. Bourgebus Ridge remained in German hands and the breakout that had been hoped for was still illusive. Losses had also been heavy with over 400 tanks lost.[478] While much of the responsibility for the defeat must be laid at the feet of British officers, it was also undeniable that VII Corps had encountered a "top class German defense" and that the *Tiger* units of 503 and SS 101 had been important parts of that defense.[479]

Although *Tiger* tanks were important to the defense against Goodwood, their performance was decidedly mixed. Its easy to praise the actions of the SS battalion and the 2nd Company, Heavy Tank Battalion 503. Their well-executed counterattacks saved the German right flank and denied the British the Bourgebus Ridge while continuing to demonstrate the strength of the *Tiger* when used in its intended role. The 3rd Company, Heavy Tank Battalion 503 also has to be commended for its quick recovery after the devastating bombardment. Because of it, the company played a key role in the defense of the Cagny area throughout much of the day. But there was also much to criticize, especially in the attack by 1st Company, where the advantages of the *Tiger II* were squandered in a poorly supported attack against a well-prepared enemy. Thus, like the *Tiger I* in its first inauspicious employment back in September 1942, the initial use of the *Tiger II* demonstrated the vehicle's weaknesses far more than its strengths.

Further, its debut also revealed how much better prepared the Allies were for the appearance of German heavy tanks than they had been in 1942, be they *Tiger I* or *Tiger II*. Despite the fact that even their most powerful weapons bounced off the new tank's frontal armour, the defenders of Démouville learned that the *Tiger II* shared its predecessor's vulnerabilities. That knowledge helped the defenders defeat the counterattack. Consequently, while the *Tiger II* was a superior vehicle over its predecessor, the strides that the Allies had made in weapons and tactics meant that the *Tiger II* did not enjoy the dazzling success that the *Tiger I* had in 1942-1943.

Another theme reappeared in Normandy. While the overall performance of the *Tiger* had been quite good, like at Villers Bocage, the Allies' numerical advantage wiped out their gains. The 400 tanks that the British lost during Goodwood were quickly replaced and the Desert Rats, who had been handed another bloody defeat, were nevertheless fully operational and ready for Operation Spring, launched on the 25th of July, only five days after a failed Operation Goodwood.[480] In contrast, the heavy losses sustained by Heavy Tank Battalion 503, were not made good. The unit lost 13 tanks on the 18th, most of them to the preliminary bombing. Not one of the *Tiger* tanks was replaced.[481]

The next attempt to break the back of the German defence at Falaise was the Canadian Operation Totalize. Like Operation Goodwood it included preliminary attacks by the RAF, though the Canadians employed the bombers differently. This II Canadian Corps attack featured not only a preliminary bombardment, but also a second phase bombardment. This second phase followed the initial break in by the 2nd and 3rd Canadian Infantry Divisions and was designed to destroy the German second line and impede the arrival of German reserves, a bitter lesson learned during Goodwood. Once the second phase bombardment had cleared the way, two armoured divisions, 4th Canadian and 1st Polish would break through.[482]

Totalize began just after 11pm on the 7th of August. It began with 1020 bombers and 720 artillery guns striking the German 89th Infantry Division. The first phase was far from flawless, with a number of units becoming disoriented or lost. Nevertheless, by noon on the 8th, they had achieved almost all of their phase one objectives. This success opened a six-kilometer-wide hole in the German line but unlike Goodwood, there was no second German line to hold the Canadians back. Only a rapid response by the Germans reserves could save the situation.[483]

A rapid response is just what the Canadians got. Soon after the bombers began to drop their payloads on the 89th Infantry, *SS Oberführer* Kurt Meyer, commanding the SS 12th Panzer Division Hitlerjugend recognized that a Canadian breakthrough in this sector could easily reach the Route Nationale 158 connecting Caen and Falaise. He moved immediately to mobilize his division.[484] German doctrine was clear: immediately counterattack. Meyer assembled two Kampfgruppen for this purpose. The first was KG Waldmüller, consisting of 2nd Battalion, SS Panzer Regiment 12, 1st Battalion, SS Panzergrenadier Regiment 25, 1st Battalion, SS Tank Destroyer Battalion 12 and 3rd Company, SS Heavy Tank Battalion 101. Waldmüller was ordered to recapture the hills south of St. Aigan.

The second was KG Wünsche consisting of three tank companies, one each of *Panzer IV*, *Panther* and the *Tiger* of SS Heavy Tank Battalion 101, along with the 1st and 3rd Battalions, SS Panzergrenadier Regiment 26. Wünsche was to disengage from the fighting at the Grimbosq bridgehead to the south and occupy the hills to the west and northwest of Potigny.[485] Once these two Kampfgruppen were in place, the Hitlerjugend would control the two best routes into Falaise.

While the two Kampfgruppen sounded formidable, all of the units employed were understrength and could not be expected to hold against the Canadian attack for long. Meyer's hope was that they could delay the attackers long enough for the 85th Infantry to arrive on the next day, adding some much-needed depth to the German position.[486]

In the finest German tactical tradition, Meyer had reacted with great speed to the attack, but his delaying actions were inadvertently helped by the uncoordinated actions of the Canadians. The majority of the Canadian objectives were secured by noon. But many had been secured hours earlier. There had been an opportunity to press on, especially since the two exploiting armoured divisions, 4th Canadian and 1st Polish were ready to go. However, the RAF bombers could not be called off on short notice. The ground forces were obliged to wait. Thus, the second phase had to begin on schedule at 1:55 in the afternoon. It was this interlude that allowed Meyer's two Kampfgruppen to advance, and it allowed them to play a significant role in Totalize's second phase.[487]

During this interlude, Michael Wittmann, in temporary command of SS Heavy Tank Battalion 101, led eight *Tiger* tanks forward as part of KG Waldmüller. It was 12:30 PM. Waldmüller's counterattack, in keeping with the long-standing German traditions of aggression and initiative had shown initial success. But the time when those hallmarks would have carried the day were long gone. While the Germans had been assembling their forces, 2nd Canadian Infantry Division and the British 51st Highland Division (attached to II Canadian Corps), had been anticipating and preparing for a counterattack. Since the Canadians expected to find the Hitlerjugend in the German second line they had planned for an attack by that division and the remnants of the 89th Infantry

Division hours earlier. So, rather than attacking exhausted men who had just finished wresting their objectives from the enemy, the weak KG Waldmüller was attacking two infantry and two armoured brigades that had had ample time to prepare.

The defenders also enjoyed a five to one superiority in artillery.[488] To make matters worse for Waldmüller, his Kampfgruppe did not strike the British and Canadian positions simultaneously. Instead, the attack broke down into three separate minor ones, which were incapable of supporting each other. The *Panzer IV* tanks attacked Cremesnil. The panzergrenadiers attacked St. Aignan, while Wittmann's *Tiger* and the *Jagdpanzer* IV troops drove down Route Nationale 158 towards *Gaumesnil*.[489] All three attacks ultimately failed. More importantly, Wittmann's attack put to rest the belief in the invulnerability of the *Tiger*. *Hauptsturmführer* Hans Hoflinger, the battalion operations officer provided this account of the attack:

> *We drove off, Michael right of the road and I left, four others with Michael ... Approximately 800 meters to Michael's right was a small wood which struck us as suspicious and which was to prove fateful to us. Unfortunately, we couldn't keep the wood under observation on account of our mission. We drove about one to one and a half kilometers, and then I received another radio message from Michael, which only confirmed my suspicions about the wood. We began taking heavy fire from anti-tank guns and once again Michael called but didn't complete the message. When I looked out to the left [right] I saw that Michael's tank wasn't moving. I called him by radio but received no answer. Then my tank received a frightful blow and I had to order my crew to get out as it had already begun to burn fiercely. My crew and I dashed for the rear and got through. I stopped to look back and to my dismay discovered that five of our tanks had been knocked*

> *out. The turret of Michael's tank was displaced to the right*
> *and tilted down somewhat. None of his crew got out.*[490]

Hoflinger's account described the collapse of the attack well and indicated a tactical lapse on Wittmann's part. Allied accounts confirm Wittmann's poor decision-making as he came under fire from three different armoured units. In the orchards to the east of the Route Nationale were the *Shermans* of A Squadron, Northamptonshire Yeomanry.[491] On the other side of the Route Nationale, A Squadron, Sherbrooke Fusiliers also fired on the Germans.[492] Further to the north, B Squadron of the 144th Regiment, Royal Armoured Corps (144 RAC) also took KG Waldmüller under fire.[493] Between the two British units and the Canadian Sherbrooke Fusiliers, five *Tiger* tanks were destroyed.[494] Clear evidence that the attack had been launched in haste and that Wittmann had led his company down the Route Nationale into what amounted to an ambush launched from three sides. In the process Wittmann lost his own life, as well as those of his crew. He also cost his battalion five *Tiger* tanks, which the already depleted unit could ill afford.[495]

After the collapse of Waldmüller's attack and the launching of Totalize's 2nd phase, the exploitation by the 4th Canadian and 1st Polish Armoured Divisions, came last *Tiger* action of the day. As part of his response to the operation, Meyer had dispatched elements of KG Wünsche to occupy positions in the woods between Robertmesnil and St. Sylvain. Wünsche also now had the 2nd Company, SS Heavy Tank Battalion 101.[496] From these woods, the *Tiger*, *Panther* and *Panzer IV* tanks were to disrupt the advance of the 1st Polish Armoured. At 2:25 PM, just half an hour after the advance had begun, the Polish came under fire from these woods, reporting that twenty *Tiger* were firing at them. In reality only three *Tiger* tanks were available, so the majority were likely *Panther* and *Panzer IV*.[497] The exact composition of the German force aside, their fire brought the Polish advance to a standstill. Attempts to blast the Germans out of the woods proved fruitless and while the 10th Mounted Rifle Regiment, the division's reconnaissance unit and its *Cromwells* were able to blunt an attempt by the Kampfgruppe to outflank the stalled Poles, the offensive proved impossible to restart. By the end of the day the division's armoured brigade, the 10th Armoured Cavalry, had lost 57 tanks, almost a third of its strength.[498] While the Poles had taken heavy losses, the Germans did not come out of the fight without losing another *Tiger*, though that was small consolation to the Poles.[499]

The operations of the *Tiger* and the rest of KG Wünsche successfully held up an entire armoured division for a day. It was a strong tactical performance, especially given the small number of vehicles involved, and a good example of the *Tiger* phobia found in Normandy. However, claims of success for KG Wünsche should come with some caveats. The 1st Polish Armoured Division had only just arrived in Normandy and watching much of their lead units being destroyed in the open by hidden German tanks would be enough to make even hardened veterans hesitant. Also, the German position had not been struck by the Phase Two bombardment and subsequent efforts to neutralize the position with the division's own artillery had also failed.[500] Consequently, while the Kampfgruppe and its *Tiger* units had done very well, they were aided considerably by the failure of the Poles' supporting arms and their inexperience.

Despite the poor showing by the Canadian and Polish Armoured Divisions, the 8th of August was the beginning of the end for the German's eastern flank. Totalize was followed by Operation Tractable, launched on the 14th, which put II Canadian Corps over the Laison River and culminated in a drive to Falaise with units of II Canadian Corps and US V Corps.[501] This effort created the Falaise pocket on the 19th of August. The pocket contained over 100,000 German troop from eleven infantry and ten panzer divisions. A major Allied victory was in the offing but determined German counterattacks managed to keep a narrow escape route open, through which between 35,000 and 40,000 men managed to escape before the Allies sealed it off for good on the 21st.[502] Amongst the escapees were the men of the three heavy tank battalions, though only three of their tanks survived the retreat and returned to Germany with their crews.[503]

The campaign in Normandy was not only a failure for the Germans in general but also for the *Tiger*. Their victories at Villers Bocage as well as during Operation Goodwood and Totalize were overshadowed not only by the overall failure of the German defense in all three instances but also the fact that even when the Germans were able to cause significant losses, the Allies were able to quickly make them good – something the Germans could not do. Also, while Wittmann helped to spread *Tiger* phobia across the beachhead after his attack at Villers Bocage, time and time again the Allies' performance against these vehicles was not characterized by fear but rather by careful application of superior tactics. This was true in both engagements with the familiar *Tiger I* but also the new *Tiger II*, whose appearance did not seem to unduly alarm the Allied units facing them. Indeed, the Allies had no trouble applying the tactics they had prepared for the *Tiger I* against its successor. So, while Normandy is often considered to be the place where the *Tiger* was most feared, it is instead where the fear of the *Tiger* finally disappeared for good.

THE FINAL BATTLES

he Normandy Campaign had been inauspicious for
the *Tiger* and for the new *Tiger II* in particular. It
was not until a number of heavy tank battalions were
deployed to Hungary, in October of 1944, that the *Tiger
II* fully demonstrated its capabilities. Fighting in Hungary
included a series of counterattacks by Heavy Tank Battalion
503 in October of 1944 and later engagements by both
army and Waffen SS battalions from January to March of
1945, including the major offensives of Konrad I to III and
Operation Frühlingserwachen (Spring Awakening). These
operations demonstrated that even with Germany's final
defeat looming, with ample support, large-scale deployments
of *Tiger II* could be tactically successful. The Allies' numerical
and materiel superiority, which had been working against the
Tiger since 1943, was still very much in evidence and ensured
that any German victories were especially short lived. Also

working against the *Tiger* was the decline of the German army more generally, which often denied the heavy tank battalions the support they required to achieve even temporary success. Consequently, operations in Hungary better illustrated the strengths of the *Tiger II*. Nonetheless, even when these tanks were performing well, there was no way they could hope to compensate for the broader problems afflicting the *Reichsheer*.

Hungary had been a member of the Axis since 1940, and by the fall of 1944 it was one of Germany's last and most vital allies. With the defection of the Romanians on the 23rd of August 1944, the Germans had lost the support of their military along its vulnerable southern flank. More importantly, the Germans had lost access to Romanian oil. Determined to keep Hungary in the war, to keep the Soviets out of Austria, and to maintain control of Hungary's oilfields, Hitler invested considerable resources into Hungary's defense. By March of 1945, half of the armoured formations on the Eastern Front were employed in Hungary. In total, 15 panzer, four panzergrenadier, four infantry and four cavalry divisions were sent to Hungary before the war's end.[504]

By the 9th of October of 1944, before the bulk of the German reinforcements arrived, the Axis forces defending Hungary had been pushed deep into the interior. Following a succession of Soviet attacks over the summer, the German Army was defending within seventy kilometers of Budapest.[505] At this point, Heavy Tank Battalion 503, which had been completely reequipped with the *Tiger II* after their losses in Normandy, was dispatched to Budapest.[506]

After helping to stage a coup to keep Hungary in the war, the battalion was transferred to the front.[507] On the 18th, they were attached to the 24th Panzer Division for IV Panzer Corps' counterattack out of the Szolnok Bridgehead towards

Debrecen. Owing to a lack of rail transport only the *Tiger* tanks of the 1st Company and ten of the 3rd were available.[508] What followed was an operation that echoed the exploits of the panzer divisions that had swept across France in 1940. The German attack struck the 1st Romanian Army and caused its defenses to collapse almost immediately. Richard *Freiherr* von Rosen, by now a tank ace and commander of the 3rd Company, witnessed the aftermath of the successful attack:

> *We reached the next village quickly, the Romanians attempting to flee in vain. We waved them aside from behind since we had no time to bother ourselves taking prisoners. There was a barrier of anti-tank guns which we crushed and with that, as we discovered, we had gone through all the defenses to their entire depth...Enemy rear-echelon units were surprised, whole columns of traffic were swept off the roads, nothing could detain our forward thrust. We had appeared in this area totally unexpectedly, like phantoms.[509]*

The chaos was so complete that a train carrying a Soviet Guards Cavalry Division drove into the area unawares and was shot up by the *Tiger* tanks.[510] By day's end the Germans had advanced 40 kilometers. In the early years of the war, an opening attack like this would have been the prelude to a great victory as the panzers surged forward, deep into the enemy's rear. Much had changed for the Germans since those halcyon days. While the Romanians were as ill-prepared as any Allied army had been early in the war, their new Soviet allies had extensive experience fighting the Germans and would not provide their enemy any easy victories the next day.

On the 20th, the 3rd Company led the assault towards the city of Turkeve. The only available route was down a narrow causeway over a dam, flanked by marshland, which was an impenetrable obstacle for the 70-ton *Tiger II*. The tanks' thick frontal armour allowed them to survive the advance down the causeway and they were able to take Turkeve, though seven of the ten tanks were disabled in the advance on the town.[511] Without more tanks, the German advance halted outside Kisujszalls.[512] Despite being unable to take Kisujszalls, the attack had been a tremendous success. The battalion advanced 70 kilometers in two days, the deepest penetration achieved by any heavy tank battalion during the war.[513] Unfortunately this great success was followed by a rapid withdrawal. Soviet forces had captured Mezötur, a town in the German rear. With the specter of encirclement looming, the Germans turned around and began a fighting retreat back to the Theiss River, where they remained for most of the next month.[514]

The actions of Heavy Tank Battalion 503 in October demonstrated that even in 1944, these tank battalions could still find great success in their intended role. But these were the exception, not the rule. The battalion was fresh, well supported by the 24th Panzer Division, and able to employ the majority of its vehicles in the attack. They also had had the advantage of attacking the 1st Romanian Army, whose principal anti-tank gun was still an outdated pre-war 47mm gun of French design. The Germans had done little to provide their erstwhile ally with better anti-tank guns and the Soviets had not had time to upgrade the Romanians' arsenal, leaving them vulnerable to attack by virtually any late war tank, but especially the *Tiger II*.[515]

The better-equipped Soviets fared only slightly better. Even their well-constructed defensive lines were penetrated by the Germans. But the circumstances that allowed for this performance, fresh tanks, good support and weak enemy forces, were rare. It is also important to emphasize that whatever the weaknesses of the Soviet defences at Turkeve were, the Soviets still had sufficient strength to outmaneuver the Germans and force them to respond to their attacks. So even at their most successful, at this stage in the war the Soviets' materiel and numerical advantage was still decisive and could erase German gains with relative ease.

On the 24th of December, the Axis position in Hungary became even worse as the Red Army encircled Budapest.[516] With the capital threatened, the emphasis shifted towards its relief. Three operations were launched to relieve Budapest in January. These were codenamed Konrad I, II and III. Heavy Tank Battalions 503 and 509 played important roles in these operations, as did the *Tiger I* of SS Totenkopf. Konrad I saw an attack from the north using the 96th Infantry Division to cross to the Danube's southern bank, opening the way for SS IV Panzer Corps to thrust eastward along the riverbank then turn southward towards the city.[517] The initial attacks on the 1st of January, were a success, but by the 6th of January, the offensive had stalled after the capture of Bicske. Soviet numerical superiority and the mountainous terrain in the area were too much for the Germans.[518]

One of the attacking divisions was the Totenkopf, the only unit to retain its heavy tank company. The 9th Company SS Panzer Regiment 3, which was still equipped with *Tiger I*, was an important part of the division's offensive firepower, but its older tanks were more vulnerable to Soviet fire than were the new *Tiger II*. This was largely due to the growing number of 152mm guns fielded to counter the latest German tanks.[519] When the offensive began on the 1st of January, 11 of the company's 17 tanks were operational. By the 6th, only four remained. As their tanks fell like dominoes, their crews subsequently destroyed them since they could not be recovered. These losses kept the company out of Konrad II while damaged vehicles were repaired, denying the Totenkopf Division an important force multiplier for the next offensive.

The loss of seven tanks in less than week was a spectacular series of losses, especially given that during Zitadelle Totenkopf had only lost one *Tiger* in the course of that two-week operation.[520] These heavy losses were witness not only to the strength of the Soviets defenses but also to the greater abundance of weapons capable of killing the *Tiger*. These included not only a greater numbers of *ZiS-3* 76mm anti-tank guns but also the aforementioned *IS-2*, the *T-34/85*, as well as the *ISU 122* and *ISU 152*. These were casemate tank destroyers with 122mm and 152mm guns on the *IS-2* chassis, which provided them with more protection than had been afforded to the earlier *SU 122* and *SU 152*.[521] While these new vehicles struggled to penetrate the heavier armour of the *Tiger II*, they had much less trouble penetrating the flat 100mm armour plate on the front of the *Tiger I*.[522] Consequently, by 1945 it was clear that the *Tiger I* was well and truly obsolete as a breakthrough tank, given the improvements in the Soviet arsenal that had been undertaken the previous year.

Heavy Tank Battalion 503 now found itself protecting the SS Panzer Corps' right flank. After three months of fighting in Hungary the battalion had only 26 tanks and of those only ten were battle-worthy when the operation began on January 1st. The initial attack struck especially strong Soviet positions, with some key areas requiring a dozen attacks to overcome it. Given this heavy fighting, it was not surprising that the attacks took a heavy toll on the depleted unit. The next day only two *Tiger* were left in operation. While repairs would allow the battalion to field thirteen tanks on the 4th, this increase made little difference to III Panzer Corps performance. With both

III and SS IV Panzer Corps making little progress, it was clear that a second operation would be required.[523]

Konrad II shifted the main effort to III Panzer Corps, to not only gain ground but also to relieve pressure on SS IV Panzer Corps. Heavy Tank Battalion 503 was once again in the vanguard of III Panzer Corps. The 1st Company was attached to the 4th Cavalry Division while the rest of the battalion fought alongside the 23rd Panzer Division. On the 9th, the 1st Company's attack went well, resulting in the destruction of seven enemy tanks. On the 23rd Panzer's front a *Tiger* ran afoul of an *SU-152* and was destroyed. However, that was far from the only problem that 503 encountered. When the unit's tanks encountered a strong Soviet trench line, the battalion commander, *Hauptmann* von Diest-Koerber attempted to personally motivate the supporting infantry.[524]

Our own infantry remained behind our tanks and made no moves to leave that cover...Hauptmann von Diest-Koerber climbed out of his tank and, right arm gesticulating forward, tried to urge the infantry forward with him. A scene like something out of an old battle painting! ...We tried to hold the Russians down with our fire and give him cover. The infantry, however, did not follow him. He was all alone in front of the trench. He hastened back again behind our tanks.[525]

With the aid of several corporals von Diest-Koerber was finally able to rally the reluctant infantry and together they secured the Soviet trench.[526] The need to rally the infantry to continue to advance with the tanks was a sign of the weakness of the German infantry by 1945. Their unwillingness to support the attack of the tanks violated the principles of combined arms attacks laid out in the 1943 *Guidelines for Employment of Panzers in Cooperation with an Infantry Division*. The manual emphasized that the close support of the infantry was absolutely vital to the success of any combined effort. The tanks reduced strong points and suppressed enemy infantry. In return, the infantry eliminated enemy anti-tank guns and warned of other obstacles. This effort placed great demands on the infantry, which the manual acknowledged, "You must then give up your last strength to take advantage of the paralysis of enemy weapons by the tanks and follow them quickly. Better to shed sweat than blood!"[527]

After six long years of war not only was there a shortage of infantry, but those available were tired, worn out, and unwilling to act in the aggressive manner that had been the hallmark of the German Army earlier in the war. It also demonstrated that the *Tiger* was only one part of a larger combined arms system. Even if the tanks themselves performed well, they were incapable of achieving their objectives alone. As Herman Balck said in his memoirs, in a criticism of this late-war tendency that could just as easily act as an assessment of this attack:

> *Tactics is the coordinated effect of all arms in space and time onto one objective, with the emphasis being on all arms and one objective. The armoured units on their own could not handle the Russian infantry. One type of arm by itself is doomed to failure, and this iron-clad principle had been violated.*[528]

For 503, the highlight of Konrad II had been the attack on Zamoly on the 11th of January. The battalion deployed 13 *Tiger* tanks for the operation and while it was a success, it was a costly one as von Rosen recalled:

> *The Russians had very skillfully positioned some SU-152 [or ISU-152s which would have been more common at this time, though distinguishing between the two at combat ranges would have been difficult*[529]*] self-propelled*

*assault guns in the vineyard...We had not even spotted
them when suddenly a 1 Company panzer went up in
flames... Half an hour later the same thing happened to
a second panzer. We withdrew a little. Apparently the
crews of these guns observed us from hiding. When they
saw a panzer they came into the open, aimed and fired
one round, and withdrew into cover immediately. This
deprived us of the opportunity to return fire and knock
them out... After another half- hour a third panzer,
standing to my left, was hit, killing the crew. We were at
a loss how to deal with these assault guns since we had no
idea where they were.*[530]

Von Rosen's *Tiger II* was the next to fall victim. His encounter
with the *SU-152s* outside Zamoly was an excellent example of
how the Soviets had learned to effectively counter the *Tiger
II*. The assault guns not only had the firepower to overcome
the tank's formidable armour. They had the tactics to avoid
retaliation. By this stage in the war, the Allies in both the east
and the west had become quite adept at countering *Tiger* tanks.
But the Soviets didn't have it all their way. They lost the town,
and according to German records, lost 21 tanks and 20 anti-
tank guns. But as was the norm by this point in the war, these
materiel losses were ones that the Soviets quickly replaced. By
contrast the three *Tiger* lost by the battalion, with a further
seven, including von Rosen's badly damaged one, were not
so easily replaced. Indeed, the attack at Zamoly was its last
operation in Konrad II. The depleted unit, which only had 23
tanks, of which only three were operational, was withdrawn to
repair and refit. So even when the Soviets lost the battle, their
ability to inflict losses on the battalion was a greater victory, as
a key German supporting element was removed from battle for
some time, weakening the German offensive.[531]

The loss of the *Tiger* unit was a blow, but the great
success of the operation was obtained not by the *Tiger*

supported III Panzer Corps, but by SS IV Panzer Corps. The 711th Infantry Division managed to break into the Soviet lines to the southeast, allowing the 5th SS Panzer Division to break through. This attack caught the Soviets off guard and allowing the division to continue until it was just 17 kilometers from Budapest before being withdrawn on the 12th. for fear that the limited German penetration would be cut off and destroyed.

Even in the last months of the war, the *Tiger* was proving its worth. More importantly, the fundamental principles of armoured warfare that the Germans had developed in the interwar period were still more than capable of delivering victory without the *Tiger*.[532]

In the end, Konrad II had been another failure, but 5th SS Panzer's success placed the Germans tantalizingly close to Budapest, so Konrad III was authorized. For this operation, IV SS Panzer Corps was once again going to lead the offensive, but rather than launching another attack in the north along the Danube, the new plan was to strike further south between Lake Balaton and Lake Velence, driving straight on to Budapest. The Soviets had noticed the movement of IV SS Panzer Corps but believed that the corps was going north to Prague rather than spearheading another attack on Budapest. Consequently, the Germans achieved total surprise when the attack was launched on the 18th of January [533].

This day was particularly auspicious for Heavy Tank Battalion 509. The battalion had been all but wiped out fighting on the Vistula River in September of 1944 and had been rebuilt and re-equipped with the *Tiger II*, arriving in Hungary on the 15th of January, just in time for Konrad III.[534] They would be spearheading the IV SS Panzer Corps attack, specifically that of the Totenkopf. The 9th Company, Totenkopf had nine *Tiger I* ready, but after their poor showing in Konrad I, these vehicles were employed in a supporting role. Leading the attack would be the new *Tiger II* of Battalion 509.[535]

The first day of Konrad III offered a rare opportunity to see a heavy tank battalion performing exactly as envisioned, at full strength, rather than attacking piecemeal and at reduced strength as had been the norm throughout the war.[536] The initial attack was a success, but extensive minefields and the usual Soviet defense in depth took a heavy toll with only 18 tanks still operational by the end of the morning.[537] At 2 PM the attack on the town of Szabadbattyan began. The town was captured but the Soviets destroyed the town's bridge over the Sarviz Canal when the lead *Tiger* was just fifty meters away. Nevertheless, they penetrated the Soviet lines to a distance of 19 kilometers, an excellent demonstration of their offensive capabilities at full strength. As impressive as the achievement was, a number of other factors must be considered which make their success one that comes with significant caveats.

The battalion suffered heavy losses in the attack. Seven tanks were destroyed by Soviet fire and a further 16 were disabled.[538] Losing half of the unit in one day, even if most of the vehicles could be recovered and restored was a serious loss, especially since the offensive was far from over. These losses were also a reflection of the fact that the *Tiger II* was unable to escape the problems that had hobbled the *Tiger I* in previous offensives, most notably at Kursk. As in that great 1943 battle, the combination of strong Soviet defenses and the tank's poor mechanical reliability led to rapid and significant losses in fighting power, which meant that it was very difficult to sustain the momentum of an advance once the initial break in had been achieved. The desired breakthroughs did not happen.

The other two *Tiger* units in Konrad III, 9th Company, Totenkopf and Heavy Tank Battalion 503 started the operation badly depleted. Battalion 503 was once again employed in support of III Panzer Corps, and began the operation with just eight tanks, which was the greatest number it would field during the operation. The average was just five tanks.[539] Totenkopf's *Tiger* units supported the division throughout the operation, but the 9th Company never had more than five operational tanks. By the time Konrad III was called off on the 26th they had just one operational *Tiger* in the whole of SS Panzer Regiment 3. In addition to its lone *Tiger*, they also had only one operational *Panzer IV* and one operational *Panther*, a far cry from the 176 tanks the regiment should have had.[540]

The poor state of the Totenkopf panzer regiment on the 26th of January was echoed across the divisions participating in the operation and Balck ended it on that day for lack of offensive power. When they stopped, the Germans were just 20 kilometers from Budapest but as the strength of the *Tiger* units indicated quite starkly, actually reaching the city was far outside the capabilities of the forces employed.[541] With the failure of the relief effort, Budapest's fate was sealed, though the city did not fall until an abortive and ill-advised breakout attempt by the city's defenders failed on the 11th of February.[542] The efforts to relieve Budapest were demonstrated that while even at the end of the war the *Wehrmacht* in general and the *Tiger* units in particular could still enjoy an occasional victory, their wider ability to capitalize on those victories was severely diminished.

The fall of Budapest was not the end of the fighting in Hungary, but it did represent the last glimmers of German operational success in the theatre. The final German offensive, Frühlingserwachen, launched in March of 1945 met with little success. The operation's goal was to encircle and destroy Soviet forces west of the Danube and north of the Drava rivers with the aim of recovering the Nagykanizsa oil fields, one of Germany's last remaining potential sources of oil.[543]

The duties of spearheading this German offensive fell to SS Heavy Tank Battalion 501 (previously SS Heavy Tank Battalion 101, having been renamed in September 1944[544]) and Heavy Tank Battalion 509. The SS battalion started the operation with just four operational tanks, the result of losses in Operation Südwind (Southwind), completed just nine days prior to the start of Frühlingserwachen on the 6th of March. It was also diminished due to unrecovered losses from the unit's involvement in Battle of the Bulge in January. While the 501 could only muster a single platoon, the 509 had spent its time since the conclusion of Konrad III back in January on the defensive, permitting it to come to the operation with 32 *Tiger* tanks.[545]

Even before it started, Frühlingserwachen suffered from a number of serious problems. The initial movement of 6th Panzer Army had been conducted in secret but the presence of new panzer divisions in Südwind let the metaphorical cat out of bag and the Soviets prepared for renewed German attacks. Also, the spring thaw had come early to Hungary. By the time the operation began, the ground had turned to mud, severely restricting the movement of the tanks.[546]

The effect of these factors became apparent on the first day as the attacking formations, I and II SS Panzer Corps as well as I Cavalry Corps, advanced just two kilometers. On their right flank, the supporting III Panzer Corps, to which Heavy Tank Battalion 509 was attached, also made little progress but the *Tiger* troops were integral to what success they did have. When the advance was stalled by a group of *IS-2s* at Seregelyes, two *Tiger II* were brought forward and dispatched six of the Soviet heavy tanks allowing the advance to continue.[547] By the 10th of March, I SS Panzer Corps had advanced to the Sió Canal in the south but the advance to the Danube by III Panzer Corps had stalled at the Sarviz Canal. By the 12th, both I SS Panzer Corps and I Cavalry Corps had managed to cross the Sió Canal, but it was clear that the offensive was running out of momentum. At this stage, with Frühlingserwachen coming to a halt, Battalion 509 had its last great battle. A group of 24 *ISU-52* protected by a minefield were holding up the German advance and all 16 of the unit's *Tiger* tanks were brought forward to remove this threat. Every one of them was severely damaged and three were destroyed, but once lanes had been cleared in the minefield every *ISU-152* was destroyed. The battalion then returned to the corps reserve to rebuild.[548]

The battalion's attack on the 13th was among the last offensive efforts carried out by the *Tiger* tanks and certainly the last carried out by the heavy tank battalions in Hungary. Events further north brought the offensive to an end on the 14th. Since the Soviets had known about Frühlingserwachen beforehand, they recognized an opportunity. While 6th Panzer Army drove south and east towards Budapest, they continued preparations for an attack of their own on Vienna, to start on the 15th of March. By the time the Soviet attack began, the Germans' armoured reserves had been badly depleted. They were in no condition to counter any attack from the north. The Soviet attack also threatened 6th Panzer Army with encirclement.[549]

This clever Soviet plan unfolded largely as intended, though they were unable to encircle the 6th Panzer Army. The Germans had become aware of the impending offensive on the 14th and covertly began to reorient their forces north to break out of the planned encirclement. It was in this effort that Battalion 501 became important. Previously, they had been held back as part of the I SS Panzer Corps reserve, partly because of the small number of available vehicles and partly because the bridge over the Sió Canal that the Germans constructed could not carry the weight of the unit's heavy armour.[550] With the corps now working to withdraw, battalion's nine *Tiger II* became an integral part of the corps once again. The tanks were split among different elements of the Leibstandarte, which while a violation of *Klotzen nicht kleckern*, was a necessary concession to the small number available.

On the 20th, while much of the battalion was committed near Peremontor-Berhida, two *Tiger II* of the 3rd Company assisted Leibstandarte Panzers in skirmishes outside Inota. Towards midnight this force dashed through the village to breakout towards Varpalota. The next day one *Tiger II*, commanded by *Hauptsturmführer* Heinz Birnschein, with two *Panther*, claimed to have destroyed 17 enemy tanks on the road between Öskü and Hajmasker. The battalion had successfully spearheaded the Leibstandarte's breakout, that victory came at a heavy cost. While only two of the operational *Tiger* tanks were lost in this period, the battalion destroyed the majority of its tanks which had been under repair since there was no way to evacuate them, turning much of this tank battalion into an infantry unit, leaving them to take a long march to safety.[552]

Heavy Tank Battalion 509 also found itself spearheading the efforts of III Panzer Corps to help their escape from the Soviet encirclement but with only 20 operational tanks it was employed a whole, rather than parceled out in packets. Nevertheless, the two units' actions during this period remained thematically similar with the *Tiger* working to break through Soviet forces and being forced to abandon many of its vehicles. On the 25th, due to lack of fuel, 14 of the unit's 27 *Tiger* tanks were destroyed. The remaining 13 *Tiger* tanks made it back to the Reich on the 31st of March.[553] In the retreat, their fighting capabilities once again shone, but their mechanical unreliability and demand for large quantities of fuel proved to be serious liabilities that left the units with few vehicles in the war's final month. Despite their losses, the fact that both battalions returned to German soil was the lone bright spot at the end of Germany's last offensive, which had come to a halt 20 kilometers from the Danube.[551]

Tactically, the heavy tank battalions that fought in Hungary from October 1944 to March 1945 did not entirely share Germany's strategic weakness. When an adequate number of the *Tiger* tanks with good support attacked the Soviets, they succeeded. But the demands placed upon them, their lack of mechanical reliability, and the poor state of the army in general made it difficult to create favorable conditions. The success of the initial operations of Heavy Tank Battalion 509 in Konrad III and the attack of Heavy Tank Battalion 503 on the 1st Romanian Army were outnumbered by failures. Frühlingserwachen was perhaps the most dramatic but it was the failed rallying of the infantry by *Hauptmann* von Diest-Koerber and the depletion of Heavy Tank battalion 509 after their initial success in Konrad III that were emblematic. They demonstrated not only the decline in the army's strength and will, but also the unreliability of the *Tiger*, which led to the rapid decline in the fighting power of the heavy tank battalion as operations progressed. Hungary provided a better showcase of *Tiger II* capabilities than Normandy, but it could not duplicate the fairly consistent ability of its predecessor to salvage the local situation, as the army it supported became weaker and its enemies became stronger.

THE TIGER
VARIANTS IN COMBAT

hile the *Tiger I* and *II* were the most famous members of the Tiger series, the other three variants built upon their chassis demonstrated the effectiveness and limitations of the specialized AFVs fielded by the *Reichsheer* in the second half of the war. Obviously, the vehicles bore a number of similarities. All three were heavy vehicles, ranging from 65 tons to 75 tons, which severely limited their mobility. The *Ferdinand* proved to be best of them when it was used as a long-range tank destroyer, the role for which it had been designed. That said, the fluid nature of the war in this period and the German shortage of AFVs meant that they were often lost in retreat and used as assault guns, a role for which they were ill-suited. The *Sturmtiger*, was an urban assault gun. As demonstrated in the Warsaw Uprising, it proved to be of limited utility even in its intended role. The *Jagdtiger* likewise proved to be of limited use since its extreme weight and the burden this put on the drivetrain meant that the vehicles were often out of commission, awaiting spare parts, leaving them with few opportunities to employ their formidable 128mm guns. The *Ferdinand* proved to be the best of the variants, but this was a dubious distinction as all three vehicles had proven to be overspecialized, or ill-conceived and ill-suited to the situations in which they were engaged.

After losing the *Tiger* contract to Henschel in July of 1942, 90 of the 100 Porsche *Tiger* hulls that had been completed by Nibelungenwerk were converted into tank destroyers.[552] The new *Ferdinand* vehicles, which had been manufactured by May 1943, shared only the hull, and running gear with the original *VK 45.01 (P)*. The *Ferdinand* sported an additional 100mm of frontal armour, for a total of 200mm, as well as the 88mm gun.[553]

This new 68.5-ton vehicle was even more radically differentiated from its origins by its look and role. Rather than being fitted with a turret, the vehicle's 88mm gun was mounted in an armoured casemate placed on the rear of the hull. While this arrangement made it easier to fit the larger gun, it meant that the gun could fire only in an arc in front of the vehicle, denying it the combat flexibility of a turreted tank. The lack of a turret was not a serious problem when the vehicle was being used in its intended role. The *Ferdinand* was a tank destroyer, meant to engage enemy tanks at long range, up to 2,800 meters.[554] Engagements at these ranges made a turret redundant. All the *Ferdinand* needed was a good firing position and enemy tanks could be comfortably dispatched long before they could outmaneuver it. However, if enemy tanks or infantry approached the vehicle from its flanks, the entire vehicle had to be moved to engage them, a serious weakness in close quarters combat.[555]

Before digging into the operational history of the *Ferdinand*, a brief overview of German tank destroyer doctrine, and the place *Ferdinand* held within it, is beneficial. The Germans' first tank destroyer, the *Panzerjäger I,* which mounted a captured Czech 47mm anti-tank gun onto a *Panzer I* chassis, was created after the Battle of France to provide German units with additional mobile anti-tank fire power.[556] These vehicles were the first in a line of open-topped tank destroyers, the most famous and prolific of which was the *Marder III* (Marten), which mounted either a captured Soviet *Zis-3* 76.2mm gun or the German 75mm Pak 40.[557] While these vehicles provided much needed anti-tank capabilities to an army chronically short of tanks, their open-top design made them dangerous to use in combat. By 1943, the *StuG* had proven to be a superior option. Initially designed for infantry support, with a short barreled 75mm gun like that on the early *Panzer IV,* by 1942 the *StuG III* had, like the *Panzer IV,* been fitted with a long-barreled 75 mm gun. This high velocity gun, combined with the vehicle's mobility, low profile and enclosed fighting compartment transformed it into a highly capable tank destroyer.[558]

The use of the *StuG,* and later tank destroyers of a similar design, like the *Jagdpanzer IV* and *Jagdpanzer 38(t)* in the anti-tank role was laid out well in the *Brief Introduction about the Management and Combat of the Assault Gun for Orientation with other Weapons Leaders,* published by the Panzer Training School in Paris in July 1943. The document did not neglect the vehicle's original role, referring to the vehicle as "the infantry's immediate support weapon against hostile pockets of resistance and tanks."[559] Nonetheless its anti-tank role was emphasized. The manual stated that "the assault gun is particularly capable of fighting tanks," a firm indication of the shift in the *StuG* role.[560]

In combat terms, *StuG* and other vehicles like it, displayed its tank-fighting capabilities by firing from ambush, then quickly relocating. In this way enemy tank attacks could be efficiently worn down by fast moving vehicles with powerful guns.[561] This combination of mobility and firepower was in keeping with the design priorities of the early German panzers and just as the heavy armour on the *Tiger* upset these priorities in tank design, the *Ferdinand* upset them in the tank destroyers. Its emphasis on armour and firepower over mobility meant they had formidable anti-tank capabilities but lacked the tactical flexibility afforded to the lighter tank destroyers. This capability shift complicated and limited their deployment.

The combat debut of the *Ferdinand* was Operation Zitadelle. For this operation, 90 *Ferdinand* were divided between two battalions, Heavy Tank Destroyer 653 and 654. These two battalions made up Heavy Tank Destroyer Regiment 656.[562] Rather than employing the regiment as a whole, its battalions were assigned to separate corps in the 9th Army. XLI Panzer Corps got Battalion 653 and XXIII Panzer Corps was given Battalion 654.

Battalion 653's objective on the 5th of July was an area nicknamed Panzer Hill. The feature was cleared by close assault, which Denis Showalter describes as "a polite euphemism for a series of vicious fights in which bayonets were civilized weapons."[563] This kind of close-quarters combat, was no place for a vehicle like the *Ferdinand*, but it was employed in the assault gun's traditional role, to supplement available *StuG* battalions. It proved a poor supplement. The great size of the vehicle and lack of a turret were not its only weaknesses. It was highly vulnerable to enemy infantry because it lacked a close-in defense weapon, like the hull-mounted and coaxial machine guns mounted on the *Tiger*.

While the lack of a machine gun was a major fault, the real problem lay elsewhere. Cooperation between the tank destroyers and the infantry had broken down.[564] Guderian summed up the consequence of this breakdown in his memoir this way: "Once they had broken into the enemy's infantry zone they literally had to go quail shooting with cannons."[565] Thus, while the Germans took Panzer Hill, the losses to the battalion were exceptionally high. They started the day at full strength with 45 vehicles. By the end of the day only 12 were still operational.[566] By the 7th of July, following two days of heavy fighting around the fiercely contested town of Ponyri, where the vehicles were once again employed in close support roles, the battalion had no operational vehicles left. The unit was withdrawn to rebuild.[567]

Battalion 654 did not fare much better during Zitadelle. Their vehicles proved just as vulnerable to attack by Soviet infantry on their own advance towards Ponyri[568]. By the 7th of July, they were reduced to 25 vehicles, having lost almost half its strength in just three days.[569] On the 9th of July the entire Heavy Tank Destroyer Regiment could only call upon ten operational vehicles. The next day, Battalion 654 lost another four vehicles inside Ponyri. After these losses, it was also withdrawn to be rebuilt.[570]

Returning to Kursk, Operation Zitadelle was called off on the 12th of July. At that time, Heavy Tank Destroyer Regiment 656 reported the loss of 19 vehicles across its two battalions. These losses were significantly higher than that of the *Tiger I* with only ten being lost out of 146 deployed. The higher losses for the tank destroyer were the result of their poor employment, being thrust into the role of assault guns, and while their armour and armament were up the task, their poor mobility, and the lack of cooperation with the infantry left them exceptionally vulnerable, leading to a very costly operation for the new vehicle. By contrast, the *Tiger* had been deployed in accordance with its design, leading to lower casualties and a more successful operation for the heavy tank.[571]

The rapidly diminishing combat power of the *Ferdinand* regiment also reflected a malady that the vehicles shared with the *Tiger*, mechanical unreliability. A number of problems were encountered with its engines, including bent or torn valves, shattered piston heads, broken piston rods and cracked cylinder heads. These were all the result of the engine overheating, not surprising given the vehicle's 68.5-ton weight.[572]

While Zitadelle had been a disappointing start for the *Ferdinand*, its next employment allowed it to be used as intended. As Zitadelle ended, the Soviets launched Operation Kutuzov with the aim of cutting off the Orel Salient. Among the forces trapped by this Soviet encirclement was Model's 9th Army.[573] The regiment had been in reserve when the Soviets attacked. It was quickly dispatched to help defend against the new Soviet offensive. The regiment remained in the Orel Salient until the end of July.

In this defensive fighting, the regiment's vehicles were dispersed amongst the German defenders. Their actions alongside the 36th Infantry Division on the 14th of July were typical. On this day, 14 *Ferdinand*, mostly from Battalion 653 were attached to the division, being dispersed around the division's frontage at platoon strength. Most of these vehicles were acting as part of the division's static defence. One platoon was employed differently, and the results spoke for themselves. The *Ferdinands* were deployed alongside a number of *StuG* and the division's pioneer battalion in an attack on a group of dug-in enemy tanks in Shelyabug. This attack, carried out with sufficient infantry support, was successful and resulted in no *Ferdinand* losses, a far cry from the fighting at Kursk.[574]

Properly employed, the *Ferdinand* proved to be potent tank destroyer. Engaging Soviet tanks at range maximized the advantages provided by the 88mm gun and the vehicle's heavy armour, while avoiding the many disadvantages that afflicted the vehicle in close combat. Overall, the fighting on the 14th was a success for the regiment and over the course of the fighting during both Zitadelle and the Orel Salient they claimed to have destroyed over 500 tanks, more than 200 anti-tank guns and 100 field guns. While these numbers are certainly exaggerated, it was nevertheless clear that the *Ferdinand* could be very successful – when used as intended.

Nevertheless, things did not always go their way. By the end of July, when the unit was withdrawn from the Orel Salient, they had lost another 20 vehicles, most of which were destroyed by their crews to prevent their capture – a demonstration to the difficulties of recovering the 68.5-ton vehicle. The fluid tactical situation in the salient just exaggerated these difficulties. By then, the badly depleted regiment was recovering in Briansk where Battalion 654 handed over their remaining vehicles to its sister battalion before returning to Germany to be re-equipped with the *Jagdpanther*.[575]

Thanks to this transfer, Battalion 653 was once again at full strength. It next saw service in October of 1943, in the Zaporozhe Bridgehead. The bridgehead was one of the last German positions on the eastern bank of the Dnieper. In mid-September *Generalfeldmarschall* Erich von Manstein had finally secured Hitler's permission to withdraw behind the mighty river in the face of continued Soviet attacks against

Army Group South.[576] When the battalion arrived on the 1st of October, it was a battalion in name only. Although nominally overstrength with 50 AFVs, the necessity of conducting most of the unit's movement by road marches owing to shortage of rail transport had taken a serious mechanical toll. Only ten tank destroyers were available for immediate use. After a week, the battalion was able to field 20 vehicles.[577]

The shortage of operational vehicles aside, Battalion 653 in the Zaporozhe Bridgehead was generally successful, particularly in the defense of the town of Novo-Alexandrovka on the 10th of October, with nine *Ferdinand* accounting for 48 Soviet tanks with no losses to themselves.[578] The 16th Panzergrenadier Division was supported by the *Ferdinand* throughout their operations in the bridgehead. Their assessment of the vehicle's strengths helps to explain their success in this encounter. The *Ferdinand's* heavy armour made it all but impervious to enemy tank fire. It also possessed "a gun with unbelievable shooting performance. Its shots [left] every *T-34* and *KV-1* in ruins, even at the longest possible range [of 3,000 meters]."[579]

The 16th Panzergrenadier Division's report was not all glowing praise however, as it also highlighted the same problems that the *Ferdinand* had shown at Kursk. It emphasized once again the vehicle's lack of close defense weapons, concluding that "it is therefore completely unsuitable for driving into the enemy alone."[580] This warning was one that was worth repeating, but it was hardly a revolutionary insight. More interesting was the report's discussion of the *Ferdinand* as an "Infantry Escort Tank", which indicated that they employed it in a direct support role, when attacking the enemy front line, though the task of exploitation was still to be handled by the *Panzer III* and *IV*.[581] Their use in this role was in violation of the rules that both the division and the members of the unit knew.[582] That they did it anyway is less a reflection of poor decision making than an indication of the chronic shortage of AFVs on the Eastern Front, which necessitated using the *Ferdinand* more like a tank or assault gun, rather than as a tank destroyer.

It also must be said that while this employment went against the vehicle's intended role, the results were nowhere near as disastrous as they were at Kursk, with Bataillon 653 noting only two losses. One *Ferdinand* was so badly damaged that it was returned to the Nibelungenwerk, and one was destroyed by its crew because it could not be recovered. These small losses were all the more remarkable given the tenuous situation of the Zaporozhe Bridgehead. This suggests that the majority of the combat engagements were consistent with its intended use and that even when it was incorrectly, the supporting divisions were careful to keep the vehicles far away from enemy infantry.

Despite the successes and minimal losses that the 653 had in the fighting in the Zaporozhe Bridgehead, it was not enough to salvage the situation. On the 10th of October, when the battalion successfully defended Novo-Alexandrovka, elsewhere in the bridgehead, the larger offensive by the Soviet 3rd and 8th Guards Armies as well as the 12th Army was successful and, on the 13th the battalion was evacuated. Regardless of Hitler's, wishes the bridgehead could not be held. By the 14th, Zaporozhe itself was liberated. On the 15th, the last German units leaving the eastern bank of the Dnieper destroyed the bridges.[583] Like with the *Tiger*, the excellent performance of the *Ferdinand*, which in the words of the regiment's commander, *Oberstleutnant* Ernst von Jungenfeld, "made it a household name for both friend and foe" were not sufficient to compensate for the Germans' overall weakness and counter the Soviets great strength.[584]

In December of 1943, the battalion was dispatched to another Dnieper Bridgehead, this one at Nikopol. : The fighting there mirrored its earlier performance, with the vehicles proving highly effective in their intended role, with the unit losing only four vehicles. Nevertheless, with an average of just ten operational vehicles, they were once again only able to delay the inevitable, with the bridgehead falling on February 8th, 1944.[585]

By that point, all the *Ferdinand* vehicles had been withdrawn and returned to the Nibelungenwerk for much needed overhaul.[586] The vehicles were modified with a hull-mounted machine gun, as well as the implementation of other crew requests, including a commander's cupola, instead of the periscopes provided previously.[587] They also underwent a name change. On the 1st of February 1944, the *Ferdinand* was renamed, the *Elefant*, a reflection of Porsche's fall from favour the previous year.[588]

The operations of the new *Elefant* in 1944 were very poor, marked by heavy losses and few successes. Heavy Tank Destroyer Battalion 653 was split to deal with multiple new crises that had developed. In February of 1944, the 1st Company was sent to the Anzio Beachhead. In March, the rest of the unit was dispatched to Army Group North in Ukraine to assist in the relief of Tarnopol. The fighting at Anzio was in response to Operation Shingle, an Allied amphibious landing on the 22nd of January 1944. Once ashore, the Allies were less than a hundred kilometers from Rome.[589] To protect the Italian capital, the Germans rushed in reinforcements to the Anzio beachhead. The battalion took the eleven *Elefanten* that were ready for combat, leaving them three vehicles short of a full company, but this was considered an acceptable risk, given the situation. By the time the company arrived in Rome on the 24th of February, the situation at the beachhead had become a stalemate.[590]

The *Elefanten* saw service in the second German effort to destroy the beachhead, launched on the 29th of February, Operation Seitensprung (Escapade), focusing on the Allied positions around Isola Bella, just south of the town of Cisterna.[591] The first and strongest attack fell on the American left flank, defended by the paratroopers of the 504th Parachute Infantry Regiment and A Company, 601st Tank Destroyer Battalion. The 601st was equipped with the *M10 Motor Gun Carriage*, a turreted tank destroyer which mounted a 3-inch (76mm) M7 gun. With standard armour piercing ammunition, it could penetrate 93mm of armour at 457 meters, making it more than a match for the *Panzer IV*, but not for the *Tiger* or the *Ferdinand*.[592] The two *M10s* defending the American position were taken under fire by five *Tiger* tanks of Heavy Tank Battalion 508 and two *Elefanten*. One of the *M10s* was caught in the open and was immobilized, though its gun still fired. This *M10*, assisted by its still mobile comrade, fired furiously at the advancing Germans. This barrage of fire knocked out two *Tiger* tanks, crippled the other three and drove off the *Elefanten*.[593] Elsewhere 3rd Platoon, B Company of the 601 was attacked by another mixed battle group of *Tiger* and *Elefanten*. While the 3-inch rounds from the *M10* bounced off of the *Elefanten* at a distance of 229 meters, flanking fire from other tank destroyers disabled two *Tiger* and an *Elefant*[594]

According to German records, the vehicles lost to the Americans on the 29th were recovered.[595] Irrespective, the counterattack had failed, despite the superior armour of the German vehicles. Part of the problem was the terrain, which was mostly reclaimed marshland that kept the heavy German tanks confined to roads and offered few opportunities for maneuvering, negating their numerical advantage. Also, while the *M10* 3-inch gun may have lacked the means to penetrate the thick frontal armour of the *Tiger* and *Elefant*, once again superior Allied tactics proved to be decisive, whether it was the sheer weight of fire or the ability of the tank destroyers to outmaneuver their foes, striking at their thinner side armour.

Things would not get much better for the *Elefant* when the attack was resumed on the 1st of March. For the new attack they were attached to Kampfgruppe Stein, which was principally made up of the *Tiger I* tanks from Heavy Tank Battalion 508. Owing to the marshy terrain that defined so much of the Anzio battlefield, they attacked down the road from Cisterna towards Isola Bella, with the *Elefant* in the lead, followed by the *Tiger*. The attack quickly faltered as the bridge in front of Isola Bella was out. When the crew commander attempted to turn his *Elefant*, it fell into the ditch at the side of the road. The *Tiger* attempted to pull it free while under heavy artillery fire but failed and the *Elefant* was abandoned. The *Tiger* was itself disabled in the recovery attempt and was also abandoned. A further attempt to salvage the *Elefant* was launched that night, but it too failed amid a "rain of steel and phosphorus."[596] A second *Elefant*, was lost just 200 meters up the road, when it struck a mine. Like the first vehicle, heavy Allied artillery fire made it impossible to recover so it was destroyed by its crew.[597]

This use of the *Elefant* lacked the heavy casualties that defined the initial engagements of the *Ferdinand* at Kursk, but the overall results were much worse, with two vehicles lost far from their objective. It once again reflected the unsuitability of the Anzio area for armour. The *Elefant* was the best protected vehicle to ever serve in the Italian theatre, but the poor terrain left the vehicles very vulnerable to the Allies' overwhelming fire superiority, which may have struggled to destroy the *Elefant* outright but was more than capable of disabling it. After this demonstration of the vehicle's shortcomings the company was withdrawn from the front line and waited at Cisterna until the Allied breakout from the beached in May of 1944.[598]

After the Allied breakout, German forces in the area began a steady retreat first to Rome and then further north. The withdrawal caused steady attrition. The *Elefanten* that had survived the fighting in Anzio were steadily reduced in number by Allied fire, shortage of spare parts, and in one case by falling through a bridge never designed to handle the 68.5-ton vehicle. The vehicles were used in a number of rearguard actions as the Germans withdrew and while they were more than capable of destroying *Shermans*, their employment either singly or in small groups meant that they made little impression on their foes. By the 13th of June, only three *Elefanten* remained.[599] These three vehicles were ultimately withdrawn in August of 1944, after which they were sent to Vienna and the surviving crews rejoined the rest of the Battalion.[600]

In the Ukraine, the *Elefant* had a similarly limited impact on events. While their initial effort, supporting the attack of the SS 9th Panzer Division Hohenstaufen, saw them reach the Strypa River as planned, they were unable to reach the encircled city of Tarnopol, which fell to the Soviets on the 14th of April.[601] Losses were light, with only four *Elefanten* destroyed, but they had once again had little impact on events. In another parallel with Italy, the failure of the battalion in front of Tarnopol was followed by another devastating retreat in June which cost the unit 22 vehicles.[602]

Owing to these heavy losses, with only 12 *Elefanten* left by the 1st of August, the majority of the unit returned to Germany to reunite with the 1st Company and begin training on the *Jagdtiger*.[603] The 2nd Company remained in the East however, since the AFV shortage was too acute to lose them. The unit, renamed Heavy Tank Destroyer Company 614 in December of 1944, lost almost all of its vehicles in retreats from the Kielce area in January of 1945.[604] In an interesting side note, four of the unit's surviving *Elefanten* were involved in the Battle for Berlin. Two were lost in the Zossen Training area outside the city and two were captured by the Soviets inside the city in the Karl-August Platz on the 1st of May 1945, making them possibly the only German vehicles fighting in the German capital which were also veterans of Kursk.[605]

The fighting in Italy and the unit's actions in the Ukraine in 1944 demonstrated that while the *Elefant* still had a gun and armour that was formidable, its lack of mechanical reliability was a fatal weakness, especially in the retreats that became more and more common as the war dragged on. Like the *Tiger*, when deployed in favorable conditions, it could be highly effective, but those circumstances were becoming ever rarer, and the vehicle's weaknesses increasingly came to the fore.

The surviving veterans of the 653 finished the war in yet another tank destroyer variant of the *Tiger*, the *Jagdtiger*. It mounted Krupp's 128mm gun, which was so large that, like the *Ferdinand* before it, the *Jagdtiger* was designed as a casemate tank destroyer, the only way to mount such a large gun. The vehicle also featured a 250mm front armour plate, angled at 75 degrees. As a consequence, the *Jagdtiger* was the heaviest AFV fielded during the war with a weight of 75 tons.[606] The *Jagdtiger* was both one of the most formidable AFVs of the Second World War and one of the weakest. Unsurprisingly, its armour and firepower fell into the former category. With 250mm of well slopped frontal armour, none of the common Allied tanks of the late war period, including the *Sherman* with the M3 75mm gun, the *T-34/85* and the *IS-2* could penetrate the *Jagdtiger* armour at anything more than 100 meters. Conversely the *Jagdtiger* 128mm gun could penetrate an *IS-2* at a range of 2,500 meters and penetrate the armour of every other Allied tank at a range of 4,000 meters.[607] Otto Carius, who commanded a *Jagdtiger* right at the war's end, provided a practical example of "the monstrous penetrating capability of our cannon."[608] On one of the few opportunities he had to fire it, a *Sherman* drove behind a building to escape from their fire. Carius had his gunner put one round through the house, demolishing a portion of it and the second round destroyed the rest of the house and the *Sherman*.[609]

The strengths and weaknesses of the *Jagdtiger* were amply demonstrated in their combat performance in the final months of the war. Only two heavy tank destroyer battalions used the *Jagdtiger*, the 653 as previously mentioned and the 512, though it is the old veterans of the 653 that will be discussed in detail, since the 512 only fought in the Ruhr Pocket in April of 1945 and its experiences mirrored those of the more experienced unit.[610]

The experiences of Heavy Tank Destroyer Battalion 653 were defined largely by its poor mechanical reliability, which accounted for far more losses than Allied arms. In January 1945, the unit had just finished two months of service, spending most of its time driving around western Germany in an abortive effort to join Operation Wacht am Rhein. This placed a great toll on the vehicles, which were forced to conduct long road marches for lack of rail transport. The result was a steady drain on the unit's operational vehicles. By the end of January only four *Jagdtiger* had been destroyed but 19 needed repairs and by the end of March, after two months of steady retreat through the Rhineland the unit had been reduced to 28 vehicles of which only eight were operational.[611]

Jagdtiger combat performance proved to be little better than its mechanical reliability. As with the *Tiger*, the *Jagdtiger* was often employed in small numbers to shore up German defenses. There were instances where the *Jagdtiger* succeeded in having a tactical impact, including a successful rearguard action by seven of them from the 1ˢᵗ Company on the 16ᵗʰ of March:

> *Oberleutnant Haberland...received a mission while operating with the 47ᵗʰ Volksgrenadier Division on March 16ᵗʰ, 1945, in the area between Hagenau and Weißenburg, to deploy his company's 7 Jagdtiger to prevent the enemy from crossing the Sauer River and screen an orderly withdrawal of friendly elements. The enemy attack, with exceptionally powerful armour and infantry elements along the Laubach-Gunstett road, halted when the tank destroyers immediately opened fire. During this operation, Oberleutnant Haberland knocked out a Sherman with his gun and destroyed an enemy howitzer as it was moving into position shortly thereafter with a direct hit. The enemy then pulled his tanks and infantry forces back over a hill to renew the attack on Kampfgruppe Haberland from the north and southeast. A timely warning by radio to the group's elements positioned on both those flanks prevented the enemy from crossing the Sauer there as well. This prevented the enemy from successfully advancing into withdrawing friendly forces from the south. Thanks to the unprecedented aggressiveness and perseverance of Oberleutnant Haberland and his Kampfgruppe, the extremely dangerous enemy penetration was delayed, so that the friendly withdrawal was conducted according to plan and without enemy interference on the following night.[612]*

It was far more common for the vehicles to be involved in poorly supported counterattacks for which they were ill-suited, leading to ever more losses of vehicles that could not be replaced.[613] Continued retreats across western Germany in March took a great mechanical toll. The unit's limited stock of vehicles was able escape from the Ruhr before the closing of the Ruhr Pocket on the 5th of April. The battalion was withdrawing to Stuttgart in order return to the factory to restore their damaged vehicles and receive new ones. At the end of the war, the last two operational *Jagdtiger* were in Lieaen, (now Liezen) Austria, having competed the journey across the Reich, but with little to show for their efforts.[614] Ultimately the *Jagdtiger* proved too unreliable for mass deployment and was too specialized to be useful in the fluid defensive fighting the Germans were engaged in at the end of the war.

The *Sturmtiger* likewise proved ill-suited to the circumstances in which it was employed. It represented the final iteration of an assault gun specifically designed for urban combat. When the citizens of Warsaw rose up against their German occupiers in August of 1944, the situation seemed to be tailor-made for the *Sturmtiger*, with the formidable armour of the *Tiger I* and a 380mm *Raketenwerfer*. Production had only just begun in August of 1944, so only two vehicles were ready for service.[615] Nevertheless, their arrival in the city caused a stir. One *Sturmtiger* was filmed on the 19th of August operating around the Kierbedz Bridge. The camera showed an "entire building crumble to dust", under the weight of the 380mm rockets.[616] It was a dramatic showcase of the vehicle's firepower, but it actually had an almost insignificant role in the German suppression of the uprising. This was partly because of the few employed but also because of the nature of the fighting. The *Sturmtiger* could certainly level buildings but that was never enough in Warsaw. As Norman Davies wrote in *Rising 44: The Battle for Warsaw*:

> *Every day, usually at dawn, the Germans would return to their chosen sectors like workmen returning to a building site. Unable to dislodge their adversary by standard infantry tactics, they would call up the bombers and the heavy guns, pound the insurgents' positions into mounds of rubble, demolish a few barricades, and gain a few yards or a couple of streets. Next morning, they would find that half the barricades had been rebuilt during the night and booby-trapped, and the shattered buildings provided perfect cover for unseen snipers and grenade throwers. In this way practically every building and crater had to be fought over time and time again before the Germans could secure a disputed sector.*[617]

In this *Rattenkreig* (War of the Rats), the *Sturmtiger* was more liability than asset.[618] Its armour was formidable, but the tightly packed and rubble choked streets of Warsaw made the vehicle difficult to maneuver, and if it should become stuck, the 65-ton *Sturmtiger* would be difficult to recover. They were also exceptionally vulnerable to infantry anti-tank weapons, including captured German *Panzerfaust* (a short-range rocket launcher) and Molotov Cocktails. Finally, as Davies indicated, the leveling of buildings looked impressive, but did little to overcome the Poles' determined resistance. They simply turned the ruins into even more formidable defensive positions. So, the *Sturmtiger* saw little use, in what was ostensibly the very environment for which they were designed. Indeed, in the long term, the citizens of Warsaw did not remember the massive German assault tank but did remember the Germans heavy use of the *Nebelwerfer* (rocket launcher). Thousands were launched into the city and were nicknamed *Krowa* (Bellowing Cow), after the sound they made.[619]

After their disappointing initial employment, the vehicles saw little use and references to them are few and far between, proof of the absence of circumstances in which these highly specialized vehicles could be successfully employed. *Oberst* Helmut Ritgen, of the Panzer Lehr Division recalled that his Kampfgruppe had one at the Vouziers Bridgehead, just north of Falaise at the end of August 1944. The vehicle had been sent for use in Paris but was diverted to him after the collapse of the German front in Normandy. Its only noteworthy contribution to the German defense came on the 31ˢᵗ of August, when it was used to demolish a windmill outside Vouziers that was being used by American artillery observers. Ritgen did not mention its fate but given the demise of the other *Tiger* tanks retreating from France and the decimated state of the Panzer Lehr generally, it is very likely that the vehicle was destroyed by its crew in the subsequent German retreat back into the Reich, either due to mechanical failure or a lack of fuel.[620]

The last recorded deployment of the *Sturmtiger* came in April of 1945, where four were attached to the 116ᵗʰ Panzer Division fighting in the Ruhr Pocket. In addition to the *Sturmtiger*, the division could only field another fourteen *Panther*.[621] While their armour and armament made them theoretically formidable, their 12-round ammunition capacity, poor mobility, and the great clouds of dust and smoke that accompanied their firing made them poorly suited for defensive fighting. They added little to the division's fighting strength at the end of the war. Consequently, the *Sturmtiger* proved to have the worst combat career of any of the *Tiger* variants, being too heavy even for its intended role and too specialized to be effective in any other role.

Overall, the tale of the *Tiger* variants is one of failure. All three vehicles proved to be too specialized to adapt to the mobile defensive war the Germans were waging from 1943 to 1945. They were technically impressive vehicles with heavy armour and awe-inspiring guns, that lacked the flexibility required to be truly successful. This was especially true of the *Sturmtiger* and *Jagdtiger*. The *Ferdinand* enjoyed more success than the others when employed as part of a static defense, but it too proved too specialized to adapt to the vast majority of situations in which it was placed, where more flexible vehicles like the *Tiger* themselves were still effective.

CONCLUSION

ith the end of the Second World War in Europe on the 8ᵗʰ of May 1945, the story of the *Tiger* tank and its variants came to an end. The heavy tank battalions were disbanded, and their vehicles were largely sent to the scrap heap. All that remained was their complex legacy as examples of German technological superiority and testaments to the folly of the weapons engineers who created such unreliable behemoths. But beyond that, the question remained regarding the effectiveness of these vehicles to the German war effort. As has been demonstrated time and again, the *Tiger* really did earn much of its legendary reputation. There were plenty of instances between 1942 and 1945 where *Tiger* tanks shrugged off enemy fire and destroyed everything in their paths. Nevertheless, the overriding conclusion of the *Tiger* story is one of failure.

From the start, the various vehicles of the so-called *Tiger* "family" were not created to fill any pressing doctrinal need. Although true that the *Waffenamt* had been thinking of a heavy tank since 1935, no firm plan for such a weapon existed until Adolf Hitler established his own parameters in May of 1941. The resultant *Tiger I* set the precedent for the rest of the *Tiger* variants that followed. Rather than continuing to embrace the doctrinal emphasis on mobility and firepower, which had guided previous tank designs like the *Panzer III* and *IV*, Hitler placed his emphasis on armoured protection and firepower. This willful deviation from almost a century of successful Prusso-German doctrinal thinking negated the strengths of traditional German way of war. For the first time, new weapons were not designed to operate within the doctrine of *Bewegungskreig*. Thus, a new trend in German weaponry and AFV design was created, with ever heavier vehicles and increasingly large guns entering service, culminating in the 75-ton *Jagdtiger*, which possessed 250mm of frontal armour and a 128mm gun.[622] These massive vehicles were certainly technically impressive, but they created substantial economic burdens even before they fired a shot in anger.

Production of the *Tiger* and its variants was in some limited respects quite successful. German industry was able to produce the vehicles in the quantities set by the *Reichsheer* for most of the war, continuing production even in the midst of concerted Allied bombing campaigns. Only in the fall of 1944, when the Allied bombing offensive reached its zenith, and the Germans began to run out of both manpower and raw materials, did production finally suffer serious delays and eventual collapse. That said, the success of the tank production process was overshadowed by larger problems.

The great technical complexity of the *Tiger* led to a limit on the number that could be produced. Consequently, it prevented the Germans from producing larger numbers of cheaper, less powerful vehicles. This compromise was considered acceptable as a means to counter the Allies' quantitative superiority with the qualitative superiority of heavier German tanks. Sadly for the Germans, no tank had the necessary qualitative superiority to overcome the Allies' overwhelming numerical superiority. Given that Germany produced only 44,688 AFVs compared with the Allies 239,750 the qualitative leap required to close such a yawning gap staggers the imagination. [623] German efforts to compensate for the Allied materiel superiority were further undermined by poor economic management. A lack of consistent prioritization and the constant conflicts between competing economic agencies ensured that for the duration of the war the term "German efficiency" remained a contradiction in terms. Subsequently, while the production of individual *Tiger* vehicles was relatively efficient, it took place against a backdrop of chronic industrial inefficiency and a wider quantitative gap between the two sides that no vehicle, regardless of its quality could possibly bridge.

The true mark of the *Tiger* success story was tactical. Success came not in its development or production, but upon the many battlefields over which the tanks fought. But even there, its success was limited and relatively brief. The *Tiger I* initial operations in the Soviet Union and North Africa in 1942 and 1943 created the *Tiger* legend. A legend of an undefeatable tank with impenetrable armour and a deadly gun. It was also at this time that the vehicle's faults first became apparent. In these operations it began to earn its other reputation as mechanically unreliable, which often left units with too few vehicles to be truly effective. Their lack of mobility was also demonstrated well, especially in the operations of Panzerbataillon 503 with Army Group Don in January 1943. In that instance, with the army group threatened with encirclement the *Tiger* units lacked the numbers or the mobility to save the day. Instead, it was Herman Balck's 11th Panzer Division, with the *Panzer III* and *IV*, which saved Army Group Don, demonstrating that the traditional emphasis of panzer design on mobility and firepower that was so compatible with the traditions of *Bewegungskrieg* was still a potent and decisive combination. These early operations also gave the Allies ample opportunities to examine the new German heavy tank, especially since both the British and the Soviets would quickly secure their own captured examples to analyze. With captured examples of the *Tiger* in hand, the British and the Soviets began to create new tactics and weapons to meet the new threat, ensuring that the German tank's superiority would be short-lived.

Operation Zitadelle seemed tailor-made for the *Tiger* and its breakthrough role. Strong Soviet defences needed to be smashed to allow the panzer divisions to surge through the gaps and deliver victory. Unfortunately, the Soviets had planned their defence well and were ready to combat the *Tiger*. While *Tiger* losses were low – with only ten of the 146 deployed being lost – the rapid depletion of their units to combat or mechanical damage meant that the heavy tanks often lacked the strength to secure the breakthroughs for which they had been designed.[624]

On the defensive, from the summer of 1943 to the summer of 1944 the *Tiger* again had decidedly mixed results. Their use as *Korsettstange* was one that stretched the already mechanically unreliable tanks to their limits as they worked to reinforce depleted and demoralized infantry formations. However, even in this period the *Tiger* tanks had a number of successes against long odds. While these successes were impressive, they could not disguise the fact that the Germans were steadily retreating and no success against the odds in local combat between the heavy tanks and the Red Army could change that. Additionally, this period saw a slew of new Soviet AFVs entering the fight, from the *IS-2* tank to numerous tank destroyers including the *SU-100* and *ISU-152*, all of which were capable of combating the *Tiger I* and *II* on a relatively equal footing – especially since they tended to be deployed in larger numbers than the *Tiger*.

Normandy cemented the legendary reputation of the *Tiger I*, especially with Michael Wittmann's actions at Villers

Bocage on the 7th of June 1944. Wittmann did his fair share to ensure the lasting nature of the *Tiger* legend. The tank's overall performance in Normandy was fairly poor. In Normandy, the *Tiger* was unable to help maintain the Germans' positions in the face of the Allies' materiel superiority. Further, the *Tiger* units were also increasingly vulnerable to Allied air power and new anti-tank weapons, especially the British 17-pounder, which turned the *Sherman* into a tank more than capable of defeating the *Tiger*.

Normandy also saw the first inauspicious deployment of the *Tiger II*. While the new tank had little success in France, its operations in Hungary from October 1944 to March 1945 did demonstrate that it was a worthy successor to the *Tiger I* in every way. Its armour and armament were even more formidable, but it also proved to be just as unreliable as its predecessor. In Hungary the *Tiger II* had a number of successes, including the attack of Heavy Tank Battalion 503 against the Romanian 1st Army in October 1944. These operations demonstrated that even with the war coming to an end, the underlying principles of panzer doctrine – the massed use of tanks, well supported by other weapons – could still lead to tactical and even operational success. However, these victories were few and far between. The Germans were generally unable to muster sufficient numbers of the *Tiger II* and adequate support for their operations. So, while the *Tiger II* did have its share of victories in Hungary, they were totally insufficient to tip the balance in a war that the Germans had already lost.

The *Tiger* variants, the *Ferdinand*, the *Sturmtiger* and the *Jagdtiger*, shared many similarities with the *Tiger I* and *II*. They were all heavily armoured and armed to their detriment, robbing them of the mobility so prized by German doctrine. They were also mechanically unreliable. There were plenty of distinguishing features in their stories. The *Ferdinand* was the most successful of the variants, but only when used as intended. When doctrinally employed, as a long-range tank destroyer in the Orel Salient as well as the Zaporozhe and Nikopol Bridgeheads in 1943, the *Ferdinand* was highly successful. When employed outside of that role, especially when pressed into service as an assault gun during its debut during *Zitadelle* and in the fighting in the Anzio beachhead in February 1944, it performed very poorly. Its lack of mobility and dearth close-range defensive weapons proved to be insurmountable handicaps.

By contrast the *Sturmtiger* and *Jagdtiger* did not enjoy the same success. The *Sturmtiger* 380mm rocket launcher was an awe-inspiring weapon, but the vehicle proved too heavy to be used effectively. Thus, it saw only limited use in the Warsaw Uprising, which should have been the vehicle's finest hour as the uprising was defined by the kind of urban warfare for which the vehicle was designed. But that was not the case. The *Jagdtiger*, too, had an impressive 128mm gun, but its unreliability and lack of mobility meant that it contributed very little to the final defense of western Germany in the final months of the war.

Taken all together the *Tiger* and its variants represented an enormous technical achievement. The development and production of a succession of ever-heavier vehicles in the midst of one of the greatest conflicts of all time, and under the shadow of Allied strategic bombing, was an accomplishment of note. Unfortunately, the performance of these vehicles was worthy of less celebration. While they did have their share of successes, especially the *Tiger I* and *II*, arguably the most famous tanks of the Second World War, their achievements were overshadowed by their failures. They did not fit into German doctrine and were never capable of fulfilling their intended roles.

In the end, as impressive as the *Tiger* and its variants were, it is clear that they never quite lived up to the expectations placed upon them. They were ultimately ineffective weapons when placed in the context of the wider war.

ENDNOTES

Chapter 1

1 F.M von Senger and Etterlin, *German Tanks of World War II: The Complete Illustrated History of German Armoured Fighting Vehicles 1926-1945.* Translated by J. Lucas, ed. Peter Chamberlain and Chris Ellis, (Munich: Lionel Leventhal ltd, 1969), 68-74.

2 Hereafter *schwere Panzer Abteilungen* will simply be referred to as *Panzerbataillonen* or tank battalions.

3 Christopher W. Wilbeck, *Sledgehammers: Strengths and Flaws of Tiger Tank Battalions in World War II,* (Bedford: Aberjona Press, 2004), 19, 30.

4 Alexander Hill, *The Red Army and the Second World War,* (Cambridge: Cambridge University Press, 2019), 440. Artem Drabkim, *Panzer Killers: Anti-Tank Warfare on the Eastern Front,* translated by Stuart Britton, (Barnsely: Pen & Sword Books, 2013), ebook, 352-353.

5 Stephen A. Hart, *Sherman Firefly vs Tiger: Normandy, 1944,* (London: Osprey Publishing, 1997), 14-15, 24

6 James S. Corum, *The Roots of Blitzkrieg: Hans von Seeckt and German Military Reform,* (Lawrence: University of Kansas Press, 1992), 112-114.

7 Peter Chamberlin, and Hilary L. Doyle, *Encyclopedia of German Tanks of World War Two: A Complete Illustrated Directory of German Battle Tanks, Armoured Cars, Self- Propelled Guns and Semi- Tracked Vehicles, 1933-1945,* (London: Arms and Armour Press, 1993), 147. Von Senger and Etterlin, *German Tanks,* 108. Thomas Jentz, *Panzertruppen: The Complete Guide to the Creation & Combat Employment of Germany's Tank Force 1933-1942,* (Atglen: Schiffer Military History, 1996), 114-115.

8 Army Weapons Office. While the name of this organization remained the same in translation, in German *Reichsheer* refers specifically to the

German Army under the Nazis as opposed to the *Reichswehr* of the Weimar Republic.

9 Thomas Jentz, and Hilary Doyle. *Germany's Tiger Tanks: D.W. to Tiger I: Design, Production & Modifications,* (Atglen: Schiffer Military History, 2000), 9.

10 Bryan Perrett, *Panzerkampfwagen IV Medium Tank 1936-45,* (London: Osprey Publishing, 2001), 4-5.

11 Jentz, and Doyle, *Germany's Tiger Tanks: D.W. to Tiger I,* 9.

12 Ibid, 10.

13 Kwk or *Kampfwagenkanone,* fighting vehicle gun, was the designation for a tank gun, while the L represented the length of the barrel. Henceforth, only the caliber will be cited. Also, while the Germans measured caliber in centimeters, caliber will instead be given in millimeters to conform to both Allied and modern practice.

14 Jentz, and Doyle, *Tiger Tank,* 10-11.

15 Ibid.

16 Franz-Wilhelm Lochmann, Alfred Rubbel and Richard Freiherr von Rosen, *The Combat History of the German Tiger Tank Battalion 503 in World War Two,* (Mechanicsburg: Stackpole Books, 2008, ebook), 120.

17 Jentz, and Doyle, *Tiger Tank,* 17-18.

18 David Doyle, *The Complete Guide to German Armoured Vehicles: Panzers, Jadgpanzers, Assault Guns, Antiaircraft. Self- Propelled Artillery, Armoured Wheeled and Semi- Tracked Vehicles, and More,* (New York: Skyhorse Publishing, 2019, ebook), 341.

19 Jentz, and Doyle, *Tiger Tank,* 23-24.

20 Hans von Luck, *Panzer Commander: The Memoirs of Colonel Hans von Luck,* (New York: Praeger Publishing, 1989), 197.

21 The *Waffen SS* was separate from the *Reichsheer.* During the Second World War, the SS fielded 38 divisions. They were usually placed under command of an army general, but not always. The Totenkopf was formally the 3rd Waffen SS.

22 Ibid, 41. Lloyd Clark, *Blitzkrieg: Myth, Reality, and Hitler's Lighting War- France, 1940,* (New York: Atlantic Monthly Press, 2016), 264. Peter McCarthy and Mike Syron, *Panzerkrieg: The Rise and Fall of Hitler's Tank Divisions,* (London: Constable, 2002), 85.

23 Thomas Jentz and Hilary Doyle, *Kingtiger Heavy Tank 1942-45,* (London: Osprey Publishing, 2002), 4.

24 Walter J. Spielberger and Hilary L. Doyle, *Tigers I and II and their Variants,* (Atglen: Schiffer Publishing, 2007), 27.

25 Steven Zaloga, *Armoured Champion: The Top Tanks of World War II*, (Mechanicsburg: Stackpole Books, 2015), ebook, 206.

26 Rheinmetall acquired August Borsig GmbH in 1933 and changed its name to Rheinmetall-Borsig AG in 1936. Henceforth simply Rheinmetall.

27 Dennis Showalter, *Hitler's Panzers: The Lighting Attacks that Revolutionized Warfare*, (Toronto: Penguin Group, 2007), 230.

28 Spielberger, and Doyle, *Tigers I and II and their Variants*, 27. Jentz, and Doyle, *Germany's Tiger Tanks: D.W. to Tiger I*, 18.

29 Thomas Jentz and Hilary Doyle. *Tiger I: Heavy Tank 1942-1945*, (London: Osprey Publishing, 1993), 5.

30 Jentz, and Doyle, *Tiger I: Heavy Tank*, 5.

31 Showalter, *Hitler's Panzers*, 231.

32 Jentz, and Doyle, *Germany's Tiger Tanks: D.W. to Tiger I*, 31. Spielberger, and Doyle, *Tigers I and II and their Variants*, 39.

33 Spielberger, and Doyle, *Tigers I and II and their Variants*, 76. Bruce Culver, *Tiger in Action* (Carrollton: Squadron/Signal Productions, 1989), 5. Spielberger, and Doyle, *Tigers I and II and their Variants*, 76. Culver, *Tiger in Action*, 5.

34 Spielberger, and Doyle, *Tigers I and II and their Variants*, 94.

35 Spielberger, and Doyle, *Tigers I and II and their Variants*, 94. Heinz Guderian, *Panzer Leader*, translated by Constantine Fitzgibbon, (London: Michael Joseph Ltd, 1952), 218.

36 In the German system 1.503 refers to the 1st Company, *Panzerbatallion 503*. Each battalion had three Kompanien, or companies, numbered successively as 2.503 and 3.503.

37 Lochmann, Rubbel and von Rosen, *The Combat History of the German Tiger Tank Battalion 503 in World War Two*, ebook, 159.

38 Ibid, 159-160.

39 Spielberger, and Doyle, *Tigers I and II and their Variants*, 98, 104.

40 Walter J. Spielberger, Hilary L. Doyle and Thomas L. Jentz, *Heavy Jagdpanzer: Development, Production, Operations*. (Atglen: Schiffer Publishing, 2007), 59.

41 Jentz and Doyle, *Kingtiger Heavy Tank*, 35. Jentz and Doyle, *Tiger I*, 20.

42 Hilary Doyle, & Tom Jentz, *StuG III Assault Gun 1940-1942*, (Oxford: Osprey Publishing, 1996), 15.

43 Spielberger, Doyle and Jentz, *Heavy Jagdpanzer*, 58, 63-64. Doyle, *The Complete Guide to German Armoured Vehicles*, ebook, 518, 530.

44 Spielberger, Doyle and Jentz, *Heavy Jagdpanzer*, 63-64, 76.

45 Jentz and Doyle. *Germany's Tiger Tanks: D.W. to Tiger I*, 23, 25.

46 Ibid, 20.

47 Spielberger, and Doyle, *Tigers I and II and their Variants*, 10-14.

48 Ibid, 18, 22-23.

49 Zaloga, *Armoured Champion: The Top Tanks of World War II*, ebook, 597-604.

50 Guderian, *Panzer Leader*, 238.

51 Spielberger, and Doyle, *Tigers I and II and their Variants*, 169.

52 Doyle, *The Complete Guide to German Armoured Vehicles*, 442-445.

53 Ibid, 451-454.

54 Doyle, *The Complete Guide to German Armoured Vehicles*, 454-456. Spielberger and Doyle, *Tigers I and II and their Variants*, 169, 172.

55 Robert Kirchubel, *Hitler's Panzer Armies on the Eastern Front*, (Barnsley: Pen and Sword Military, 2009), 134. Oberkommando des Heeres. Merkblatt des OKH den 1.6.41. Betr. Die wichtigsten Panzerkampfwagen der UdSSR. TsAMO f.500. o.12451. d. 452.

56 Erhard Raus, *Panzer Operations: The Eastern Front Memoir of General Raus, 1941-1945,* complied and translated by Steven H. Newton, (Da Capo Press: Cambridge, 2003), ebook, 72-76.

57 Raus, *Panzer Operations*, 76-88.

58 Hans Schäufler, *Panzer Warfare on the Eastern Front,* (Mechanicsburg: Stackpole Books, 2012), 52.

59 Doyle, *The Complete Guide to German Armoured Vehicles*, 127.

60 Ibid, 206-207. Perrett, *Panzerkampfwagen IV Medium Tank*, 8.

61 Albert Speer, *Inside the Third Reich,* translated by Richard and Clara Winston. (Toronto: The Macmillan Company, 1970), 233.

62 Jentz, and Doyle, *Kingtiger Heavy Tank*, 5.

63 Thomas Jentz and Hilary Doyle. *Germany's Tiger Tanks: VK45.02 to Tiger II: Design, Production & Modifications,* (Atglen: Schiffer Military History, 1997), 10-11.

64 Jentz and Doyle, *Germany's Tiger Tanks: VK45.02 to Tiger II*, 8-10.

65 Jentz and Doyle, *Germany's Tiger Tanks: VK45.02 to Tiger II*, 16-18.

66 Jentz and Doyle, *Germany's Tiger Tanks: VK45.02 to Tiger II*, 10, 15.

67 Ibid, 18.

68 Jentz, and Doyle, *Tiger I: Heavy Tank 1942-1945*, 20. Raus, *Panzer Operations,* 191.

69 Richard Freiherr von Rosen, *Panzer Ace: The Memoirs of an Iron Cross Panzer Commander From Barbarossa to Normandy,* translated by Geoffrey Brooks, (South Yorkshire: Greenhill Books, 2018), ebook, 378.

70 Otto Carius, *Tigers in the Mud. The Combat Career of German Panzer Commander Otto Carius,* translated by Robert J. Edwards, (Mechanicsburg: Stackpole Books, 1992), 3.

71 Guderian, *Panzer Leader,* 217.

72 Ibid, 217, 247. Showalter, *Hitler's Panzers,* 238.

73 Jentz, and Doyle, *Kingtiger Heavy Tank,* 7-8.

74 Ibid, 11.

75 Spielberger, Doyle and Jentz. *Heavy Jagdpanzer,* 126.

76 Spielberger, Doyle and Jentz. *Heavy Jagdpanzer,* 126-127. Spielberger, and Doyle, *Tigers I and II and their Variants,* 153.

77 Spielberger, Doyle and Jentz. *Heavy Jagdpanzer,* 141.

78 Spielberger, Doyle and Jentz. *Heavy Jagdpanzer,* 149.

79 Ibid, 149, 168.

Chapter 2

80 Niklas Zetterling, *Blitzkrieg: From the Ground Up,* (Philadelphia: Casemate Publishers, 2017), 140-141. Erich von Manstein, *Lost Victories: The Memoirs of Hitler's Most Brilliant General,* translated and edited by Antony G. Powell. (St. Paul: Zenith Press, 2004), 97, 99-100, 104.

81 Hermann Balck, *Order in Chaos: The Memoirs of General of Panzer Troops Hermann Balck,* edited and translated by Major General (ret) David T. Zabecki and Lieutenant Colonel Dieter J. Biedekarken, (Lexington: University of Kentucky Press, 2017), 445.

82 Robert M. Citino, *The German Way of War: From the Thirty Years War to the Third Reich,* (Lawrence: University Press of Kanas, 2005), XIV. Clark, *Blitzkrieg,* 32. See also Colonel Charles S. Oliviero, *Auftragstaktik: The Birth of Enlightened Leadership*, (Toronto: Double Dagger Books, 2022).

83 Zetterling, *Blitzkrieg: From the Ground Up,* 17-18.

84 G. W. L. Nicolson, *Canadian Expeditionary Force, 1914-1919: Official History of the Canadian Army in the First World War,* (Montreal & Kingston: McGill- Queen's University Press, 2015), 168-169.

85 Showalter, *Hitler's Panzers,* 7.

86 Ibid.

87 Ibid

88 Ibid, 7-8.

89 Father of *General der Panzertruppen* Hermann von Balck

90 Corum, *The Roots of Blitzkrieg,* 22.

91 Ibid, 8.

92 Corum, *The Roots of Blitzkrieg,* 8.

93 Ibid, 30.

94 Robert M. Citino, *The Path to Blitzkrieg: Doctrine and Training in the German Army, 1920-1939,* (London: Lynne Rienner Publishers, 1999), 120-121.

95 Mary R. Habeck, *Storm of Steel: The Development of Armour Doctrine in Germany and the Soviet Union, 1919-1939,* (New York: Cornell University, 2003), 85.

96 Habeck, *Storm of Steel,* 97.

97 Ibid, 136.

98 Ibid, 138.

99 Corum, *The Roots of Blitzkrieg,*112-114.

100 Ibid, 125, 135.

101 Citino, *The Path to Blitzkrieg,* 202.

102 McCarthy and Syron, *Panzerkrieg,* 83. Thomas Jentz, *Panzer Truppen Vol. I,* 76-77.

103 Guderian, *Panzer Leader,* 19.

104 Ibid, 28, 90.

105 Citino, *The Path to Blitzkrieg,* 231.

106 David Doyle, *The Complete Guide to German Armoured Vehicles,* ebook, 26-29.

107 Ibid, 56-59.

108 Ibid, 91,98,154-155, 164.

109 Jentz, *Panzer Truppen Vol. I,* 77.

110 Ibid, 83.

111 Heinz Guderian, *Achtung- Panzer!: The Development of Armoured Forces, their Tactics and Operational Potential,* translated by Christopher Duffy, (London: Brockhampton Press: 1999), 155-157.

112 Chamberlin, and Doyle, *Encyclopedia of German Tanks of World War Two: A Complete Illustrated Directory of German Battle Tanks, Armoured Cars, Self- Propelled Guns and Semi- Tracked Vehicles, 1933-1945,* 147.

von Senger and Etterlin, *German Tanks of World War II: The Complete Illustrated History of German Armoured Fighting Vehicles 1926-1945,* 108.

113 Jentz, and Doyle, *Germany's Tiger Tanks: D.W. to Tiger I,* 9.

114 Ibid, 10-11.

115 Wilbeck, *Sledgehammers,* 202-204.

116 Habeck, *Storm of Steel,* 288. Jürgen E. Förster, "The Dynamics of Volksgemeinschaft: The Effectiveness of the German Military Establishment in the Second World War", *Military Effectiveness.*

Volume III: The Second World War, edited by Allan R. Millett and Williamson Murray, 204, (Winchester: Allen & Unwin Inc., 1988). Zetterling, *Blitzkrieg: From the Ground Up*, 139-140.

117 Showalter, *Hitler's Panzers*, 109.

118 Ibid, 109.

119 Ibid, 110.

120 Ibid, 109-110.

121 von Luck, *Panzer Commander*, 41. Clark, *Blitzkrieg: Myth, Reality, and Hitler's Lighting War- France, 1940*, 264. McCarthy and Syron, *Panzerkrieg*, 85.

122 McCarthy and Syron, *Panzerkrieg*, 71-72.

123 Showalter, *Hitler's Panzers*, 119.

124 Doyle, *The Complete Guide to German Armoured Vehicles*, 132-133.

125 Jentz and Doyle, *Germany's Tiger Tanks: D.W. to Tiger I*, 17-18, 23-24.

Chapter 3

126 Jentz and Doyle, *Germany's Tiger Tanks: D.W. to Tiger I*, 68.

127 Ibid.

128 Jentz and Doyle, *Germany's Tiger Tanks: D.W. to Tiger I*, 68.

129 Jentz and Doyle, *Germany's Tiger Tanks: D.W. to Tiger I*, 69-70.

130 Donald Caldwell, and Richard Muller, *The Luftwaffe over Germany: Defence of the Reich*, (London: Greenhill Books, 2007), 31-33. Robin Neillands, *The Bomber War: The Allied Air Offensive Against Nazi Germany*, (Woodstock: The Overlook Press, 2001), 36.

131 Tammi Davis Biddle, "British and American Approaches to Strategic Bombing: Their Origins and Implementation in the World War Two Combined Bomber Offensive", *Airpower: Theory and Practice*, edited by John Gooch, (London: Frank Cass & CO Ltd., 1995), 91.

132 Richard Overy, *The Bombers and the Bombed: Allied Air War over Europe, 1940-1945*, (New York: Penguin Press, 2013), 93.

133 Overy, *The Bombers and the Bombed*, 281. William Manchester, *The Arms of Krupp 1587-1968*, (Toronto: Little, Brown and Company, 1968), 449.

134 Jentz and Doyle, *Germany's Tiger Tanks: D.W. to Tiger I*, 69-70.

135 Jentz and Doyle, *Germany's Tiger Tanks: D.W. to Tiger I*, 68. Overy, *The Bombers and the Bombed*, 153.

136   Phillips Payson O'Brien, *How the War was Won: Air-Sea Power and Allied Victory in World War Two*, (New York: Cambridge University Press, 2015), 287.

137 Jentz and Doyle, *Germany's Tiger Tanks: D.W. to Tiger I*, 68.

138 Adam Tooze, *The Wages of Destruction: The Making and Breaking of the Nazi Economy,* (New York: Penguin Group, 2006), 358-359, 513.

139 Ibid, 640.

140 Jentz and Doyle, *Germany's Tiger Tanks: D.W. to Tiger I,* 70.

141 Lieutenant Mancur Olson, "The Economics of Target Selection for the Combined Bomber Offensive," *Royal United Services Institution Journal 107,* No. 218 (1962), 311, doi 10.1080/03071846209428669.

142 Hilary Doyle & Thomas Jentz, *StuG III Assault Gun 1940-1942.* (Oxford: Osprey Publishing, 1996), 15.

143 Spielberger, Doyle and Jentz, *Heavy Jagdpanzer,* 58, 63-64. Doyle, *The Complete Guide to German Armoured Vehicles,* 518, 530.

144 Spielberger, Doyle and Jentz, *Heavy Jagdpanzer,* 76. Jentz and Doyle, *Germany's Tiger Tanks: D.W. to Tiger I,* 28.

145 Spielberger, Doyle and Jentz, *Heavy Jagdpanzer,* 76-77, 81.

146 Doyle, *The Complete Guide to German Armoured Vehicles,* 454-456. Spielberger and Doyle, *Tigers I and II and their Variants,* 169, 172.

147 Jentz, and Doyle, *Germany's Tiger Tanks: VK45.02 to Tiger II,* 60-62.

148   Ibid, 59, 62.

149 Jentz, and Doyle, *Germany's Tiger Tanks: VK45.02 to Tiger II,* 59-62.

150 Overy, *The Bombers and the Bombed,* 184, 189. Speer, *Inside the Third Reich,* 194, 284.

151 Jentz and Doyle, *Germany's Tiger Tanks: VK45.02 to Tiger II,* 61.

152 Ibid, 59.

153 Tooze, *The Wages of Destruction,* 650.

154 Jentz and Doyle, *Germany's Tiger Tanks: VK45.02 to Tiger II,* 60-61.

155 Tooze, *The Wages of Destruction,* 342. O'Brien, *How the War was Won,* 351, 353.

156 O'Brien, *How the War was Won,* 354-355.

157 Jentz and Doyle, *Germany's Tiger Tanks: VK45.02 to Tiger II,* 59.

158 Ibid, 59.

159 Tooze, *Wages of Destruction,* 652-653.

160 Jentz and Doyle, *Germany's Tiger Tanks: VK45.02 to Tiger II,* 60.

161 *The Combat History of Schwere Panzer Abteilung 508: In Action in Italy with the Tiger I,* edited by Kurt Hirlinger, translated by David Johnston, (Winnipeg: J.J. Fedorowicz Publishing Inc., 2001), 37.

162 Spielberger and Doyle, *Tigers I and II and their Variants,* 154. Spielberger, Doyle and Jentz, *Heavy Jagdpanzer,* 149, 153.

163 Spielberger, Doyle and Jentz, *Heavy Jagdpanzer,* 168.

164 Ibid, 168.

165 Spielberger, Doyle and Jentz, *Heavy Jagdpanzer,,* 169-170.

166 Ibid, 169-170.

167 Manchester, *The Arms of Krupp 1587-1968,* 329.

168 Ibid, 335.

169 William L. Shirer, *The Rise and Fall of the Third Reich: A History of Nazi Germany,* (New York: Simon and Schuster, 1960), 282, 625.

170 Tooze, *The Wages of Destruction,* XXIII.

171 Ibid, XXIII.

172 Bernhard R. Kroener, Rolf- Dieter Müller, Hans Umbreit, *Germany and the Second World War. Volume V/I Organization and Mobilization of the German Sphere of Power: Wartime Administration, Economy, and Manpower Resources 1939-1941,* translated by John Brownjohn, Patrica Crampton, Ewald Osers and Louise Willmot, (Oxford: Clarendon Press, 2000), 410-413.

173 Ibid, 704. Tooze, *The Wages of Destruction,* 225.

174 Jentz, *Panzer Truppen* I, 22, 28, 90

175 Tooze, *The Wages of Destruction,* 230-231.

176 Tooze, *The Wages of Destruction,* 237, 240-41.

177 Ibid, 301-302.

178 Jentz, *Panzer Truppen* I, 88, 90-91.

179 Doyle, *The Complete Guide to German Armoured Vehicles,* 91-108, 162-176.

180 Tooze, *The Wages of Destruction,* 334-335. Balck, *Order in Chaos,* 445.

181 Richard J. Evans, *The Coming of the Third Reich,* (New York: Penguin Books, 2004), ebook, 394, 395. Volker Ullrich, *Hitler: Downfall 1939-1945,* translated by Jefferson Chase, (New York: Alfred A. Knopf, 2020), 610-611.

182 Kroener, Müller and Umbreit. *Germany and the Second World War. Volume V/I Organization and Mobilization of the German Sphere of Power,* 688.

183 Ibid, 688.

184 Ibid, 688.

185 Showalter, *Hitler's Panzers,* 60.

186 Gegory P. Liedtke, *Too Few to Fight? The German Army and the Issue of Force Maintenance on the Eastern Front, June 1943 to May 1944,* Masters Thesis, (Kingston: Royal Military College of Canada, 2006), 66.

187 Liedtke, *Too Few to Fight,* 67.

188 Speer, *Inside the Third Reich,* 193.

189 Tooze, *The Wages of Destruction,* 47.

190 Tooze, *The Wages of Destruction,* 349.

191 Martin Kitchen, *Speer: Hitler's Architect,* (Yale: Yale University Press, 2015), 109.

192 Kitchen, *Speer: Hitler's Architect,* 109.

193 Tooze, *The Wages of Destruction,* 350-351. Bernhard R. Kroener, Rolf-Dieter Müller, Hans Umbreit, *Germany and the Second World War. Volume V/II Organization and Mobilization of the German Sphere of Power: Wartime Administration, Economy, and Manpower Resources 1942-1944/5,* translated by Derry Cook-Radmore, Ewald Osers, Barry Smerin and Barbara Wilson, (Oxford: Clarendon Press, 2003), 339.

194 Tooze, *The Wages of Destruction,* 123-124.

195 Tooze, *The Wages of Destruction,* 434.

196 Steven Zaloga, *Armoured Champion*, ebook, 352-353.

197 Tooze, *The Wages of Destruction,* 434.

198 Zaloga, *Armoured Champion,* ebook 600.

199 Tooze, *The Wages of Destruction,* 352.

200 Zaloga, *Armoured Champion,* 364.

201 Zaloga, *Armoured Champion, 364.* Jentz and Doyle, *Kingtiger Heavy Tank,* 4-5. Citino, *The Path to Blitzkrieg,* 202. Guderian, *Panzer Leader,* 217.

202 Zaloga, *Armoured Champion, 364.* Spielberger, Doyle and Jentz, *Heavy Jagdpanzer,* 126. Showalter, *Hitler's Panzers,* 238.

203 Showalter, *Hitler's Panzers,* 230.

204 Prices listed here reflect the price the army paid for each vehicle and is an average only, but is the best available for comparison. They ignore the fact that the prices provided reflects only the cost of the hull, as many parts, including power trains and guns were provided to firms as government equipment. It also ignores variations in price from different factories, reflecting different state tax schemes and machine tool investments.

205 Zaloga, *Armoured Champion,* 92-93.

206 Zaloga, *Armoured Champion,* 97. Thomas Jentz, *Panzer Truppen: The Complete Guide to the Creation & Combat Employment of Germany's Tank Force: 1943-1945,* (Atglen: Schiffer Military History, 1996), 164.

207 Tooze, *The Wages of Destruction,* 553.

208 Speer, *Inside the Third Reich,* 166.

209 Tooze, *The Wages of Destruction,* 553.

210 Kitchen, *Speer: Hitler's Architect,* 7.

211 Kitchen, *Speer: Hitler's Architect,* 6. Tooze, *The Wages of Destruction,* 553.

212 Tooze, *The Wages of Destruction,* 557-558.

213 Ibid, 562.

214 Ibid, 559.

215 Tooze, *The Wages of Destruction,*, 559-560.

216 Kitchen, *Speer: Hitler's Architect,* 131-132. Kroener, Müller, Umbreit, *Germany and the Second World War. Volume V/II Organization and Mobilization of the German Sphere of Power,* 339.

217 Ibid, 339.

218 Kroener, Müller, Umbreit, *Germany and the Second World War. Volume V/II Organization and Mobilization of the German Sphere of Power,* 339-340.

219 Zaloga, *Armoured Champion,* 600. Jentz, *Panzer Truppen I,* 264,266. Doyle, & Jentz, *StuG III Assault Gun 1940-1942,* 13. Hilary Doyle, & Tom Jentz, *Sturmgeschütz III and IV 1942-45,* (Oxford: Osprey Publishing, 2001), 16.

220 Speer, *Inside the Third Reich,* 210.

221 Tooze, *The Wages of Destruction,* 353-557.

222 Tooze, *The Wages of Destruction,* 565.

223 Kitchen, *Speer: Hitler's Architect,* 177.

224 Ibid, 8.

225 Ibid, 210, 242.

226 Kitchen, *Speer: Hitler's Architect,* 132.

227 Tooze, *The Wages of Destruction,* 594.

228 Oberkommando des Heers. Abt. Hauptausschuß Panzerwagen und Zugmaschinen Nr. 18 den März 1943. Betr. Adolf Hitler Panzerprogramm. NARA T-78, Roll 619, frame 000081, 000085-000087.

229 Tooze, *The Wages of Destruction,* 594.

230 Oberkommando des Heers. Abt. Hauptausschuß Panzerwagen und Zugmaschinen Nr. 18 den März 1943. Betr. Adolf Hitler Panzerprogramm. NARA T-78, Roll 619, frame 0000106-0000109.

231 Tooze, *The Wages of Destruction,* 558, 595-596.

232 Speer, *Inside the Third Reich,* 272.

233 Tooze, *The Wages of Destruction,* 596-598.

234 Jentz, *Panzer Truppen The Complete Guide to the Creation & Combat Employment of Germany's Tank Force: 1943-1945,* 262.

235 Zaloga,. *Armoured Champion,* 600.

236 Kroener, Müller, Umbreit, *Germany and the Second World War, Volume V/II Organization and Mobilization of the German Sphere of Power: Wartime Administration, Economy, and Manpower Resources 1942-1944/5,* 812.

237 Zaloga, *Armoured Champion,* 600.

238 Ibid, 597-604.

239 Williamson Murray, *The Luftwaffe 1933-45: Strategy for Defeat,* (Washington: Brassey's, 1983), 54. Alexander Hill, *The Great Patriotic War of the Soviet Union, 1941-45: A documentary Reader,* (New York: Routledge, 2009), 56-57.

240 Kroener, Müller, Umbreit, *Germany and the Second World War, Volume V/II Organization and Mobilization of the German Sphere of Power: Wartime Administration, Economy, and Manpower Resources 1942-1944/5,* 455.

241 Mark Harrison, "Resource Mobilization for World War Two: The U.S.A, U.K, U.S.S.R and Germany, 1938-1945", *Economic History Review, 41:2,* 1988, 183-184.

242 Richard Overy, *Why the Allies Won,* (London: Random House Books, 2006), ebook, 27.

243 Harrison, Resource Mobilization for World War Two, 177.

244 Ibid, 177.

245 Ibid, 177. Zaloga, *Armoured Champion,* 597-604.

246 John Buckley, *British Armour in the Normandy Campaign,* (New York: Frank Crass, 2004), 36. Jentz, *Panzer Truppen: The Complete Guide to the Creation & Combat Employment of Germany's Tank Force: 1943-1945,* 164.

247 Buckley, *British Armour in the Normandy Campaign,* 36. Schneider, *Tigers in Combat I,* 133.

248 Oberkommando des Heers Abt. Gef.Std. s. Panzer-Abteilung 503 den 10.10.1943. Betr. Aufstellungen für die Zeit vom 5.7.43-21.9.43. NARA T-78, Roll 620, frame 000802.

249 "German Tank Maintenance in World War II" in *World War II German Military Studies: A Collection of 213 Special Reports on the Second World War Prepared by Former Officers of the Wehrmacht for the United States Army, Volume 23, Part X. Special Topics,* edited by Charles B. Burdick, Donald S. Detwiler and Jürgen Rohwer, (New York: Garland Publishing Inc., 1979), 21-23. Zaloga, *Armoured Champion,* ebook, 535.

250 Speer, *Inside the Third Reich,* 234.

251 Zaloga, *Armoured Champion,* ebook, 535.

252 Oberkommando des Heers Abt. Gef.Std. s. Panzer-Abteilung 503 den 10.10.1943. Betr. Aufstellungen für die Zeit vom 5.7.43-21.9.43. NARA T-78, Roll 620, frame 000789-000794,000802.

253 Lochmann, Rubbel and von Rosen, *The Combat History of the German Tiger Tank Battalion 503 in World War Two,* ebook, 55.

254 Thomas Jentz, *Germany's Tiger Tanks: Tiger I & II: Combat Tactics*, (Atglen: Schiffer Military History, 1997), 97-98. Wilbeck, *Sledgehammers*, 92.

255 Jentz, *Germany's Tiger Tanks: Tiger I & II: Combat Tactics*, 97-98. Wilbeck, *Sledgehammers*, 92-94.

256 Wilbeck, *Sledgehammers*, 92-94.

257 Wolfgang Schneider, *Tigers in Combat I*, (Mechanicsburg: Stackpole Books, 2000), 323.

258 *Tiger! The Tiger Tank: A British View*, edited by David Fletcher, (London: Her Majesty's Stationary Office, 1987), 220-221.

259 Schneider, *Tigers in Combat I*, 197, 323.

260 Harrison, Resource Mobilization for World War Two, 177. Zaloga, *Armoured Champion*, 597-604

261 Zaloga, *Armoured Champion*, 597-604. O'Brien, *How the War was Won*, 2-3.

262 Karl- Heinz Frieser, Klaus Schmider, Klaus Schönherr et al., *Germany and the Second World War Volume VIII: The Eastern Front 1943-1944: The War in the East and the Neighboring Fronts*, translated by Barry Smerin and Barbara Wilson, (Oxford: Clarendon Press, 2017), 30.

Chapter 4

263 Jentz and Doyle, *Kingtiger Heavy Tank 1942-45*, 4.

264 Wilbeck, *Sledgehammers*, 19.

265 Jentz and Doyle, *Germany's Tiger Tanks: D.W. to Tiger I*, 68. Jentz, *Panzer Truppen Vol 1*, 143.

266 Wilbeck, *Sledgehammers*, 19-20.

267 Wilbeck, *Sledgehammers*, 20-21. Jentz, *Germany's Tiger Tanks: Tiger I & II: Combat Tactics*, 25.

268 Speer, *Inside the Third Reich*, 241.

269 Guderian, *Panzer Leader*, 219. Schneider, *Tigers in Combat I*, 73.

270 Jentz, *Germany's Tiger Tanks: Tiger I & II: Combat Tactics*, 38-39. Schneider, *Tigers in Combat I*, 173-175.

271 Oberkommando des Heers. Generalinspekteur der Panzertruppen. Nachrichtenblatt der Panzertruppen, Nr.4 *Oktober, 1943*. Betr.: Russiche Anweisung zur Bekämpfung des "Tiger." NARA, T-78, Roll 623, frame 000587.

272 The SUs were a series of casemate tank destroyers and assault guns mounting a variety of weapons, with the number after the name referring to the caliber of weapon.

273 Michael Green, *Tiger Tanks,* (Osceola: Motorbooks International, 1995), 69. Hill, *The Red Army and the Second World War,* 440. Robert A. Forczyk, *Tank Warfare on the Eastern Front 1943-1945: Red Steamroller,* (Barnsley: Pen & Sword Books Ltd., 2016), 67. Schneider, *Tigers in Combat I,* 75.

274 Guderian, *Panzer Leader,* 219.

275 von Manstein, *Lost Victories,* 368-370. Robert M. Citino, *The Wehrmacht Retreats: Fighting a Lost War, 1943,* (Lawrence: University of Kansas Press, 2012), 58-61.

276 Wilbeck, *Sledgehammers,* 35. Carius, *Tigers in the Mud,* 22.

277 Wilbeck, *Sledgehammers,* 59-60. Schneider, *Tigers in Combat I,* 121.

278 Schneider, *Tigers in Combat I,* 122. Wilbeck, *Sledgehammers,* 60.

279 Oberkommando des Heers. Gen.St.d.H/ Ausb.Abt. (II). Zusammendruck der Ausbildungshinweise Nr.10-23.g.5.5.44. TsAMO f.500.o.12451.d.133.

280 Jentz, *Germany's Tiger Tanks: Tiger I & II: Combat Tactics,* 69.

281 Bob Carruthers, *Hitler's War Machine: Tiger I Official Wartime Crew Manual (The Tigerfibel),* translated by Bob Carruthers, (Havertown: Pen and Sword, 2014), 21-22.

282 Schneider, *Tigers in Combat I,* 123.

283 Forczyk, *Tank Warfare on the Eastern Front 1943-1945,* 53. Schneider, *Tigers in Combat I,* 122.

284 Showalter, *Hitler's Panzers,* 215. von Mellenthin, *Panzer Battles,* 183.

285 von Mellenthin, *Panzer Battles, 183.*

286 Balck, *Order in Chaos,* 280. von Mellenthin, *Panzer Battles,* 204-205. Forczyk, *Tank Warfare on the Eastern Front 1943-1945,* 53.

287 von Mellenthin, *Panzer Battles,* 183.

288 Schneider, *Tigers in Combat I,* 74,121-122.

289 Forczyk, *Tank Warfare on the Eastern Front 1943-1945,* 53.

290 Horst Boog, Werner Rahn, Reinhard Stumpf et al, *Germany and the Second World War: Volume VI: The Global War: Widening of the Conflict into a World War and the Shift of the Initiative 1941-1943,* translated by Ewald Osers, John Brownjohn et al, (Oxford: Clarendon Press, 2001), 1100.

291 A *Kampfgruppe* (pl *Kampfgruppen*) was a combined arms unit of indeterminant size, usually based on a battalion. The German custom was to name the *Gruppen* after their commanders.

292 Wilbeck, *Sledgehammers,* 40. Schneider, *Tigers in Combat I,* 42.

293 Jentz, *Germany's Tiger Tanks: Tiger I & II: Combat Tactics,* 42.

294 Wilbeck, *Sledgehammers,* 42-43.

295 Oberkommando des Heers. Abt.Ia/Brb.Nr.157/43 Geh- Panzer Abteilung 501 den 18.3.1943. Betr.: Tiger- Erfahrungen in Tunisen. NARA, T-78, Roll 620, frame 001239.

296 Wilbeck, *Sledgehammers*, 45.

297 Jentz, *Germany's Tiger Tanks: Tiger I & II: Combat Tactics*, 48. Schneider, Wolfgang. *Tigers in Combat I*, 43. Wilbeck, *Sledgehammers*, 45.

298 Wilbeck, *Sledgehammers*, 47.

299 *Tiger! The Tiger Tank: A British View*, 17.

300 Jentz, *Germany's Tiger Tanks: Tiger I & II: Combat Tactics*, 48. Schneider, Wolfgang. *Tigers in Combat I*, 49.

301 *Tiger! The Tiger Tank: A British View*, 17-20. Jentz, *Germany's Tiger Tanks: Tiger I & II: Combat Tactics*, 51-53.

302 Wilbeck, *Sledgehammers*, 111.

303 Jentz, *Germany's Tiger Tanks: Tiger I & II: Combat Tactics*, 49.

304 Wilbeck, *Sledgehammers*, 48. Oberkommando des Heers. Pz.Offz.b.Chef. Gen St d H Bb.Nr.945/43. Geh Kdr. Pz.Abt. (FKL) 301 den 23.7.43. Betr. Denkschrift über die weitere Verwendung der FKL-Waffe unter Auswertung der Erfarungen des Einstatzes vom 5.-8.7.43 bei Unternehmen "Zitadelle." NARA, T-78, Roll 620.

305 Schneider, Wolfgang. *Tigers in Combat I*, 44.

306 David Fletcher, *Mr. Churchill's Tank: The British Infantry Tank Mark IV*,(Atglen: Schiffer Publishing Ltd., 1999), 112-113. Schneider, Wolfgang. *Tigers in Combat I*, 194.

307 *Tiger! The Tiger Tank: A British View*, 54.

Chapter 5

308 Citino, *The Wehrmacht Retreats*, 114.

309 Schneider, *Tigers in Combat I*, 224.

310 Schneider, *Tigers in Combat II*, ebook, 71, 183, 244, 314.

311 Lochmann, Rubbel and von Rosen, *The Combat History of the German Tiger Tank Battalion 503 in World War Two*, ebook, 20. Jentz and Doyle, *Kingtiger Heavy Tank 1942-45*, 4. Oberkommando des Heers. Oberstleutnant m.d.Führ..d.Abt.beauftr. Geh- Panzer Abteilung 503 den 12.4.43. Betr. Erfahrungsbericht für die Zeit vom 2.2-2.22 1943. NARA, T-78 Roll 620, frame 001155. Oberkommando des Heers. 114/43 Geh. 13. Kompanie (Tiger Kp.) Pz. Rgt. Großdeutschland den 27.3.43. Betr. Erfaungsbericht über den Panzer VI (Tiger). NARA, T-78 Roll 620, frame 000992.

312 Schneider, *Tigers in Combat II*, 67, 178, 238, 308.

313 Schneider, *Tigers in Combat I*, 125.

314 Oberkommando des Heers. Abt.Ia/Brb.Nr.157/43 Geh- Panzer Abteilung 501 den 18.3.1943. Betr.: Tiger- Erfahrungen in Tunisen. NARA, T-78, Roll 620, frame 001235. Carius, *Tigers in the Mud*, 246-247.

315 Oberkommando des Heers. Oberstleutnant m.d.Führ..d.Abt.beauftr. Geh- Panzer Abteilung 503 den 12.4.43. Betr. Erfahrungsbericht für die Zeit vom 2.2-2.22 1943.

NARA, T-78 Roll 620, frame 001155. Oberkommando des Heers. 114/43 Geh. 13. Kompanie (Tiger Kp.) Pz. Rgt. Großdeutschland den 27.3.43. Betr. Erfaungsbericht über den Panzer VI (Tiger). NARA, T-78 Roll 620, frame 000992.

316 Oberkommando des Heers. Der Generalinspekteur der Panzertruppen Ia Org. Nr.1000/43 geh. den 14.5.43. Betr. Einzatz von "Tiger"- Einheiten. NARA, T-78 Roll 620, frame 001005.

317 Niklas Zetterling, and Anders Frankson, *Kursk 1943: A Statistical Analysis,* (New York: Frank Cass, 2000), 69. Hill, *The Red Army and the Second World War*, 440.

318 Vasiliy Krysov, *Panzer Destoryer: Memoirs of a Red Army Tank Commander,* translated by Vladimir Krouprnik, edited by Stuart Britton, (Barnsley: Pen & Sword Books Ltd., 2010), ebook, 75-80.

319 Krysov, *Panzer Destoryer,* ebook, 81

320 Krysov, *Panzer Destoryer,* ebook, 75-81. Upravlenie Komanduiushchego bronetankovimi... Krasnoi armii. Naibolee uizazvime i porazhaemie mesta nemetskogo Tanka T-VI I sposobi bor'bi s nim (Moscow: Voenizdat NKO SSSR, 1943?). TsAMO f.500.o.12480.d.145. Thanks to Dr. Alexander Hill for these Soviet materials and their translation.

321 Steven H. Newton, *Kursk: The German View: Firsthand Accounts of the German Commanders who Planned and Executed the Largest Tank Battle In History,* translated and edited by Steven H. Newton, (Cambridge: Da Capo Books, 2002), ebook., 224. Dennis Showalter, *Armour and Blood: The Battle of Kursk: The Turning Point of World War Two,* (New York: Random House, 2013), 81.

322 Schneider, *Tigers in Combat I,* 224.

323 Forczyk, *Tank Warfare on the Eastern Front 1943-1945,* 113.

324 Showalter, *Armour and Blood,* 91.

325 Showalter, *Armour and Blood,* 91-92. Schneider, *Tigers in Combat I,* 224.

326 Schneider, *Tigers in Combat I,* 224. Showalter, *Armour and Blood,* 138.

327 Showalter, *Armour and Blood,* 140. Schneider, *Tigers in Combat I,* 224.

328 Schneider, *Tigers in Combat I,* 225. Citino, *The Wehrmacht Retreats,* 202.

329 Lloyd Clark, *Kursk: The Greatest Battle, Eastern Front 1943,* (London: Headline Review, 2011), 241. Carruthers, *Hitler's War Machine: Tiger I Official Wartime Crew Manual (The Tigerfibel),* ebook, 265.

330 Schneider, *Tigers in Combat II,* 183-184, 244, 314.

331 Newton, *Kursk: The German View,* 158-161.

332 This was the AFV designator, much like a call sign. In Commonwealth regiments, up to the present, individual tanks are given names, often after battle honours.

333 Schneider, *Tigers in Combat II,* 185.

334 Frieser, Schmider, Schönherr et al, *Germany and the Second World War Volume VIII: The Eastern Front 1943-1944: The War in the East and the Neighboring Fronts,* 116-117.

335 Schneider, *Tigers in Combat II,* 315.

336 Schneider, 186.

337 Schneider, 245.

338 Valeriy Zamulin, *The Battle of Kursk: Controversial & Neglected Aspects,* translated and edited by Stuart Britton, (West Midlands: Helion & Company Limited, 2017), 294.

339 Valeriy Zamulin, *The Battle of Kursk: Controversial & Neglected Aspects,* 282.

340 Frieser, Schmider, Schönherr et al, *Germany and the Second World War Volume VIII: The Eastern Front 1943-1944: The War in the East and the Neighboring Fronts,* 131.

341 Hill, *The Red Army and the Second World War,* 452-453.

342 Showalter, *Armour and Blood,* 200-203.

343 Showalter, 210-211.

344 Ibid.

345 Erwin Bartmann, *Für Volk and Führer: The Memoir of a Veteran of the 1st SS Panzer Division Leibstandarte SS Adolf Hitler,* translated and edited by Derik Hammond, (Solihull: Helion & Company, 2013), ebook, 257-258.

346 Frieser, Schmider, Schönherr et al, *Germany and the Second World War Volume VIII: The Eastern Front 1943-1944: The War in the East and the Neighboring Fronts,* 131.

347 Hill, *The Red Army and the Second World War,* 452-453. Zamulin, *The Battle of Kursk: Controversial & Neglected Aspects,* 278, 294.

348 Showalter, *Armour and Blood* 219-220. Newton, *Kursk: The German View,* ebook, 182

349 Wilbeck, *Sledgehammers,* 23-24. Oberkommando des Heers. Der Generalinspekteur der Panzertruppen Ia Org. Nr.1000/43 geh. den

14.5.43. Betr. Einzatz von "Tiger"- Einheiten. NARA, T-78 Roll 620, frame 001005.

350 Schneider, *Tigers in Combat II,* 77.

351 Schneider, 207, 261, 404, 510.

352 Schneider, 15.

353 Schneider, *Tigers in Combat I,* 125.

354 Lochmann, Rubbel and von Rosen, *The Combat History of the German Tiger Tank Battalion 503 in World War Two,* 283.

355 Oberkommando des Heers. Ia Nr. 1549/43 geh. Der Kommandierende General des III.Panzerkorps den 21.7.43. Betr. Auf Grund der Erfahrungen bei der letzten Kämpfen gebe ich folgende Hinweise für die Zusammenarbeit der Tiger mit anderen Waffen. NARA, T-78 Roll 620, frame 000919. Lochmann, Rubbel and von Rosen, *The Combat History of the German Tiger Tank Battalion 503 in World War Two,* 283.

356 Lochmann, Rubbel and von Rosen, *The Combat History of the German Tiger Tank Battalion 503 in World War Two,* 243.

357 Schneider, *Tigers in Combat I,* 125. Showalter, *Armour and Blood,* 124, 134, 147.

358 Zetterling, *Kursk 1943: A Statistical Analysis,* 69.

359 von Rosen, *Panzer Ace,* ebook, 482-485.

360 von Rosen, 515-516.

361 Showalter, *Armour and Blood,* 185. Schneider, *Tigers in Combat I,* 125..

362 Showalter, *Armour and Blood,* 186.

363 Showalter, *Armour and Blood,* 188-192.

364 Citino, *The Wehrmacht Retreats,* 138.

365 Karl- Heinz Frieser, Klaus Schmider, Schönherr et al, *Germany and the Second World War Volume VIII: The Eastern Front 1943-1944: The War in the East and the Neighboring Fronts,* 153. Hill, *The Red Army and the Second World War,* 454.

366 Schneider, *Tigers in Combat I,* 187,263. Schneider, *Tigers in Combat II,* ebook, 71-74, 223, 302, 395.

367 Frieser, Schmider, Schönherr et al, *Germany and the Second World War Volume VIII: The Eastern Front 1943-1944: The War in the East and the Neighboring Fronts,* 85.

368 Oberkommando des Heers. Ia Nr.783/43 Geh. Kommandeur 16th Panzergrenadier Division den 4.10.43. Betr. Zusammenarbeit mi Tiger-Panzern. T-78, Roll 620, frame 000836.

369 Showalter, *Armour and Blood,* 271.

Chapter 6

370 Frieser, Schmider, Schönherr et al, *Germany and the Second World War Volume VIII: The Eastern Front 1943-1944: The War in the East and the Neighboring Fronts*, 343.

371 It can be confusing. A Soviet *Front* can refer to a line of troops as well as a formation. The 1st Ukrainian Front was equivalent to an Army Group.

372 Frieser, Schmider, Schönherr et al, 362-366. Forczyk, *Tank Warfare on the Eastern Front 1943-1945*, 188-189.

373 Schneider, *Tigers in Combat I*, 345.

374 Forczyk, *Tank Warfare on the Eastern Front 1943-1945*, 189-190.

375 von Manstein, *Lost Victories*, 488. Raus, *Panzer Operations*, ebook, 531-532.

376 Forczyk, *Tank Warfare on the Eastern Front 1943-1945*, 190.

377 Schneider, *Tigers in Combat I*, 345-346.

378 Schneider, 346.

379 Schneider, *Tigers in Combat II*, ebook, 249-250. Frieser, Schmider, Schönherr et al, *Germany and the Second World War Volume VIII: The Eastern Front 1943-1944: The War in the East and the Neighboring Fronts,* 370.

380 Schneider, *Tigers in Combat I*, 346.

381 Forczyk, *Tank Warfare on the Eastern Front 1943-1945,* 191-192.

382 Schneider, *Tigers in Combat I*, 346.

383 Schneider, *Tigers in Combat II,* ebook, 252.

384 Schneider, 193-194.

385 Forczyk, *Tank Warfare on the Eastern Front 1943-1945,* 193-194.

386 Frieser, Schmider, Schönherr et al, *Germany and the Second World War Volume VIII: The Eastern Front 1943-1944: The War in the East and the Neighboring Fronts,* 371.

387 Oberkommando des Heers. Nachrichtenblatt der Panzertruppen Nr.1 g.15.7.43. TsAMO f.500.o.12473.d.197.

388 Forczyk, *Tank Warfare on the Eastern Front 1943-1945,* 69-70.

389 Frieser, Schmider, Schönherr et al, *Germany and the Second World War Volume VIII: The Eastern Front 1943-1944: The War in the East and the Neighboring Fronts,* 275.

390 Schneider, *Tigers in Combat I,* 77.

391 Oberkommando des Heers.s.Pz.Abt.502. *Merkpunkte für den Panzereinstatz.* NARA. T-78, Roll 203, frame 147056.

392 s.Pz.Abt.502.

393 Oberkommando des Heers. s.Panzer. Abteilung 506 Abt.Gef.St. den 15.1.44. Betr. Erfahrungsbericht der Tiger Abteilung 506. T-78, Roll 620, 000235.

394   s.Panzer. Abteilung 506 000236.
395 Oberkommando des Heers. Major, 25.Pz.Div. Einstaz von Panzern in dem HKL zur Unterstützung der Infanterie. NARA, T-78, Roll 203, frame 147052.
396 Frieser, Schmider, Schönherr et al, *Germany and the Second World War Volume VIII: The Eastern Front 1943-1944*, 201.
397 Frieser, Schmider, Schönherr et al, 292.
398 Carius, *Tigers in the Mud*, 63.
399 Schneider, *Tigers in Combat I*, 80. Carius, *Tigers in the Mud*, 84-88.
400 Carius, *Tigers in the Mud*, 89-90. Schneider, *Tigers in Combat I*, 80. Forczyk, *Tank Warfare on the Eastern Front 1943-1945*, 201.
401 Carius, *Tigers in the Mud*, 95.
402 Carius, *Tigers in the Mud*, 100-101. Schneider, *Tigers in Combat I*, 80.
403 Boevoi put'59 armii 15 noiabria 1944 g.18.11.44. TsAMO RF f.416.010437.d.12.1.45. Thanks to Dr. Alexander Hill for these Soviet materials and their translation.
404 Oberkommando des Heers. GenStdH/Ausb.Abt./Gen.Insp.d.Pz.Tr. Richtlinien für den Einsatz von Panzerkampfwagen im Rahmen einer Infanterie Division.g.1.10.43. TsAMO f.500.o.12480.d.145.
405 Forczyk, *Tank Warfare on the Eastern Front 1943-1945*, 226-230.
406 Frieser, Schmider, Schönherr et al, *Germany and the Second World War Volume VIII: The Eastern Front 1943-1944*, 627.
407 Wilbeck, *Sledgehammers*, 105.
408 Schneider, *Tigers in Combat I*, 83. Wilbeck, *Sledgehammers*, 107-108.
409 Wilbeck, *Sledgehammers*, 108.
410 Raus, *Panzer Operations*, ebook, 72-88. Zaloga, *KV-1 & 2 Heavy Tanks 1939-45*, 28
411 Steven J. Zaloga, *KV-1 & 2 Heavy Tanks 1939-45*, (London: Osprey Publishing, 2005), 28. Steven Zaloga, IS-2 Heavy Tank 1944-1973, (London: Osprey Publishing, 1994), 3, 8.
412 Oberkommando des Heers. Pz Offz B Chef GenStdH Anlage 7. 5.7.1944. Betr. Tiger 2. NARA, T-78, Roll 620 frame 000079.
413 Zaloga, IS-2 Heavy Tank 1944-1973, 7, Photo Insert D.
414 Oberkommando des Heers. Pz Offz B Chef GenStdH Anlage 7. 5.7.1944. Betr. Tiger 2. NARA, T-78, Roll 620 frame 000079.
415 Schneider, *Tigers in Combat I*, 84-85. Carius, *Tigers in the Mud*, 167. Wilbeck, *Sledgehammers*, 109-110.
416 Schneider, *Tigers in Combat I*, 84-85. Carius, *Tigers in the Mud*, 167. Wilbeck, *Sledgehammers*, 109-110.
417 Frieser, Schmider, Schönherr et al, 231.

418 Schneider, *Tigers in Combat I,*364.

419 Michael Green, *Tiger Tanks,* 75.

420 Oberkommando des Heers. Pz Offz B Chef GenStdH Anlage 7. 5.7.1944. Betr. NARA, T-78, Roll 620 frame 000079.

421 Oberkommando des Heers. *Nachrichtenblatt der Panzertruppen* Nr.15 den 9.44. Betr. Kampf zwischen "Tiger" und "Josef Stalin." NARA, T-78, Roll 623, frame 000720.

422 Wilbeck, *Sledgehammers,* 205-208. Victor Failmezger, *American Knights: The Untold Story of the Men of the Legendary 601st Tank Destroyer Battalion,* (New York: Osprey Publishing, 2015), ebook, 31,37.

423 Green, *Tiger Tanks,* 80-81.

Chapter 7

424 Oberkommando des Heers. Pz Offz B Chef GenStdH Anlage 7. 5.7.1944. Betr. Tiger 1. NARA, T-78, Roll 620 frame 000053. Fletcher, *Mr. Churchill's Tank,* 113.

425 David Fletcher, & Richard C. Harley, *Cromwell Cruiser Tank 1942-50,* (New York: Osprey Publishing, 1996), 13. Fletcher, *Mr. Churchill's Tank,* 120.

426 Steven Zaloga, *Sherman Medium Tank 1942-1945,* (New York: Osprey Publishing, 2004), 14. Oberkommando des Heers. Pz Offz B Chef GenStdH Anlage 7. 5.7.1944. Betr. Tiger 1. NARA, T-78, Roll 620 frame 000053.

427 Zaloga, *Sherman Medium Tank 1942-1945,* 10.

428 Fletcher, & Harley, *Cromwell Cruiser Tank 1942-50,* 36-38.

429 Fletcher, *Mr. Churchill's Tank,* 200, 202, 208.

430 Buckley, *British Armour in the Normandy Campaign,* 115-116. Ian Hogg, *Tank Killing: Anti-Tank Warfare by Men and Machines,* (London: Sidgwick & Jackson, 1996), 114.

431 Hart, *Sherman Firefly vs Tiger,* 14-15, 24.

432 Hart, *Sherman Firefly vs Tiger,* 14. Wilbeck, *Sledgehammers,* 112. Buckley, *British Armour in the Normandy Campaign,* 130-131.

433 Buckley, *British Armour in the Normandy Campaign,* 130.

434 Schneider, *Tigers in Combat II,* ebook, 406-407.

435 Schneider, *Tigers in Combat II,* ebook, 406-407. Ben. H. Shepherd, *Hitler's Soldiers: The German Army in the Third Reich,* (New Haven and London: Yale University Press, 2016), 443.

436 Buckley, *British Armour in the Normandy Campaign,* 23-24.

437 Buckley, 24.

438 Wilbeck, *Sledgehammers,* 116-117.

439 Wilbeck, *Sledgehammers,* 117. Wolfgang Schneider, *Tigers in Normandy,* translated by Battle Born Books and Consulting, (Mechanicsburg: Stackpole Books, 2011), ebook, 61.

440 Wilbeck, *Sledgehammers,* 117.

441 Showalter, *Hitler's Panzers,* 325.

442 Carlo D'Este, *Decision in Normandy: The Unwritten Story of Montgomery and the Allied Campaign,* (Toronto: Penguin Books, 2001), 183.

443 Schneider, *Tigers in Normandy,* 62. Buckley, *British Armour in the Normandy Campaign,* 25.

444 Schneider, *Tigers in Normandy,* 62-63. Wilbeck, *Sledgehammers,* 118.

445 Buckley, *British Armour in the Normandy Campaign,* 25.

446 Buckley, 25.

447 Schneider, *Tigers in Normandy,* 68.

448 Schneider, 68-69.

449 Jentz, *Germany's Tiger Tanks: Tiger I & II: Combat Tactics,* 104,107, 110. Wilbeck, *Sledgehammers,* 117.

450 Schneider, *Tigers in Normandy,* 70.

451 Wilbeck, *Sledgehammers,* 118-119. Buckley, *British Armour in the Normandy Campaign,* 26.

452 Buckley, *British Armour in the Normandy Campaign,* 125.

453 Buckley, 107.

454 Jentz, *Germany's Tiger Tanks: Tiger I & II: Combat Tactics,* 13.

455 Dmitriy Loza, *Commanding the Red Army's Sherman Tanks,* edited and translated by James F. Gebhardt, (Lincoln: University of Nebraska, 1996), 22. Canadian tank squadrons soon adopted a similar tactic whereby the troop's *Firefly* would use a normal *Sherman* as bait to lure the *Tiger* into an engagement. At that point, the remaining two tanks would engage the *Tiger* to fix it in place while the *Firefly* came in for the kill shot. Dangerous, but effective.

456 Buckley, *British Armour in the Normandy Campaign,* 92.

457 George G. Blackburn, *The Guns of Normandy: A Soldier's Eye View, France 1944,* (Toronto: McClelland & Stewart Inc., 1997), 212-213.

458 Buckley, *British Armour in the Normandy Campaign,* 92.

459 Buckley, *British Armour in the Normandy Campaign,* 33. D'Este, *Decision in Normandy,* 356, 358, 360. Colonel C.P. Stacey, *Official History of the Canadian Army In The Second World War: Volume III: The Victory Campaign: The Operations in North-West Europe 1944-1945,* (Ottawa: Queen's Printer and Controller of Stationery, 1966), 166-168.

460 Schneider, *Tigers in Combat I*, 132-133. Schneider, *Tigers in Normandy*, 266.

461 von Rosen, *Panzer Ace*, ebook, 643.

462 von Rosen, 645.

463 von Rosen, 646.

464 von Rosen, 646-647.

465 von Rosen.

466 von Rosen, 651-652.

467 *Oberst* von Luck related after the war that he had drawn his pistol and threatened the Flak gunners with execution because they had refused to level their guns to look for tanks after the bombardment.

468 von Rosen, *Panzer Ace*, ebook, 653. D'Este, *Decision in Normandy*, 375. von Luck, *Panzer Commander*, 196.

469 von Luck, *Panzer Commander*, 197.

470 von Luck, 197.

471 Wilbeck, *Sledgehammers*, 123. Lochmann, Rubbel and von Rosen, *The Combat History of the German Tiger Tank Battalion 503 in World War Two*, ebook, 709.

472 Jentz, *Tiger I & II: Combat Tactics*, 14.

473 Lochmann, Rubbel and Richard von Rosen, *The Combat History of the German Tiger Tank Battalion 503*, 709. Wilbeck, *Sledgehammers*, 123.

474 Wilbeck, *Sledgehammers*, 709.

475 Schneider, *Tigers in Normandy*, 344.

476 Showalter, *Hitler's Panzers*, 325.

477 Wilbeck, *Sledgehammers*, 123. Hubert Meyer, *The History of the 12.SS-Panzer Divisions Hitlerjugend*, translated by H. Harri Henschler, (Winnipeg: J.J. Fedorowicz Publishing Inc., 1994), 158.

478 Buckley, *British Armour in the Normandy Campaign*, 36.

479 D'Este, *Decision in Normandy*, 376.

480 Buckley, *British Armour in the Normandy Campaign*, 36.

481 Schneider, *Tigers in Combat I*, 133-134.

482 Stacey, *The Victory Campaign*, 211-215.

483 Stacey, *The Victory Campaign*, 218-220. Hubert Meyer, *The History of the 12.SS- Panzer Division Hitlerjugend*, 171.

484 Brian A. Reid, *No Holding Back: Operation Totalize, Normandy, August 1944*, (Toronto: Robin Bass Studio, 2005), ebook, 529-533.

485 Reid, *No Holding Back*, ebook, 533. Meyer, *The History of the 12.SS-Panzer Division Hitlerjugend*, 172.

486 Reid, *No Holding Back*, 541-545.

487   Kurt Meyer, *Grenadiers: The Story of Waffen SS General Kurt "Panzer" Meyer,* translated by Michael Mende and Robert J. Edwards, (Mechanicsburg: Stackpole Books, 2005), ebook, 279-280. Stacey, *The Victory Campaign,* 222. Wilbeck, *Sledgehammers,* 126.

488 Reid, *No Holding Back,* 591-592.

489 Wilbeck, *Sledgehammers,* 127.

490 Reid, *No Holding Back,* 1006-1007.

491 Reid, 597-599.

492 Reid, 599-600.

493 Reid, 600.

494 Reid, 1037.

495 Reid, 603.

496 Reid, 698.

497 Reid, 699. Schneider, *Tigers in Combat II,* 420.

498 Reid, *No Holding Back,* 702.

499 Schneider, *Tigers in Combat II,* 420.

500 Reid, *No Holding Back,* 703-704.

501 Stacey, *The Victory Campaign,* 252.

502 Horst Boog, Gerhard Krebs and Detlef Vogel, *Germany and the Second World War: Volume VII; The Strategic Air War in Europe and the War in the West and East Asia 1943-1944/45,* translated by Derry Cook-Radmore, Francisca Garvie, Ewald Osers, Barry Smerin, Barbara Wilson (Oxford: Clarendon Press, 2006), 612.

503 Schneider, *Tigers in Combat I,* 134. Schneider, *Tigers in Combat II,* ebook, 424-425, 531.

Chapter 8

504   Frieser, Schmider, Schönherr et al, *Germany and the Second World War Volume VIII: The Eastern Front 1943-1944: The War in the East and the Neighboring Fronts,* 855-856, 862-863.

505 Frieser, Schmider, Schönherr et al,, 872.

506 Wilbeck, *Sledgehammers,* 164.

507 Wilbeck.

508 Frieser, Schmider, Schönherr et al, *Germany and the Second World War Volume VIII: The Eastern Front 1943-1944: The War in the East and the Neighboring Fronts,* 873. Schneider, *Tigers in Combat I,* 135.

509 von Rosen, *Panzer Ace:* ebook, 781.

510 Frieser, Schmider, Schönherr et al, *Germany and the Second World War Volume VIII: The Eastern Front 1943-1944: The War in the East and the Neighboring Fronts* 781-782. Wilbeck, *Sledgehammers,* 155.

511 Lochmann, Rubbel and von Rosen, *The Combat History of the German Tiger Tank Battalion 503 in World War Two*, ebook, 818.

512 Lochmann, Rubbel and von Rosen, 820. Wilbeck, *Sledgehammers*, 155.

513 Hill, *The Red Army and the Second World War*, 527-528. Wilbeck, *Sledgehammers*, 155.

514 Schneider, *Tigers in Combat I*, 136.

515 Wilbeck, *Sledgehammers*, 155-156.

516 Frieser, Schmider, Schönherr et al. *Germany and the Second World War Volume VIII: The Eastern Front 1943-1944: The War in the East and the Neighboring Fronts*, 895.

517 Ibid, 905. Balck, *Order in Chaos*, 409-410.

518 Frieser, Schmider, Schönherr et al. *Germany and the Second World War Volume VIII: The Eastern Front 1943-1944: The War in the East and the Neighboring Fronts*, 906.

519 Oberkommando des Heers. Pz Offz B Chef GenStdH Anlage 7. 5.7.1944. Betr. Tiger 1. NARA, T-78, Roll 620 frame 000071.

520 Schneider, *Tigers in Combat II*, ebook, 343, 395-396.

521 Hill, *The Red Army and the Second World War*, 491.

522 Oberkommando des Heers. En Pruf (BuM) den 23.6.44. Betr. Gegenüberatellung deutscher Pz.Kfw. gegen die neuen russischen Pz.Kfw. T-34 85 und IS 122. NARA, T-78, Roll 620, frame 000043-000044. Oberkommando des Heers. Pz Offz B Chef GenStdH Anlage 7. 5.7.1944. Betr. Tiger 1. NARA, T-78, Roll 620, frame 000071.

523 Frieser, Schmider, Schönherr et al. *Germany and the Second World War Volume VIII: The Eastern Front 1943-1944: The War in the East and the Neighboring Fronts*, 907. Schneider, *Tigers in Combat I*, 138. Wilbeck, *Sledgehammers*, 164.

524 Lochmann, Rubbel and von Rosen, *The Combat History of the German Tiger Tank Battalion 503 in World War Two*, ebook, 882.

525 Lochmann, Rubbel and von Rosen.

526 Wilbeck, *Sledgehammers*, 166.

527 Oberkommando des Heers. GenStdH/Ausb.Abt./Gen.Insp.d.Pz.Tr. Richtlinien für den Einsatz von Panzerkampfwagen im Rahmen einer Infanterie Division.g.1.10.43. TsAMO f.500.o.12480.d.145.

528 Balck, *Order in Chaos*, 406.

529 Hill, *The Red Army and the Second World War*, 491.

530 von Rosen, *Panzer Ace*, 896-898.

531 Wilbeck, *Sledgehammers*, 167.

532 Frieser, Schmider, Schönherr et al. *Germany and the Second World War Volume VIII: The Eastern Front 1943-1944: The War in the East and the Neighboring Fronts,* 909-910.

533 Frieser, Schmider, Schönherr et al. *Germany and the Second World War Volume VIII: The Eastern Front 1943-1944: The War in the East and the Neighboring Fronts,* 912-913. Balck, *Order in Chaos,* 411-412.

534 Wilbeck, *Sledgehammers,* 167. Schneider, *Tigers in Combat I,* 345.

535 Schneider, *Tigers in Combat II,* ebook, 344.

536 Wilbeck, *Sledgehammers,* 169.

537 Wilbeck, 169.

538 Oberkommando des Heers. Armeegruppe Balack den 17.1.45. Betr. Fernschreiben An Heersgruppe Sud. TsAMO.f.500.o.12472.d.410. Wilbeck, *Sledgehammers,* 169-170.

539 Schneider, *Tigers in Combat I,* 138-139. Oberkommando des Heers. Armeegruppe Balck Ia den 18.1.45. Betr. Anruf von IV SS Pz.Kps. TsAMO.f.500.o.12472.d.410.

540 Schneider, *Tigers in Combat II,* ebook, 345-346.

541 Balck, *Order in Chaos,* 412. Frieser, Schmider, Schönherr et al, *Germany and the Second World War Volume VIII: The Eastern Front 1943-1944: The War in the East and the Neighboring Fronts,* 914-915.

542 Frieser, Schmider, Schönherr et al, *Germany and the Second World War Volume VIII: The Eastern Front 1943-1944: The War in the East and the Neighboring Fronts,* 919-920.

543   Wilbeck, *Sledgehammers,* 171.

544 Schneider, *Tigers in Combat II,* ebook, 430.

545 Wilbeck, *Sledgehammers,* 173.

546 Frieser, Schmider, Schönherr et al, *Germany and the Second World War Volume VIII: The Eastern Front 1943-1944: The War in the East and the Neighboring Fronts,* 929.

547 Wilbeck, *Sledgehammers,* 175.

548 Michael Reynolds, *Sons of the Reich: II SS Panzer Corps,* (Staplehurst: Spellmount, 2002), 264-272. Frieser, Schmider, Schönherr et al, *Germany and the Second World War Volume VIII: The Eastern Front 1943-1944: The War in the East and the Neighboring Fronts,* 931-940. Wilbeck, *Sledgehammers,* 175. Schneider, *Tigers in Combat I,* 354.

549 Reynolds, *Sons of the Reich,* 258.

550 Wilbeck, *Sledgehammers,* 175.

551 Frieser, Schmider, Schönherr et al, *Germany and the Second World War Volume VIII: The Eastern Front 1943-1944: The War in the East and the Neighboring Fronts,* 941.

Chapter 9

552   Spielberger, Doyle and Jentz, *Heavy Jagdpanzer,* 59, 76-77, 81.

553 Spielberger, Doyle and Jentz, 59.

554 Spielberger, Doyle and Jentz, 122.

555 Oberkommando des Heers. Abteilungsführerschule der Panzertruppen Paris den 16.8.43. Betr. Kurzemerkblatt über Führung und Kampf der Sturmgeschütze zur Orientierung für andere Waffengetttunen. TsAMO.f.500.o.12473.d.137. Showalter, *Hitler's Panzers,* 238. Bruno Friesen, *Panzer Gunner: A Canadian in the German 7th Panzer Division, 1944-45,* (Mechanicsburg: Stackpole Books, 2009), 149-151.

556 David Doyle, *The Complete Guide to German Armoured Vehicles,* ebook, 540-541. Showalter, *Hitler's Panzers,* 97.

557 Doyle, *The Complete Guide to German Armoured Vehicles,* 565,567.

558 Doyle & Jentz, *StuG III Assault Gun 1940-1942,* 15. Doyle & Jentz, *Sturmgeschütz III and IV 1942-45,* 5, 24.

559 Oberkommando des Heers. Abteilungsführerschule der Panzertruppen Paris den 16.8.43. Betr. Kurzemerkblatt über Führung und Kampf der Sturmgeschütze zur Orientierung für andere Waffengetttunen. TsAMO.f.500.o.12473.d.137.

560 Ibid.

561 Bruno Friesen, *Panzer Gunner: A Canadian in the German 7th Panzer Division, 1944-45,* 149-151.

562 Karlheinz Münch, *The Combat History of German Heavy Anti-Tank Unit 653 in World War II,* (Mechanicsburg: Stackpole Books, 2005), 45.

563 Showalter, *Armour and Blood,* 80.

564 Culver, *Tiger in Action,* 14. Showalter, *Armour and Blood,* 80. Münch, *The Combat History of German Heavy Anti-Tank Unit 653,* 65-66.

565 Guderian, *Panzer Leader,* 251.

566 Münch, *The Combat History of German Heavy Anti-Tank Unit 653,* 50.

567 Münch, 50.

568 Showalter, *Armour and Blood,* 82.

569 Spielberger, Doyle and Jentz, *Heavy Jagdpanzer,* 86.

570 Forczyk, *Tank Warfare on the Eastern Front 1943-1945,* 116. Spielberger, Doyle and Jentz, *Heavy Jagdpanzer,* 86.

571 Shepherd, *Hitler's Soldiers,* 330.

572   Oberkommando des Heers. Kommandeur Panzer-Jäger Abteilung 656 den 2.11.43. Lagebreicht über das schw. Panzer-Jäger-Regiment 656. NARA, T-78, Roll 620, frame 000775. Münch, *The Combat History of German Heavy Anti-Tank Unit 653,* 56, 66-70.

573 Frieser, Schmider, Schönherr et al, *Germany and the Second World War Volume VIII: The Eastern Front 1943-1944: The War in the East and the Neighboring Fronts,* 173.

574 Münch, *The Combat History of German Heavy Anti-Tank Unit 653,* 51.

575 Spielberger, Doyle and Jentz, *Heavy Jagdpanzer,* 42. Münch, *The Combat History of German Heavy Anti-Tank Unit 653,* 61.

576 Frieser, Schmider, Schönherr et al, *Germany and the Second World War Volume VIII: The Eastern Front 1943-1944,* 356-358.

577 Münch, *The Combat History of German Heavy Anti-Tank Unit 653,* 71.

578 Münch, 71.

579 Oberkommando des Heers. Kommandeur 16.Panzer-Grenadier-Division den 7.10.43. Betr. Zusammenarbeit mit Panzern "Ferdinand" und Sturmpanzern. NARA, T-78, Roll 620, frame 000827.

580 Oberkommando des Heers. Kommandeur 16.Panzer-Grenadier-Division den 7.10.43. Betr. Zusammenarbeit mit Panzern "Ferdinand" und Sturmpanzern. NARA, T-78, Roll 620, frame 000826.

581 Kommandeur 16.Panzer-Grenadier-Division.

582 Kommandeur 16.Panzer-Grenadier-Division.

583 Frieser, Schmider, Schönherr et al, *Germany and the Second World War Volume VIII: The Eastern Front 1943-1944,* 375.

584 Oberkommando des Heers. Kommandeur Panzer-Jäger Abteilung 656 den 2.11.43. Lagebreicht über das schw. Panzer-Jäger-Regiment 656. NARA, T-78, Roll 620, frame 000777.

585 Frieser, Schmider, Schönherr et al, *Germany and the Second World War Volume VIII: The Eastern Front 1943-1944,* 467.

586 Münch, *The Combat History of German Heavy Anti-Tank Unit 653,* 174.

587 Münch, 171-173. Spielberger, Doyle and Jentz. *Heavy Jagdpanzer,* 110-116.

588 Münch, *The Combat History of German Heavy Anti-Tank Unit 653,* 64-65. Spielberger, Doyle and Jentz. *Heavy Jagdpanzer,* 110-116.

589 Steven Zaloga, *Anzio 1944: The Beleaguered Beachhead,* (New York: Osprey Publishing, 2005), 21,36.

590 Zaloga, *Anzio 1944: The Beleaguered Beachhead,* 57. Münch, *The Combat History of German Heavy Anti-Tank Unit 653,* 175.

591 Zaloga, *Anzio 1944: The Beleaguered Beachhead,* 68.

592 Failmezger, *American Knights,*ebook, 841.

593 Failmezger, 359.

594 Failmezger, 365-368.

595 Münch, *The Combat History of German Heavy Anti-Tank Unit 653,* 185. Schneider, *Tigers in Combat I,* 322.

596 Münch, *The Combat History of German Heavy Anti-Tank Unit 653*, 177.

597 Münch, 177-178.

598 Münch, *The Combat History of German Heavy Anti-Tank Unit 653*, 178.

599 Münch, 182-183.

600 Münch, 185.

601 Münch, *The Combat History of German Heavy Anti-Tank Unit 653*, 203.

602 Münch, 215. Frieser, Schmider, Schönherr et al. *Germany and the Second World War Volume VIII: The Eastern Front 1943-1944*, 684.

603 Münch, *The Combat History of German Heavy Anti-Tank Unit 653*, 221.

604 Ibid, 221-222.

605 Spielberger, Doyle and Jentz. *Heavy Jagdpanzer*, 124. Münch, *The Combat History of German Heavy Anti-Tank Unit 653*, 227-228.

606 Spielberger, Doyle and Jentz. *Heavy Jagdpanzer*, 126-127. Spielberger, and Doyle, *Tigers I and II and their Variants*, 153.

607 Oberkommando des Heers. Pz Offz B Chef GenStdH Anlage 7. 5.7.1944. Betr. Jagdtiger. NARA, T-78, Roll 620 frame 000081.

608 Carius, *Tigers in the Mud*, 214.

609 Carius.

610 Spielberger, Doyle and Jentz, *Heavy Jagdpanzer*, 183-185.

611 Münch, *The Combat History of German Heavy Anti-Tank Unit 653*, 280,282-283.

612 Münch, 287-288.

613 Münch, 278.

614 Münch, *The Combat History of German Heavy Anti-Tank Unit 653*, 297.

615 Doyle, *The Complete Guide to German Armoured Vehicles*, 454-456. Spielberger and Doyle, *Tigers I and II and their Variants*, 169, 172.

616 Oberkommando des Heers. 76 g 31 a WaIRU...Wa Chefgruppe den 4.1.1944. Betr. Tiger Mörser. United States National Archives (NARA), T-78, Roll 619, frame 001047.

Alexandra Richie, *Warsaw 1944: The Fateful Uprising*, (London: William Collins, 2013), 416-417.

617 Norman Davis, *Rising 44: The Battle for Warsaw*, (London: Pan Books, 2018), 254.

618 Davis, *Rising 44*, 259.

619 Davis, 259.

620 Helmut Ritgen, *The Western Front 1944: Memoirs of a Panzer Lehr Officer*, translated by Joseph Welsh, (Winnipeg: J.J Fedorowicz Publishing Inc., 1995), 204.

621 Jorge Rosado and Chris Bishop, *Wehrmacht Panzer Divisions 1939-45*, (London: Amber Books, 2010), 184.

Conclusion

622 Spielberger, Doyle and Jentz. *Heavy Jagdpanzer*, 126-127. Spielberger, Doyle, *Tigers I and II and their Variants,* 153.

623 Zaloga, *Armoured Champion: The Top Tanks of World War II*, ebook, 597-604.

624 Schneider, *Tigers in Combat I,* 187,263. Schneider, *Tigers in Combat II,* ebook, 71-74, 223, 302, 395.

ABOVE: The sole surviving Sturer Emil at Patriot's Park, Moscow. (Dr. Alexander Hill.)

BELOW: A Tiger I leaves Henschel in May 1943. Note the early production "smokestack" commander's cupola. (NARA)

ABOVE: Tiger I sans outer road wheels, and with lower profile commander's cupola. Patriots Park, Moscow. (Dr. Alexander Hill.)

BELOW: The Ferdinand featured a more powerful gun and thicker armour than the Tiger I. Patriots Park, Moscow. (Dr. Alexander Hill)

ABOVE: A Sturmtiger abandoned in the Ruhr Pocket, near Minden at the end of the war. It combined the Tiger's formidable armour and a 380mm rocket launcher.(NARA)

BELOW: An Elefant captured during the fighting in Italy by the US Army. This image provides an excellent look at the main upgrades that differentiate the Elefant from the earlier Ferdinand. (NARA.)

ABOVE: A Tiger II of Heavy Tank Battalion 503, prepared for battle in Normandy. The Normandy Campaign would be an inauspicious debut for the heavy tank. (NARA)

BELOW: Two American soldiers inspect a 128mm shell from a captured Jagdtiger. The great size of the vehicle is very evident in this image, which had a negative impact on its reliability. (NARA).

LEFT: *A Panzer III of the 5th SS Panzer Division Wiking (Viking) in the east. They made up the bulk of Germany's Panzer Divisions until 1943, when they began to be phased out in favour of the Panther and the Panzer IV. (NARA)*

ABOVE: *A captured Panzer IV. One of the few tanks that was produced right up to the end of the war, it proved to be a reliable and versatile vehicle.(NARA)*

BELOW: *A knocked-out Panther. Like the Tiger, it paired strong armour with an excellent 75mm gun, even more powerful than the one mounted on the Panzer IV. (NARA)*

ABOVE: A StuG III on the move. This assault gun, based on the chassis of the Panzer III would prove to be a formidable tank destroyer thanks to a low profile and a high velocity 75mm gun. These features, combined with excellent mobility and reliability would make it vastly superior to the larger Ferdinand and Jagdtiger. (NARA)

Photo 13: The Henschel factory in Essen being inspected after the city fell to the Americans in March 1945. It was not until the second half of the war that strategic bombing reached its full destructive potential. It and German territorial losses shattered the wartime economy irrevocably. (NARA).

ABOVE: Despite the awesome destructive power of Allied bombing, the German economy still continued to function, after a fashion, until the bitter end and from the Henschel factory a trickle of production continued to flow. These Tiger II turrets, inspected on the factory floor by American soldiers in March 1945 represent the literal last vestiges of their production. (NARA)

BELOW: The M4 Sherman Production Line at the Detroit Arsenal Tank Plant in 1942. Even without the effects of strategic bombing, the best organizational efforts of Fritz Todt and Albert Speer could never hope to create an economy that could match the Allies vast industrial might. (NARA)

ABOVE: A Soviet M4 Sherman of the 8th Guards Mechanized Corps in Granbow, Germany, 3rd, May 1945. (NARA)

BELOW: A British Sherman Firefly stands watch over the Meuse River at Namur in September 1944. (NARA)

ABOVE: A M26 Pershing of A Company, 14th Tank Battalion crosses the Rhine on a pontoon bridge on 12th, March 1945. (NARA)

BELOW: A T-34, armed with the 76mm gun that was fitted from 1940 to 1943, as initially encountered by the Germans. (Dr. Alexander Hill.)

ABOVE: The KV-1 was the main heavy tank of the Red Army in 1941. It encouraged Hitler to press for the Tiger II. (Dr. Alexander Hill)

BELOW: The T-34-85 represented a significant improvement in the capabilities of the vaunted Soviet medium tank. (Dr. Alexander Hill.)

ABOVE: The SU-100 was one of several casemate tank destroyers built on the chassis of the T-34. It proved to a potent tank destroyer. (Dr. Alexander Hill)

BELOW: The ISU-152 is perhaps one of the most iconic of the Soviet "Beast Killers". It was built on the chassis of the IS-2. (Dr. Alexander Hill)

INDEX

ORGANIZATIONS

General Plenipotentiary for the War Economy), 70, 73

Hauptausschuss Panzerkampfwagen, 62, 64, 77, 79
Henschel (Henschel und Sohn), 13, 16, 18-19, 21-24, 26,
    32-33, 36, 52-53, 55, 57, 60-62, 64-66, 69, 78, 87-88,
    100
Heereswaffenamt (Weapons Office), 13-14, 16-19, 21-23,
    31-32, 37, 47, 52, 79, 213

I.G Farben, 70

Kriegsmairne, 74, 82, 84, 86
Krupp (Fredrich Krupp AG), 13, 15, 17-18, 21-22, 24,31,
    33, 35-36, 55,57, 59, 61, 66, 69-70, 75, 87-88

Luftwaffe, 72, 74, 84, 87, 166

Maybach (Maybach Motorenbau), 15, 58, 61-62, 85, 87, 93

Nibelungenwerk, 24-25, 33, 37, 53, 59, 65-68, 87, 193,
    201-202

Oberkommando des Heeres (OKH, Army High Command),
    8, 28, 35, 77, 101
Oberkommando der Wehrmacht (OKW, Armed Forces
    High Command), 70, 73, 77
Office of War Mobilization, 89
Organisation Todt, 76

Panzerkommission, 32, 79
Panzer Notprogramm, 65, 67, 69
Panzerwaffe, 39-40, 71, 101
Porsche (Dr. Ing. h.c. F. Porsche KG.), 13, 19-25, 31-33, 52

PEOPLE

Essen (see also Krupp), 55-57, 61, 88

Falaise, 170-171, 211
Fastov, 138
Friedrichshafen (see also Maybach), 55, 58

Garniai, 148
Gaumesnil, 173

Hajmasker, 191
Hagenau, 208

Inota, 191
Isola Bella, 203-204

Kassel (see also Henschel), 53, 56-57, 61, 65, 69, 88
Kazache,131
Kharkov, 119
Kielce, 206
Kiev, 135, 139-141, 151
Kirchmöser, 60
Kisujszalls, 180
Königsberg, 146
Kursk (also Operation Zitadelle), 9, 11, 27, 60, 116-118,
    120-134, 135, 187, 196-197, 200, 206, 216, 219

Lembitu, 144
Lieaen, 209
Linz (see also Eisenwerk Oberdonau), 25, 59
Luga, 143

Malinava, 147-148
Manneville, 165
Manychskaya, 107-108

UNITS BY COUNTRY

AMERICAN

BRITISH

47th Volksgrenadier Division, 208
85th Infantry Division, 172
89th Infantry Division, 171-172
96th Infantry Division, 181
116th Panzer Division, 211
205th Infantry Division, 147
346th Infantry Division, 167
352nd Infantry Division, 158
711th Infantry Division, 186

POLISH
1st Polish Armoured Division, 170, 172, 174-175
10th Armoured Cavalry Regiment, 175
10th Mounted Rifle Regiment, 175

ROMANIAN
1st Romanian Army, 179-180, 192, 217

SOVIET
1st Ukrainian Front, 136, 138
2nd Baltic Front, 149
3rd Baltic Front, 149
3rd Guards Army, 201
3rd Guards Tank Brigade, 108
5th Guards Tank Army, 124
5th Tank Army, 107
6th Guards Army, 146
8th Guards Army, 201
12th Army, 201
15th Rifle Division, 121
34th Tank Brigade, 162
35th Guards Rifle Corps, 130
59th Army, 144-145
69th Army, 130-131

WEAPONS

www.ingramcontent.com/pod-product-compliance
Lightning Source LLC
Chambersburg PA
CBHW061139120626
46546CB00005B/1857